STUDIO AN
LIGHTING

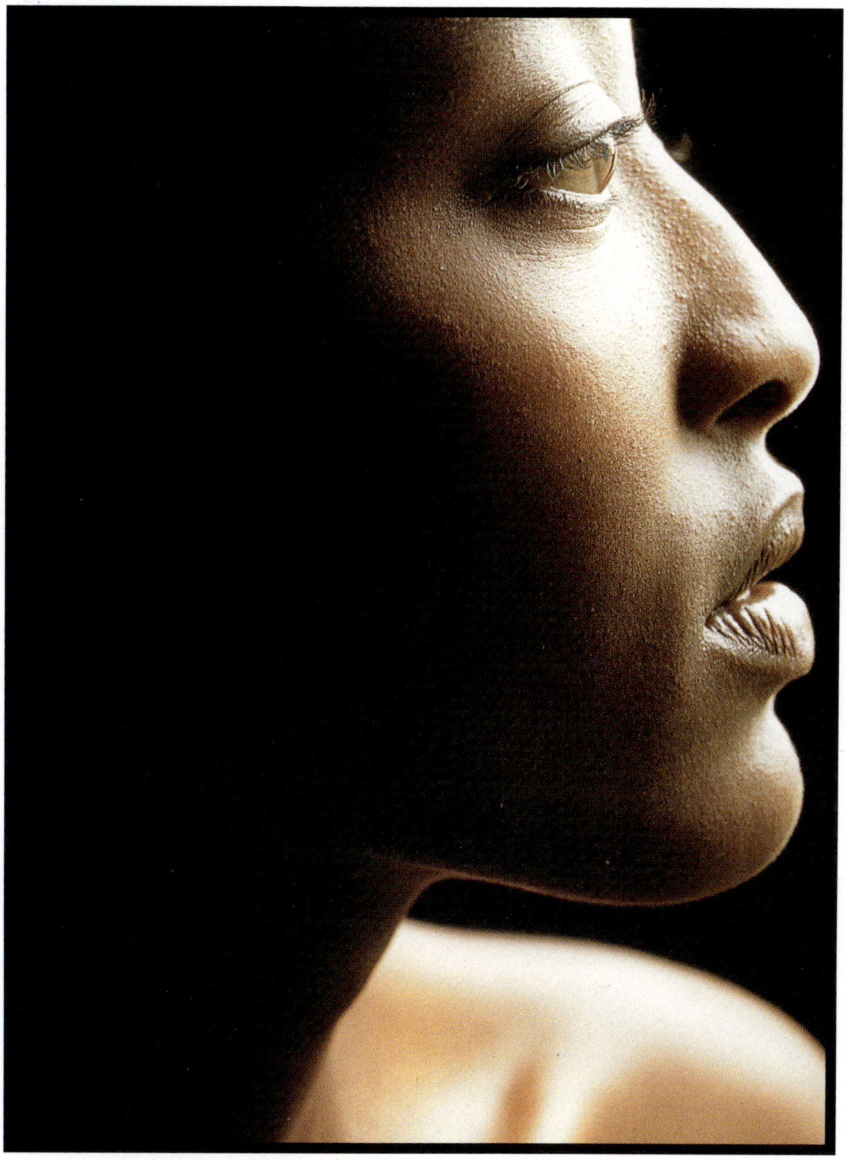

Controlling and using light

CASSELL

ACKNOWLEDGEMENTS
Front cover (main) Zefa, front cover(l) Nigel Robertson/EP, front cover(c) Zefa, front cover(r) Trevor Melton/EP, 1-4 ICL, 5 TIB, 6 Keith Johnson and Pelling, 7 Keith Johnson and Pelling, 9 John Suett/EP, 10 Patrick Llewelyn-Davies/EP, 11(t) TIB, 11(b) Zefa, 12 Zefa, 13(t) Allsport, 13(b) George Wright, 14 TIB, 15(t) Zefa, 15(b) George Wright, 16 TIB, 17-20 Steve Tanner/EP, 21(t) Trevor Melton/EP, 21(b) BFI Stills, 22 Trevor Melton/EP, 23 Simon Donnelly, 24(t) Trevor Melton/EP, 24(b) John Heseltine, 25-27 Trevor Melton/EP, 28 Retna Pictures, 29(t) EP, 29(b) Tobi Corney/EP, 30-32 Tobi Corney/EP, 33 Simon Page-Ritchie/EP, 34(t) Simon Page-Ritchie/EP, 34(b) Adam Eastland, 35 Rapid Eye Baskets, 36(t) Simon Page-Ritchie/EP, 36(b) Michael Freeman, 37(tl) Trevor Melton/EP, 37(tr) Simon Page-Ritchie/EP, 37(b) Zefa, 38 Simon Page-Ritchie/EP, 39(t) Trevor Melton/EP, 39(b) TIB, 40(t) Alastair Scott, 40(b) Simon Page-Ritchie/EP, 41(t) Zefa, 14(b) Trevor Melton/EP, 42-44 Trevor Melton/EP, 45 Eugene Doyen, 46-48 Nigel Robertson/EP, 49 The Photographers Library, 50 Tobi Corney/EP, 51 Alastair Scott, 52(t) Action Plus, 52(b) Philip Dunn, 53(t) Trevor Melton/EP, 53(b) Jonathan Knowles, 54-55 Trevor Melton/EP, 56 Jonathan Vince, 57-60 Trevor Melton/EP, 61-64 Trevor Melton/EP, 65-68 Jane Brown, 69 Seamus Ryan, 70(t) Seamus Ryan, 70(b) Trevor Melton/EP, 71 The Photographers Library, 72(t) Trevor Melton/EP, 72(b) TSI, 73(t) Scott Acee, 73(b) Trevor Melton/EP, 74-76 Trevor Melton/EP, 77-80 Trevor Melton/EP, 81-84 Harry Ormesher/EP, 85-88 Seamus Ryan/EP, 89-92 Seamus Ryan/EP, 93-94 Seamus Ryan/EP, 95(t) Trevor Melton/EP, 95(b) Seamus Ryan/EP, 96 Seamus Ryan/EP.

Key: EP - Eaglemoss Publications; ICL - Images Colour Library; TIB - The Image Bank; TSI - Tony Stone Images

Consultant editor: Roger Hicks

First published 1994 by Cassell
Villiers House, 41/47 Strand, London WC2N 5JE

Distributed in Australia
by Capricorn Link (Australia) Pty Ltd
2/13 Carrington Road, Castle Hill, NSW 2154

British Library Cataloguing-in-Publication Data
A catalogue record for this book is available from the British Library

ISBN 0-304-34401-X

Printed in Spain by Cayfosa Industria Grafica

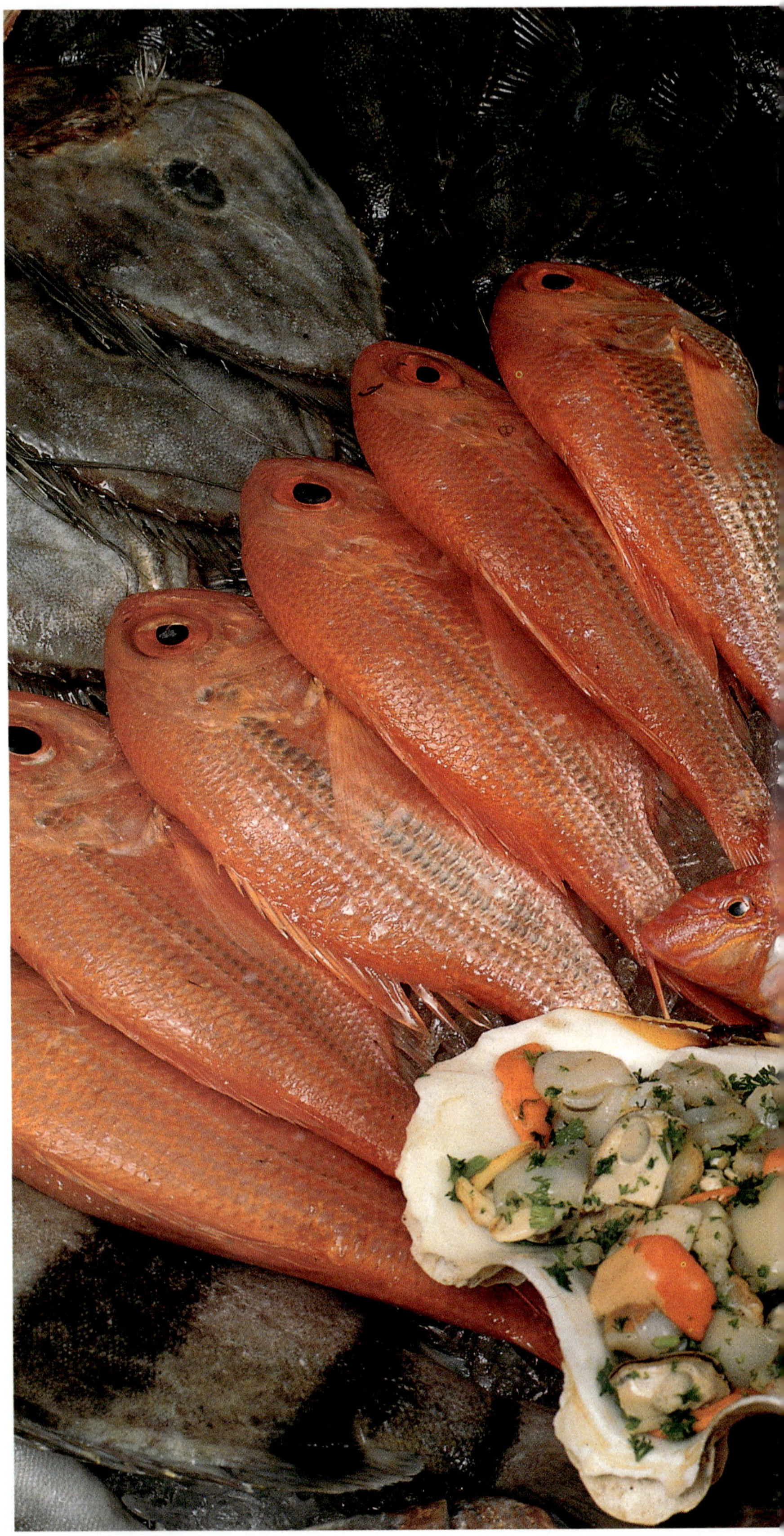

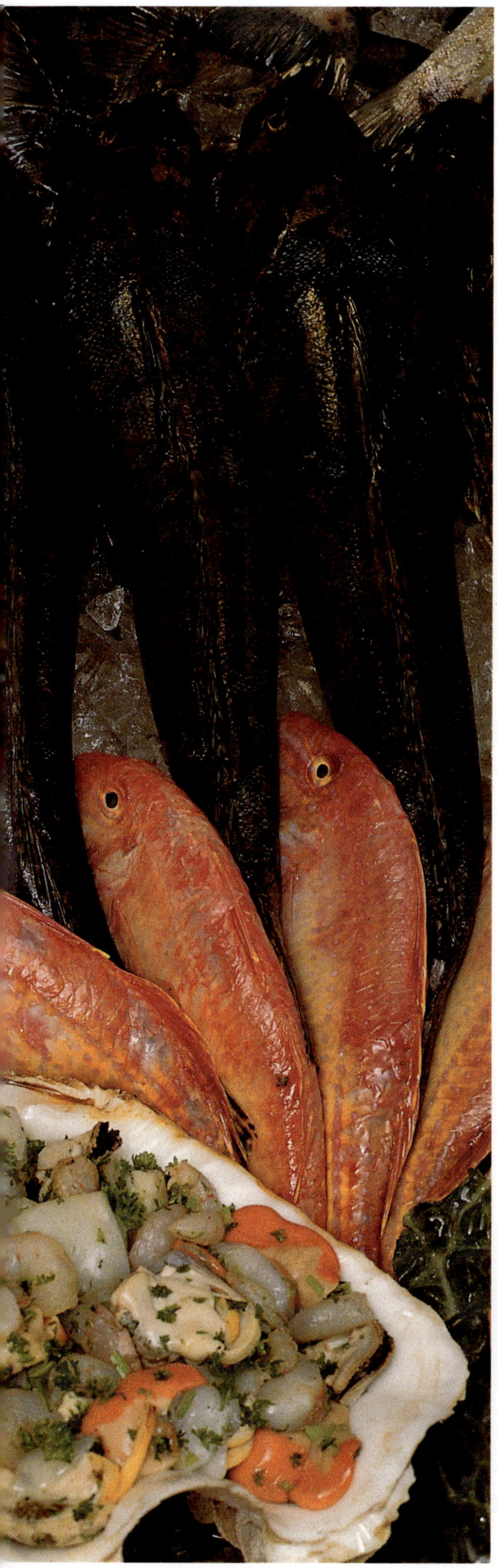

CONTENTS

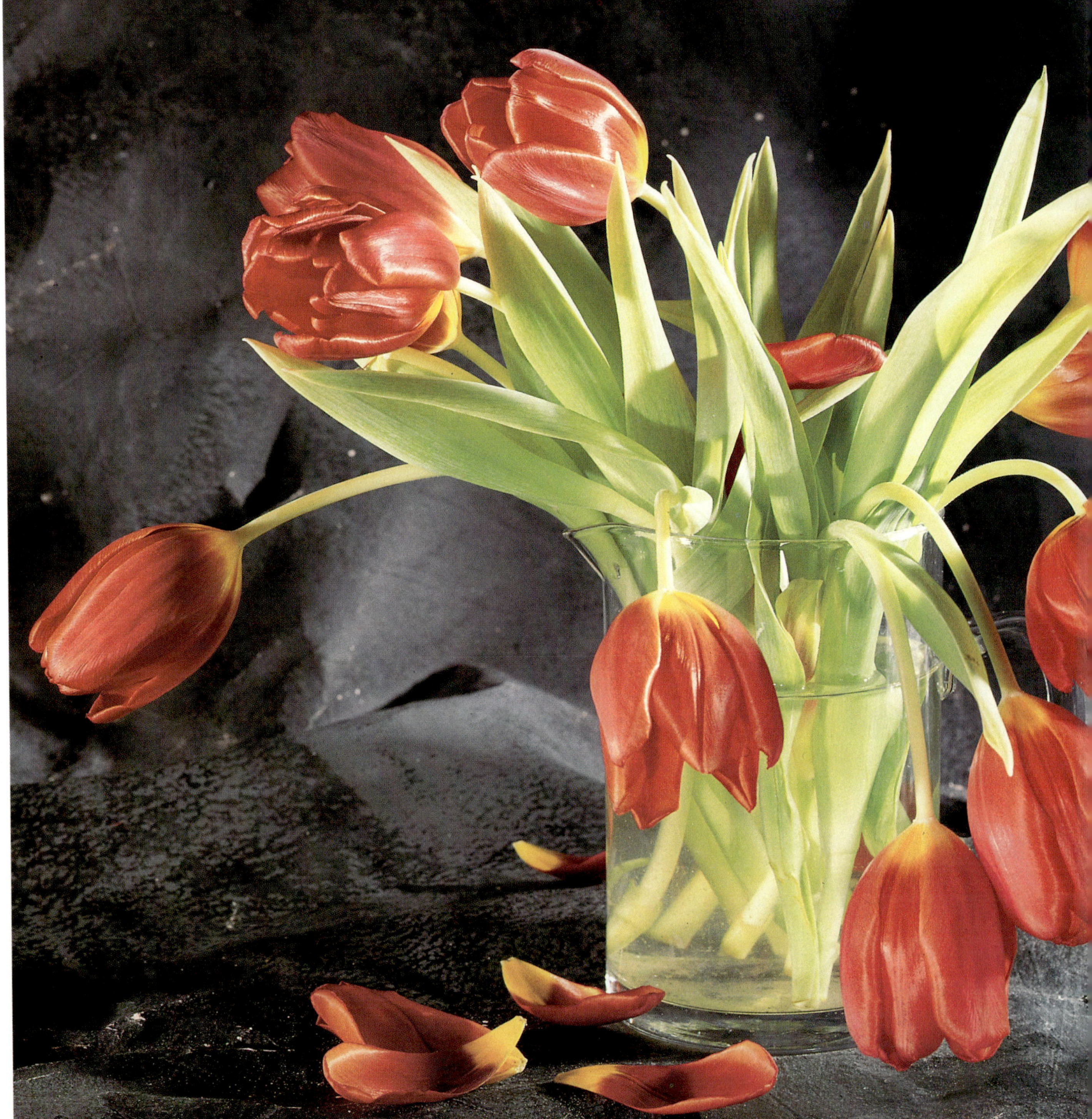

INTRODUCTION

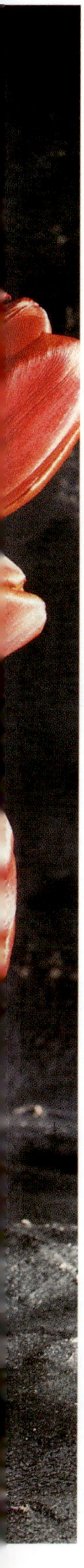

PROFESSIONAL photographers take certain skills for granted: how to control light and shadow, how to choose and use backgrounds and props effectively. It's all a question of control, the kind of control that you get when you stop simply taking pictures, and start making them. The basic techniques are surprisingly easy to learn – and they don't have to remain the exclusive preserve of professional photographers.

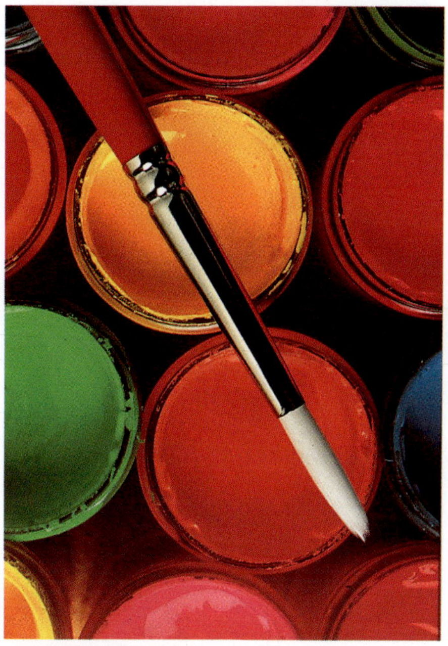

It is of course possible to take excellent pictures on location by using only available light, but you can enormously increase your photographic scope and versatility by learning to control light and work in a studio. Frequently, the two disciplines of studio and non-studio photography interact: where most people would take a snap, you can make a really great shot by knowing how best to use natural light, while in the studio you can make even a formal portrait look natural and un-contrived. On these pages, you will find clear step-by-step instructions alongside examples of the work of top professionals such as Jane Bown and Tobi Corney.

You don't have to have a fully-equipped permanent studio. Surprisingly often, you can adapt a spare room or a garage to allow you to tackle a wide range of subjects; and even if your 'studio' has to be set up on a temporary basis in a bedroom or garage, you can achieve much more than you might think possible. Even food photography, which is a notoriously difficult subject, can be tackled in a surprisingly small space.

It's a commonly held myth that you need to spend a fortune to achieve professional-quality results. In fact, the reverse is often true and the quality of the photographs you take is as much a question of know-how as of equipment. And even where special equipment is required, it's often possible to improvise and make it by yourself. Admittedly, there are times when you do need to spend money on buying it or hiring special equipment, but there are plenty of tips in these pages which tell you how to get the best value for your money. Where professional tools are needed, we pull no punches in telling you: there is no point in pretending that a food photographer would use a compact camera.

This book also contains many insights into the subtle touches which lift a picture out of the ordinary. Some of them (how a background is lit, for example) are things which most of us notice only unconsciously, if at all. Other sections deal with areas of special interest, such as double exposures and food photography.

It may be an exaggeration to say that unless you understand studio lighting, you cannot call yourself a photographer, but it is no exaggeration to say that mastering studio and lighting techniques will almost certainly make you a better photographer.

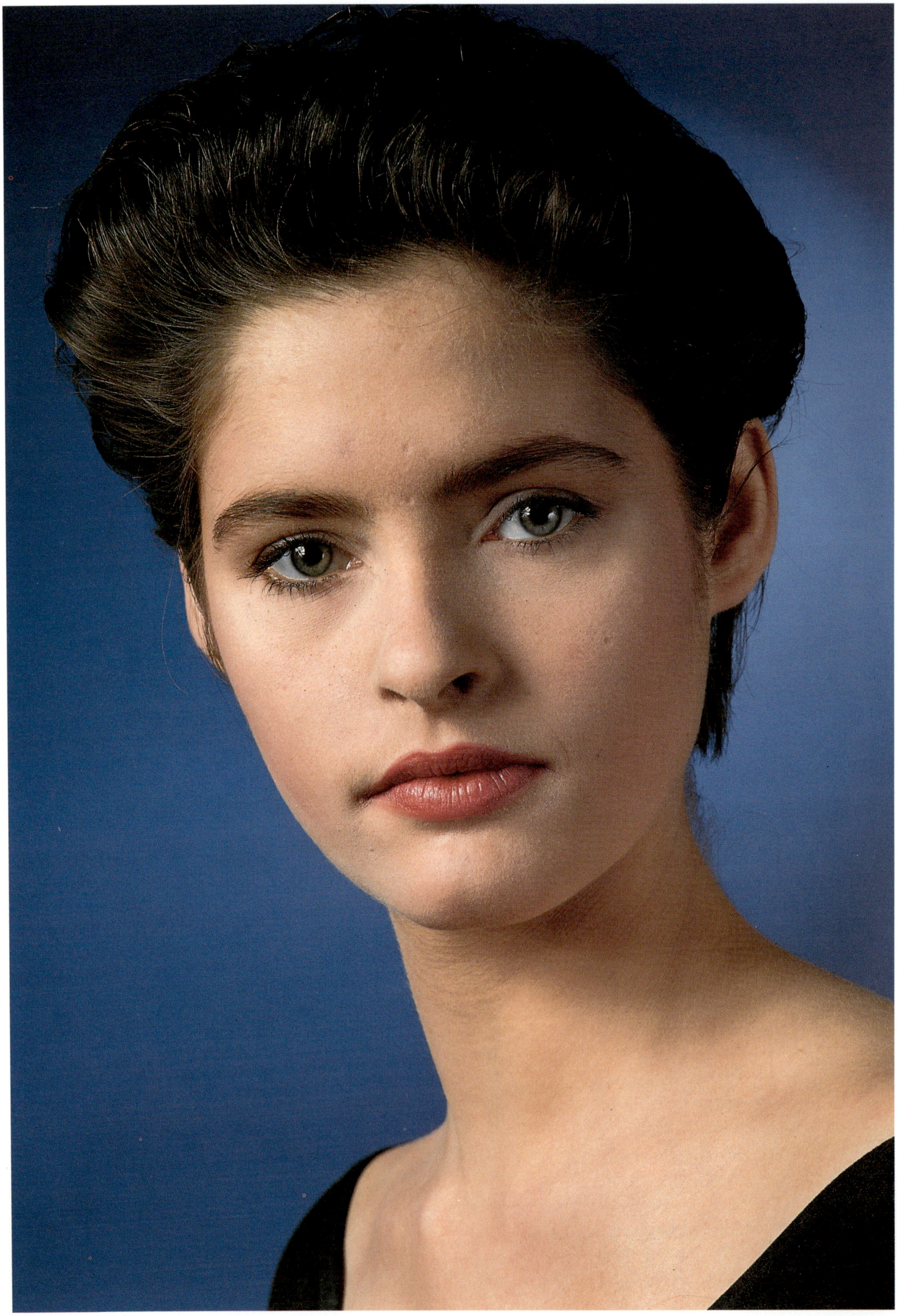

An improvised studio at home

A home studio opens up a new photographic world, giving you much greater control over both lighting and background effects. It is particularly useful for still life and portrait photography.

A temporary studio is quick to set up and is well worth doing because it leaves you free to create the images you want whenever you want.

Selecting a room

Choose a room that's not in constant use. If possible, the walls should be a neutral colour – white, grey or cream – because light which is reflected from colourful walls might cause a colour cast. The room should be as far away as possible from the vibrations of traffic, to avoid camera shake.

A studio doesn't have to fill a whole room, but make sure there's space for a tripod, light stands and the subject you're shooting and allow enough room to walk around the set easily. Plywood boxes or old chests of drawers fitted with castors are very useful for storing all your equipment and props. You can slide them under a table to save space.

Light

If you're aiming to use natural light, choose a room with as large a window as possible. North facing rooms (south facing in the southern hemisphere) are best, because their light levels and the direction of the shadows are most constant. If your room faces south, cover the window with tracing paper to soften the light.

You'll probably use artificial light more often as you can control precisely the amount and direction, but you'll need a room you can black out easily. Any heavy curtain does the job, but if you don't have one, black card will do. You don't need to make the room totally lightproof unless it's doubling as a darkroom.

▼ A studio enables you to take photos at any time, without having to wait for favourable weather and lighting conditions outside. Here, a temporary studio is set up in the corner of a living room. The background, reflector and light stands are collapsible, so that they can be packed away out of sight between shoots. The top class portrait opposite illustrates the polished results which you can achieve using a similar studio set up in your own home.

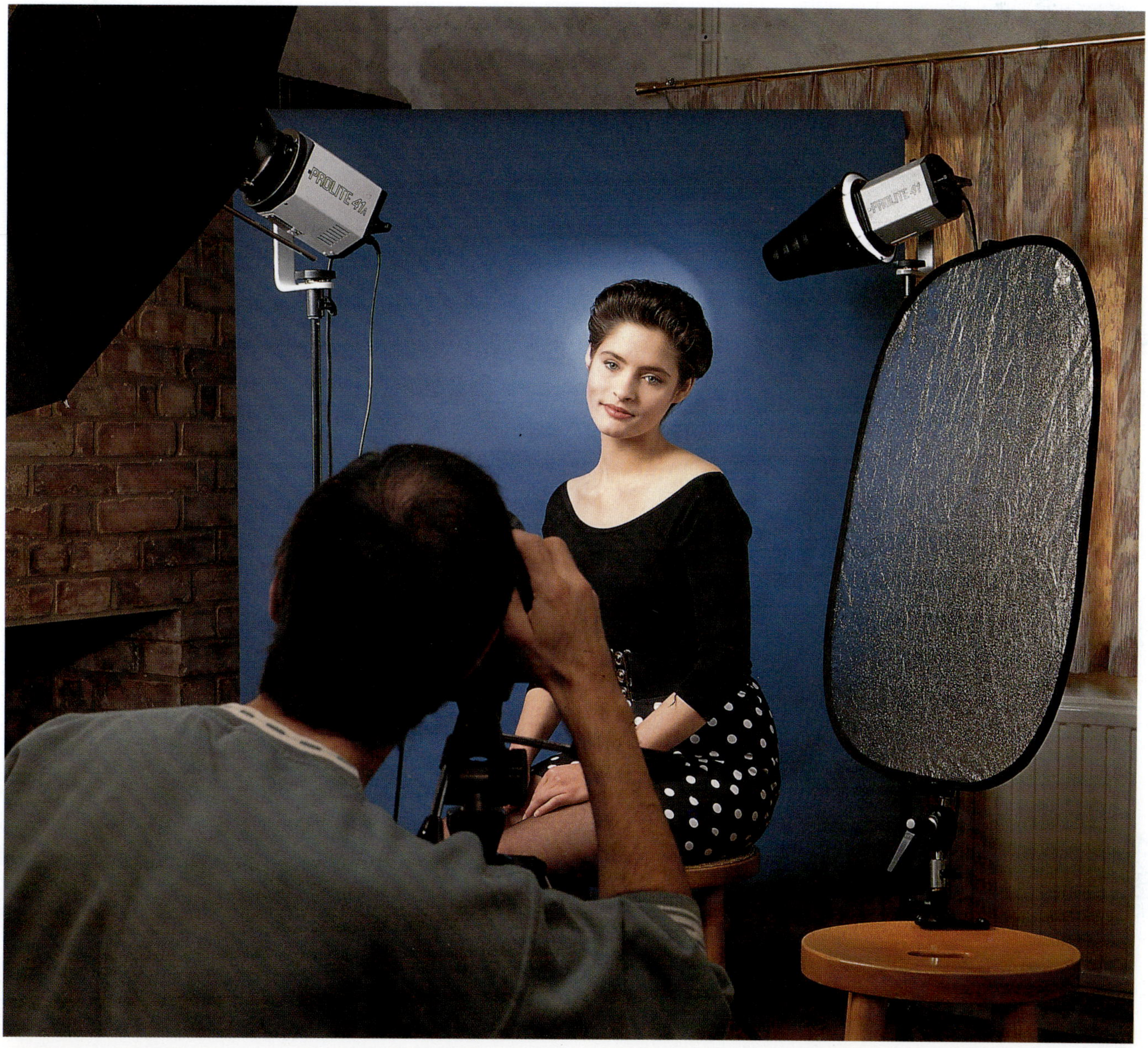

Size of studio

Length The room must be long enough for you to set up the camera at the correct distance from the subject, depending on the lens length. For example, to shoot a full-length portrait with a 105mm lens on 35mm film, you'll need a studio at least 6 metres long. If your subject is seated you need a much shorter studio – or shoot through an open door for extra studio length.

Width Ideally, the room should leave enough space on either side of your subject so that you can place lights for sidelighting without them showing in the photo.

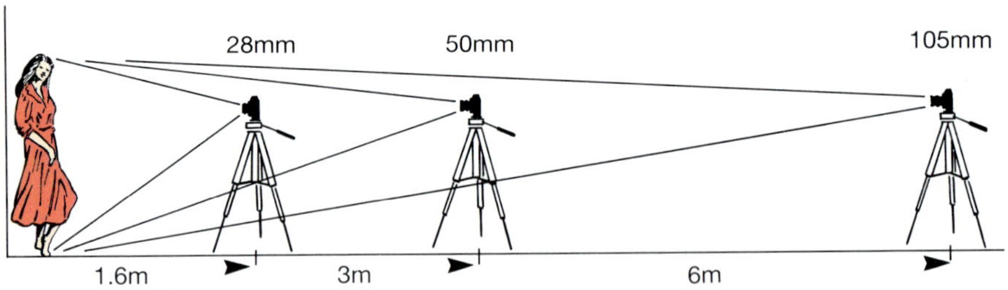

Height A low ceiling restricts your camera angles and placement of lights. If possible, choose a high-ceilinged room so that you can position lights above your subject without the risk of heat from them scorching the ceiling – and so that you can take shots from above.

▲ Here are three examples of studio lengths – the length you need varies depending on your lens and the height of the model. Look through the viewfinder before you set up the shoot and check that you can get everything in. Though a 28mm lens allows you to use a shorter studio, take care : a wide angle lens may include unwanted detail at the edges of the frame.

Preparing the room

Setting up the room takes a little time. Begin by stacking any furniture at one end of the room, out of view of the shot. Don't forget to allow time at the end of the session to restore the room to its original state.

The floor should be clean and clear of clutter. The surface should be hard, so you have a steady base for tripods and light stands – tiles or floorboards are ideal. If the room is carpeted, lay hardboard on top to provide a firm base for background paper.

The backdrop Special photographic backdrop paper is quite expensive, but it is easier to use than alternatives such as bed sheets or wallpaper. To shoot small subjects, drape your backdrop over a chair. For larger subjects, fix it to the wall or to a board held up with chairs or clamps.

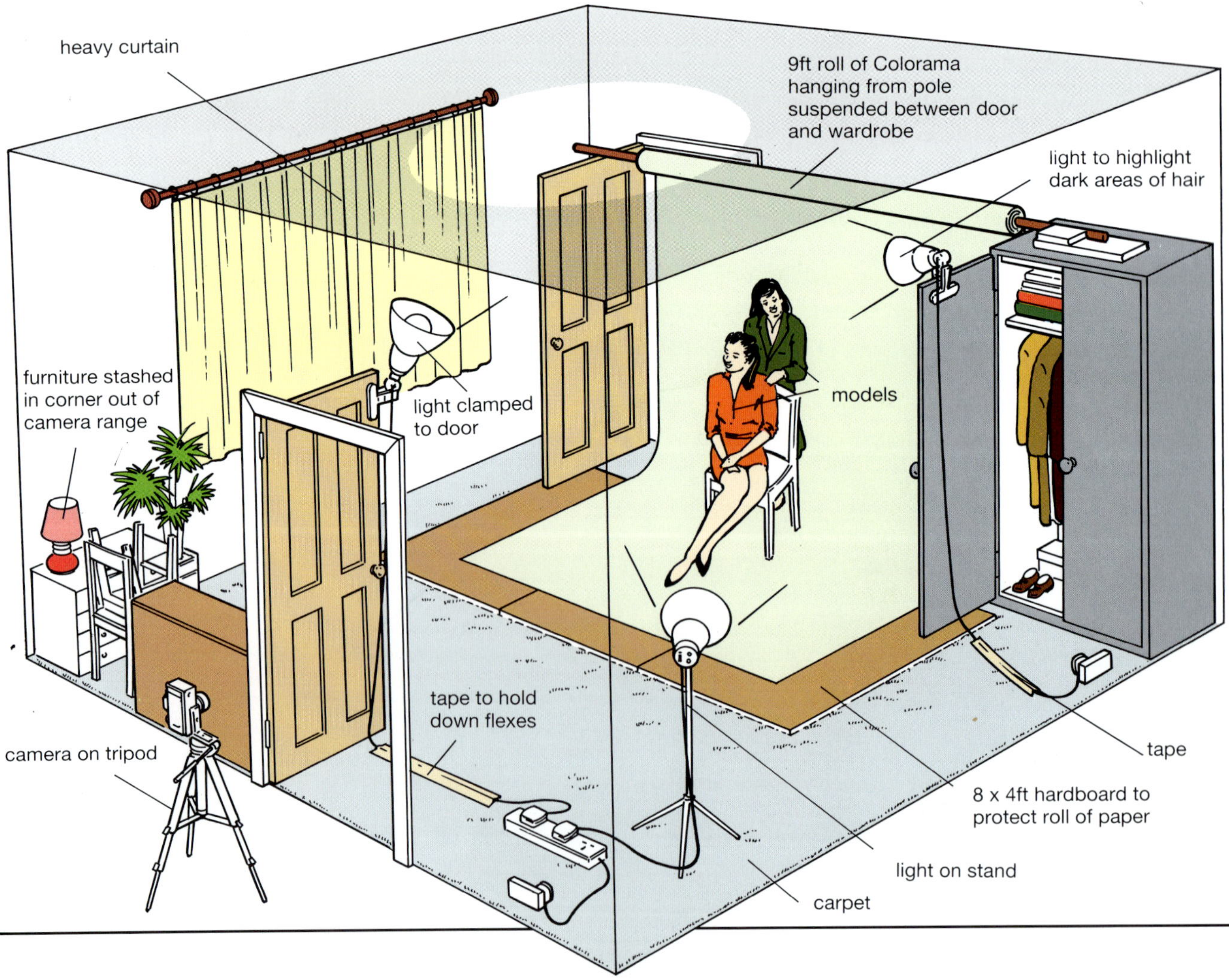

Tip: Studio safety

❑ Make sure you don't leave cables trailing on the floor where you might trip over them.
❑ Tape any loose leads to the floor with insulation tape.
❑ Buy a socket board to avoid overloading extension cables.
❑ Remember to turn off all the lights at the end of a session, and wait for them to cool down before you touch them.

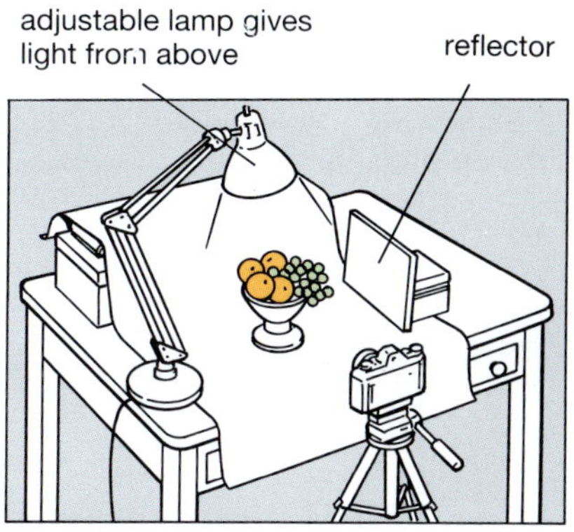

SIMPLE SET UP
For a very simple lighting set up, all you need is an adjustable desk lamp, a reflector and a large sheet of seamless paper. If you're shooting a small subject, you could rest the backdrop on books piled on a table top.

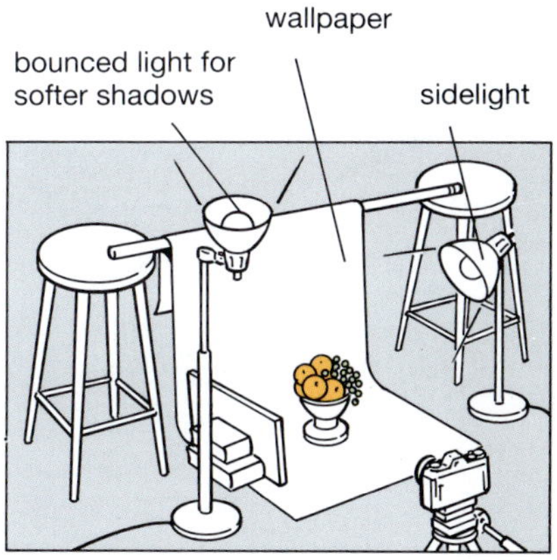

SUSPENDED BACKDROP
If you plan to shoot your subject from above, you could suspend your backdrop material from a pole or broom resting on two stools or chairs.

Artificial lighting

The simplest form of lighting is an adjustable desk lamp. Start with just one mobile light and a lamp stand to fix it on. A step ladder, the top of a door or any sturdy free standing object you happen to have makes a good alternative to a light stand, provided you can secure the light with clamps.

Most professional studios use mains-powered electronic flash as a light source.

Studio flash units provide a brief but intense burst of light. They also feature a modelling light: a tungsten bulb that imitates the effect of the flash so you can preview the shot to see what it will look like. Studio flash units are too costly for occasional use, but there are several cheaper alternatives.

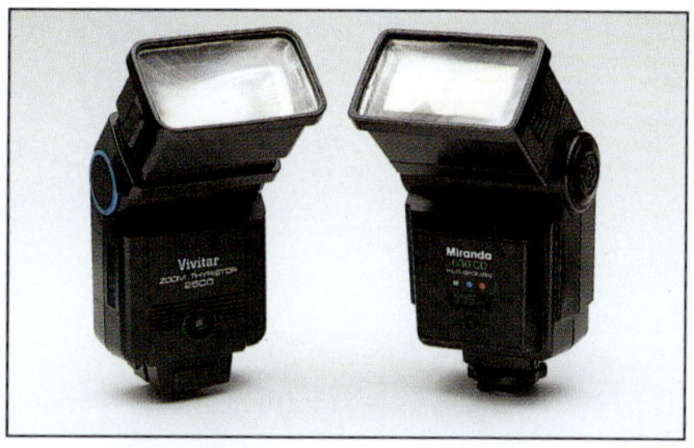

▲ ***Portable flash units***

Portable flash units These can do much of the work of the studio flash unit. However, they are much less powerful, recycle more slowly and have no modelling light. You could try using a small desk lamp to preview the lighting; simply replace the lamp with flash when you are ready to shoot.

Tungsten photoflood lights allow you to judge the kind of effect you'll get from flash. They fit into normal light sockets but are three to five times brighter than ordinary light bulbs. However, they're also three to five times hotter, and could melt the light fitting. For this reason you should use them in special ceramic bulb holders. You could use ordinary light fittings as long as you remember to switch on the photoflood for only a few seconds at a time.

Look for lights with large reflectors because the larger the reflector, the softer the shadow will be. Shallow and white or matt reflectors produce softer results than highly polished reflectors and

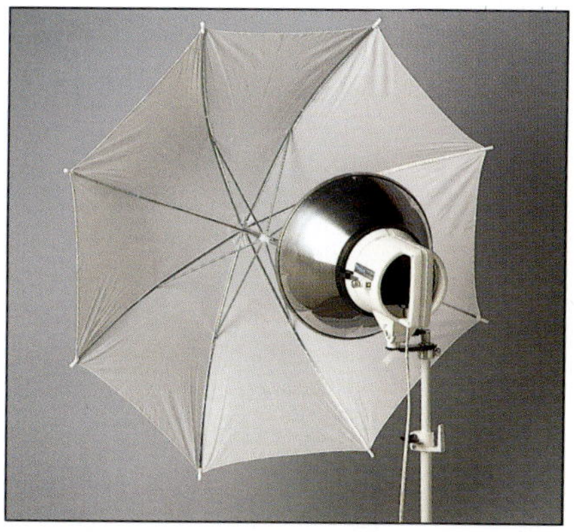

▲ ***Tungsten photoflood light used with umbrella to soften and diffuse light.***

those that are deeply dished, and should be used in preference.

Use special photographic bulbs which are very much brighter than conventional light bulbs. They also have a bluer light that closely matches the colour sensitivity of tungsten light-balanced film. The commonest bulbs produce either 375 or 500 watts, making them three to five times more powerful than ordinary light bulbs.

In non-heatproof bulb holders, these powerful lights should be switched on for no more than a few seconds at a time. However, in a ceramic bulb holder, the lamp can be left burning more or less continuously.

You will need an extension sync lead so you can take the flash off the camera, or a G-clamp to fix the flash to a chair.

With your lighting set up, use a reflector to bounce light into shadow areas. A large piece of white card or polystyrene does the job. Kitchen foil mounted on a piece of card provides stronger light – if the foil is scrunched up and then smoothed out, it will reflect the light more softly.

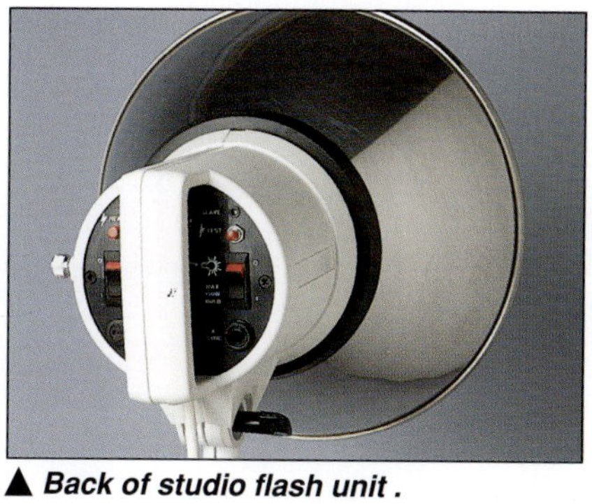

▲ ***Back of studio flash unit .***

A soft touch

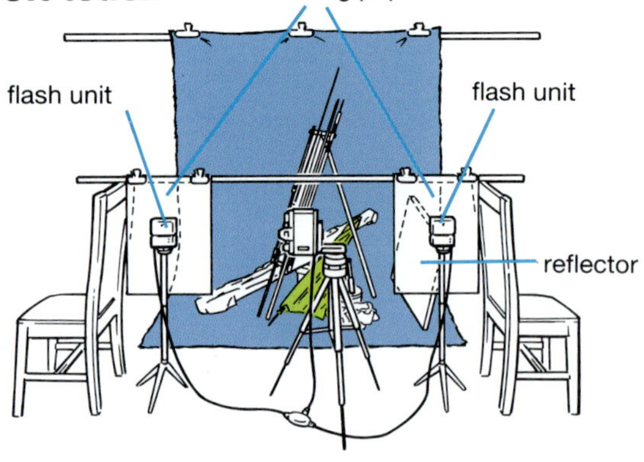

To create soft lighting for shots such as the still life on the right, try positioning a couple of regular battery-powered flash units each side of the camera, diffusing their hard-edged beams with sheets of tracing paper held at least half a metre in front of the flashgun.

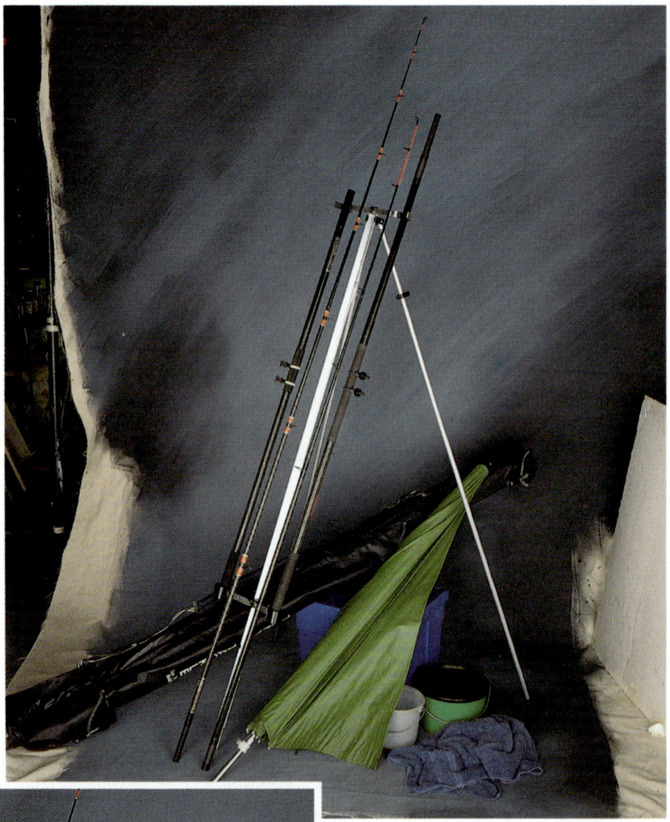

▲ ***Your studio doesn't have to look good to work hard: remember that nobody who looks at your photographs will know what was just beyond the edges of the frame. Cluttered surroundings and improvized reflectors all disappear when you press the shutter release.***

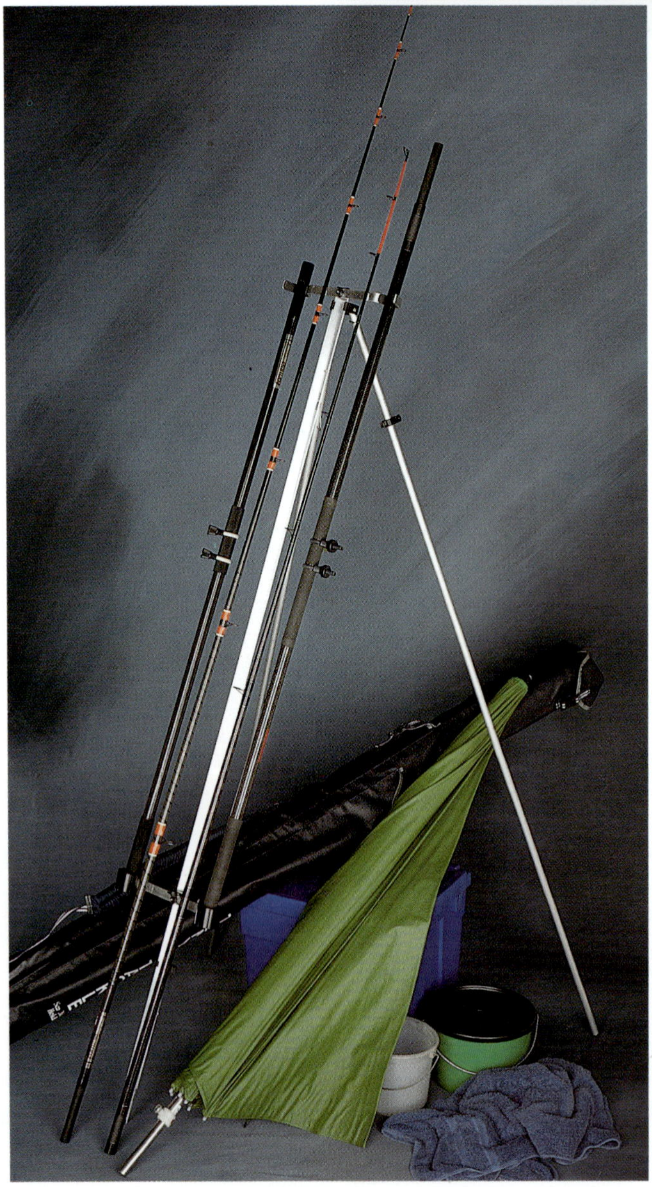

What you need:

Before buying special studio equipment from a camera shop, think about cheaper options. By buying secondhand or improvising with household objects, you can greatly lower the cost – or leave out odd items until you can afford them.

Basic equipment:

- ❑ **Tripod**
- ❑ **Light and light stand**
- ❑ **Extension cable and socket board**
- ❑ **Insulation tape**
- ❑ **Masking tape**
- ❑ **Blacking out material** (such as a curtain), unless using natural light
- ❑ **Backdrop materials** (such as a sheet)
- ❑ **Reflectors** (such as white card)
- ❑ **String, bulldog clips and pegs** to hold reflectors and props in place
- ❑ **Extension sync lead**

Useful extras:

- ❑ **Kodak Wratten 80A filter**
- ❑ **Cable release**
- ❑ **Grey card**
- ❑ **Spirit level**
- ❑ **Thin pieces of wood, wire and G-clamps**
- ❑ **Studio umbrella**

Tip: Choosing the right film

Use daylight balanced film if you shoot in natural light or with flash. If you use tungsten light, you'll need tungsten balanced film (your local camera shop should have some) or a blue Kodak Wratten 80A filter over your lens to avoid an orange colour cast with daylight balanced film.

10 tips for better portrait photography

Whether you are shooting in the studio or on location, lighting portraits requires considerable care. Once you have mastered the art of portraiture, you will understand the basics of all types of lighting.

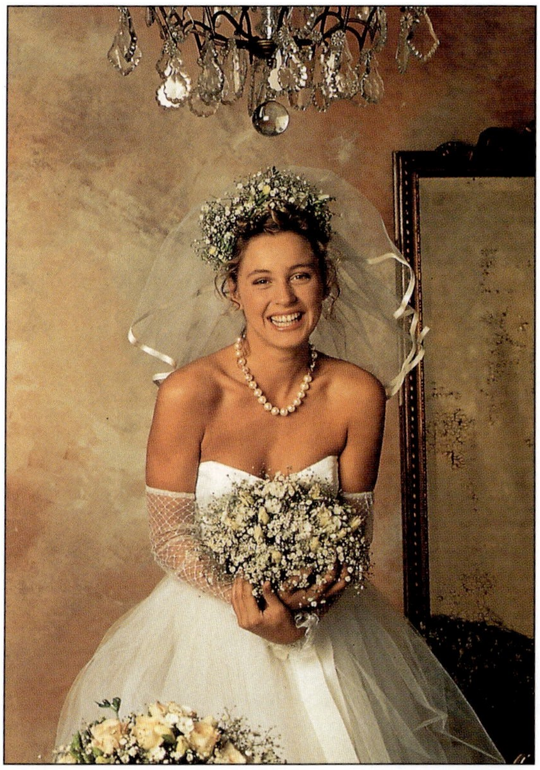

◀ **WEDDING DAY**
Telling a few jokes to the bride ensured that she looked happy and relaxed. A pastel background and carefully selected props helped create an appropriately romantic setting.

1 Relax your subject

Your first priority should be to put the sitter at ease. Subjects who feel inhibited and self-conscious in front of the camera will never reveal their true character. Music and conversation often help, but above all the photographer should appear relaxed and confident.

Prepare as much as possible in advance. Have any props you might need near at hand and all the necessary equipment set up before the session begins. A person who is forced to wait around is liable to become a restless and unco-operative subject.

Use a medium telephoto lens – by keeping a comfortable distance you are less likely to intimidate your subject. A tripod used in conjunction with a cable release is also a good idea. Not only does it prevent the risk of camera shake, but it also allows you to walk around freely and talk to your subject face to face without being hidden behind the camera.

2 Consider the background

Your choice of background should be determined by the effect you are trying to convey in the portrait. Select a simple backdrop such as a roll of cartridge paper, a large piece of velvet or a plain wall to provide a neutral background and concentrate all attention on the subject.

Alternatively, enhance the mood of a picture by including a more elaborate backdrop. Draped pastel coloured curtains, for example, can help create a soft, atmospheric effect. Or inject energy into the composition with bright colours behind the sitter – but make sure they aren't too distracting.

If you are photographing outdoors, look for appropriate settings beforehand. As with indoor backgrounds your choice should be in harmony with the mood you are trying to produce. For instance, it would upset the balance of the picture if you were to use a fussy and detailed backdrop of trees when you really wanted to capture a straightforward portrait of your subject's face.

▼**PRETTY GIRL**
By setting a wide aperture the photographer threw the background out of focus and fixed attention on the young girl's face.

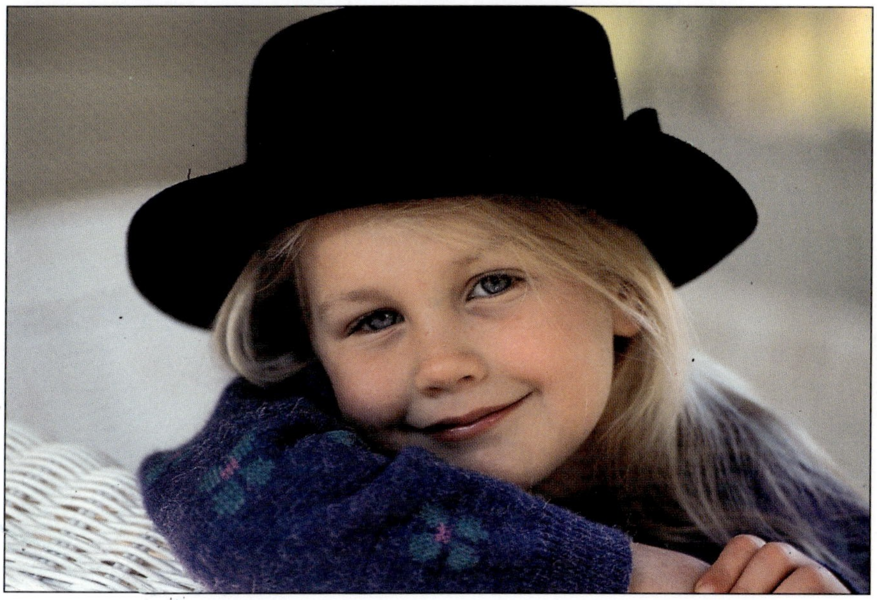

3 Add props

Use props to enhance the composition. A carefully positioned house plant or item of antique furniture, for example, can add variety to a portrait and even make the scene come alive.

Props can also be used to tell you something about the subject. Find out if they have a particular hobby and pose them with a prop related to that interest.

For instance, a portrait of a man placed next to an easel and paints, or a young girl holding a violin, provides more clues to their personalities than a simple head and shoulder shot.

▼BALLOON BOY
The strong colours of the props and background make this portrait come alive. A slow speed film gives excellent colour saturation.

4 Check the composition

Fill the frame with your subject's face to emphasize every change of expression. Remember that in close-up blemishes and wrinkles show up very clearly so the results may not necessarily be flattering. Make sure that the eyes are sharply focused as they are often a person's most expressive feature.

If you decide on a three quarter length portrait, it's best to crop just above the knees rather than on or below them. Otherwise the result tends to look unnatural. Pay particular attention to the hands. Their form and position can give an insight into a subject's personality.

Explore different viewpoints to affect how a viewer responds to your sitter. A low viewpoint exaggerates the stature of a person. This can be appropriate for a successful business person, emphasizing their power and control. A high viewpoint makes a subject look smaller and more vulnerable , which can be useful if you trying to emphasize fragile beauty or extreme youth.

▶THE BOOKMAKER
The photographer explored a variety of viewpoints before deciding on a low position to inject some drama into this portrait shot against a background of clouds. Fill-in flash was used to light the subject – a bookmaker taking bets for the famous Grand National race at Aintree.

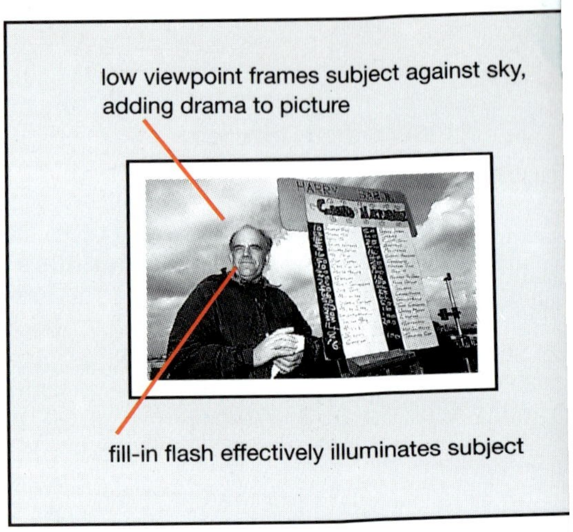

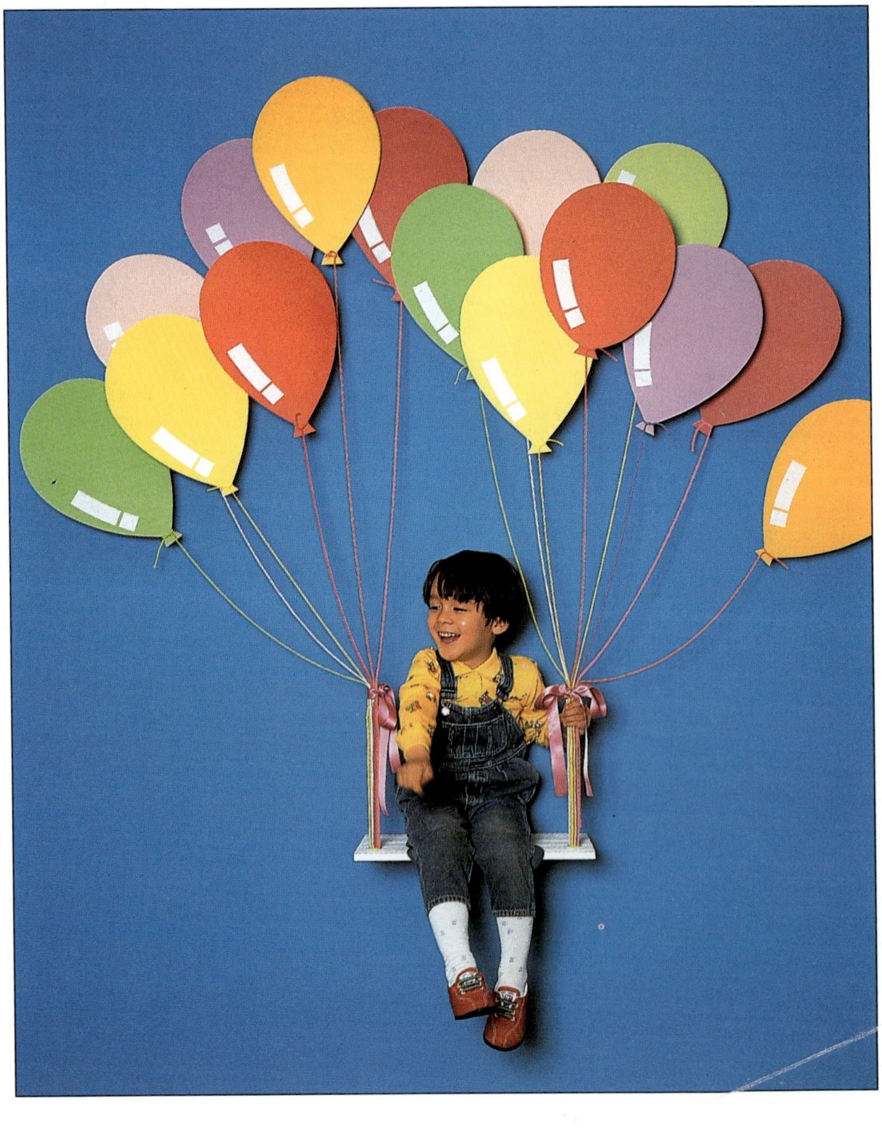

5 Choose appropriate lighting

The quality of lighting can radically affect the appearance of a person. Strong, oblique lighting, for example, brings out lines and wrinkles, whereas they tend to disappear under more diffused light.

Select lighting which compliments your subject. If you are photographing a bride, for instance, you should use soft, diffused light to create a romantic and gen mood. For a portrait of a boxe the other hand, use hard, c lighting. This produces shar lines and harsh, deep sh which accentuate the asserti aggressive nature of the subj

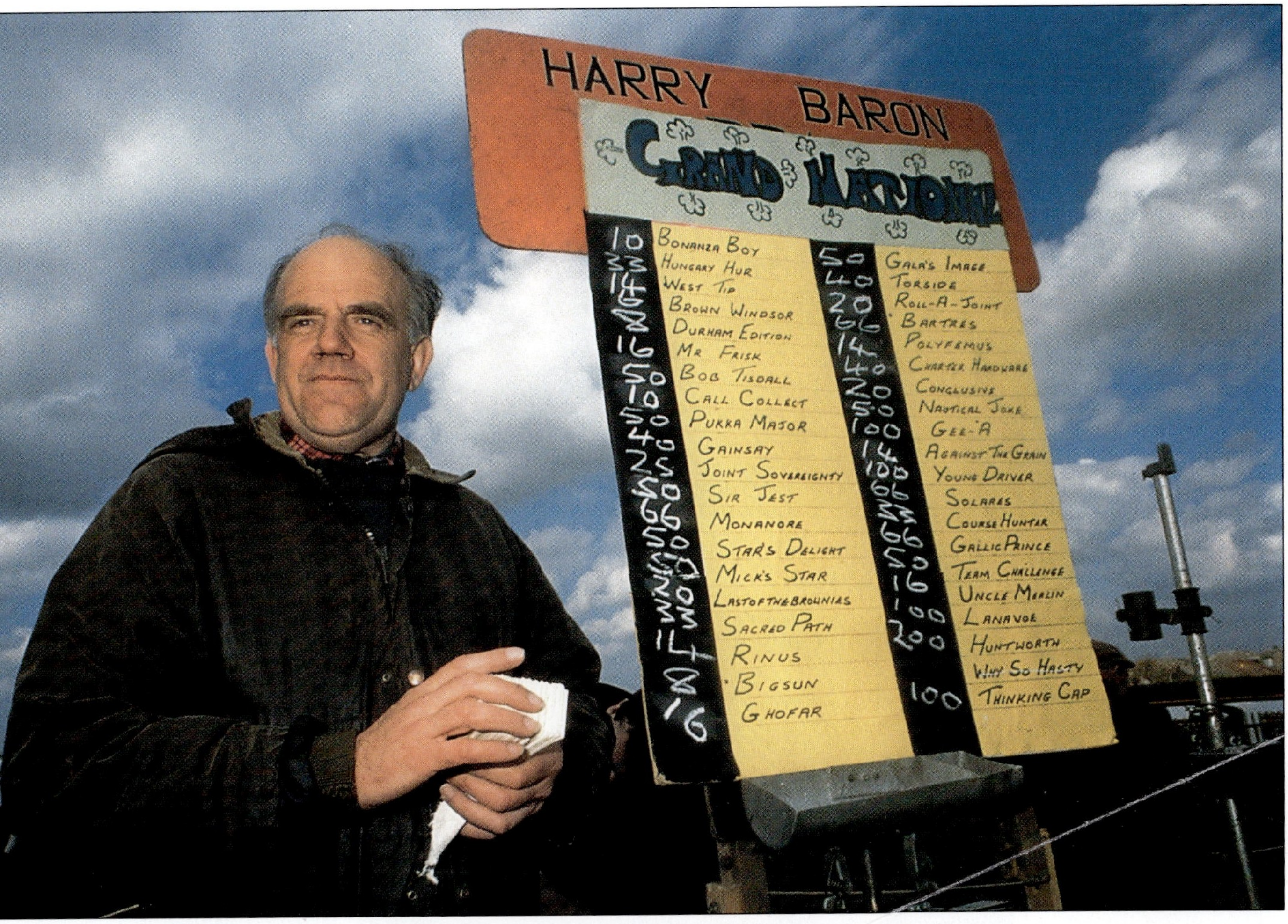

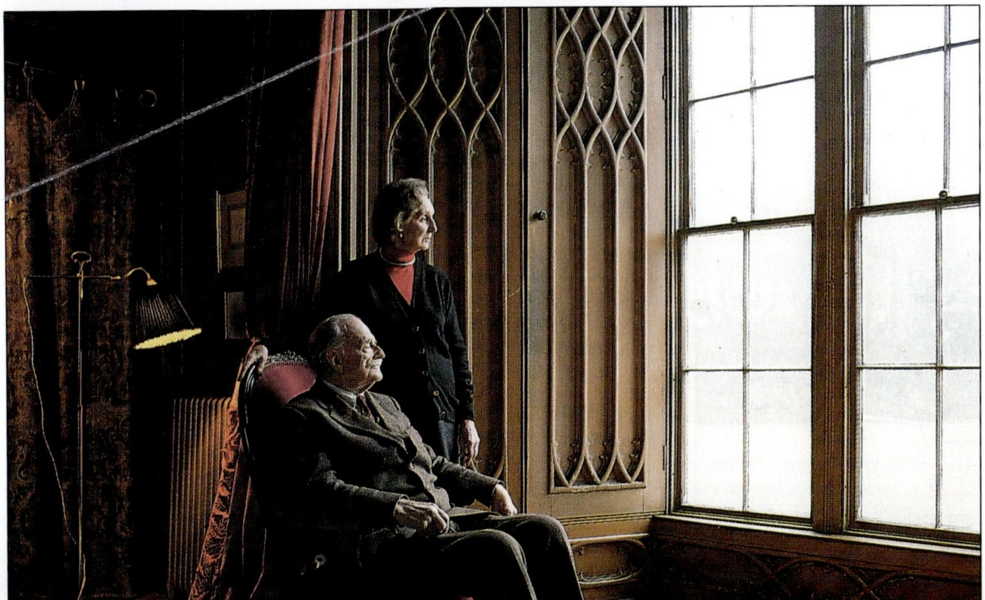

▶ **DISTANT LONGINGS**
A combination of window lighting and the warm illumination from a lamp light this intriguing study of a thoughtful looking couple. The setting and pose imply that the figures are looking out at their country estate. Intentionally exposing for the interior means that the utdoor scene beyond the dow is overexposed and esn't distract from the

6 Strike the right pose

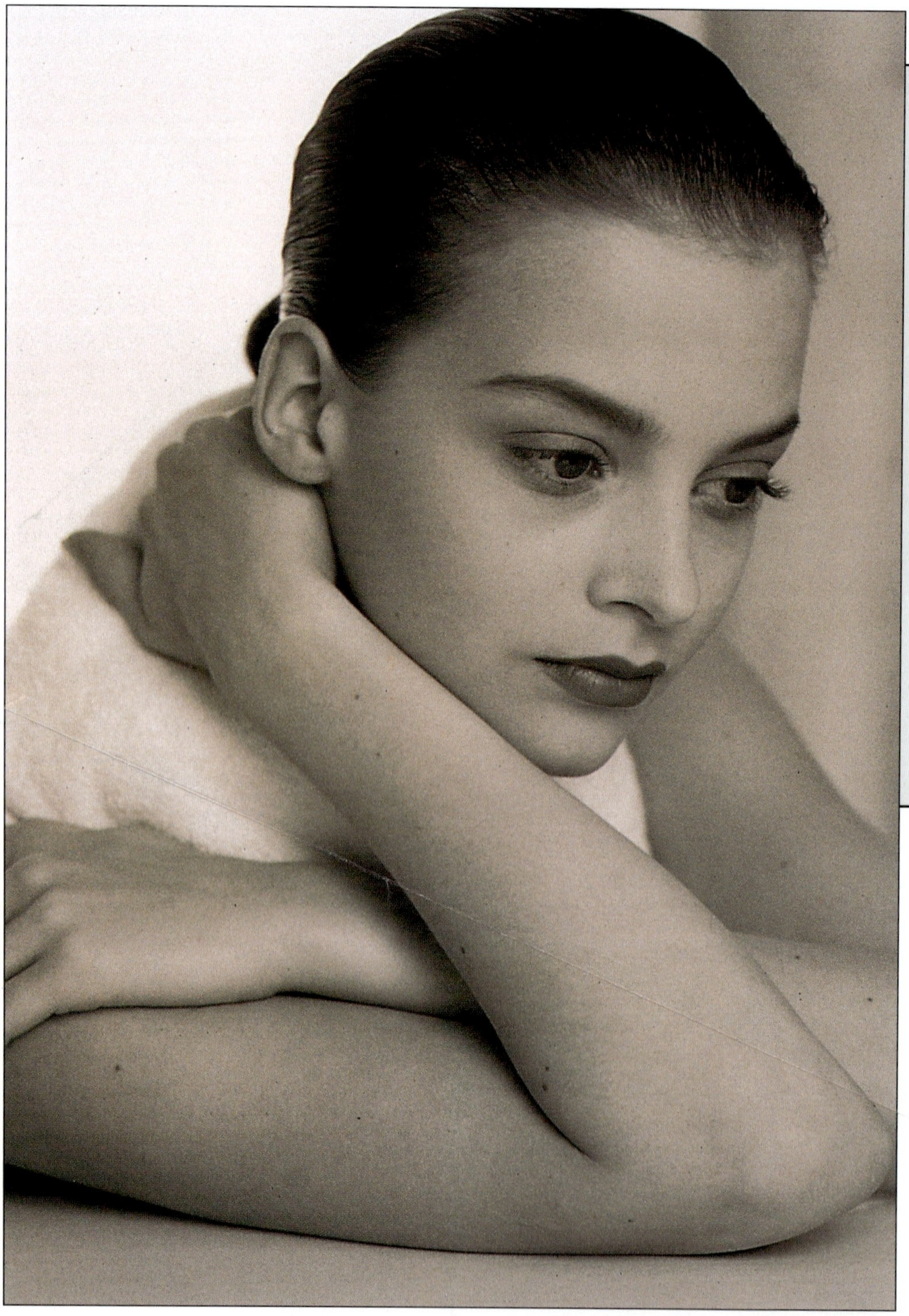

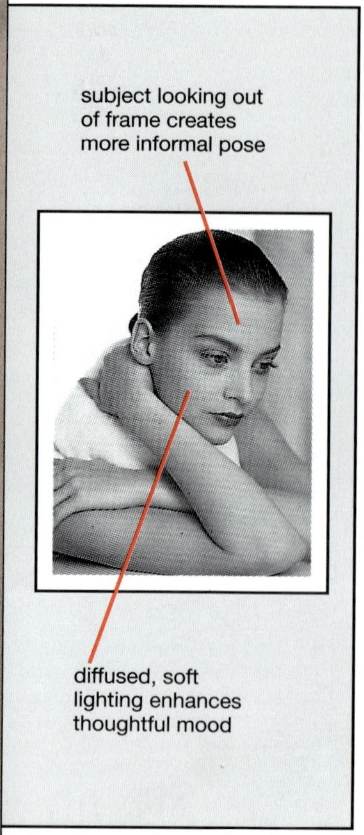

◀ **DAYDREAMING**
The use of black and white film and an unusual pose has produced a dreamy, gentle mood for this picture.

Select a pose which brings out the best in your subject. Extrovert people may be happy to look straight into the lens – this usually conveys an air of formality. For a more informal approach and for those who are camera shy, try asking them to look out of the frame.

Never direct your sitter to hold a pose with which they feel uncomfortable because this results in stilted looking pictures. If a pose looks awkward, allow your subject to move around within a predetermined area until you see through the viewfinder a pose which makes a good composition. If you are photographing the whole figure, check the position of fingers and hands, elbows, legs and feet, to ensure that all are shown to their best advantage.

Once the session has warme
and a rapport has been esta
you can experiment w
unusual poses. An un
posture like lying
instance, or us
unusual way
catching a

7 Shoot a double portrait

Convey the relationship between two individuals by taking a double portrait. Some subjects require little prompting to find the right poses, such as a mother protectively holding her baby. Others require more directing, but always bear in mind how they behave together naturally rather than attempting to impose anything on them.

You can produce an interesting and dynamic composition by placing the faces of your subjects so that they fall on a diagonal. One could be slightly to the left and above the centre of the frame, and the other below and to the right.

Any physical contact between people can have a profound influence on how their relationship appears to the viewer. A man and his son standing together without contact might mean very little but ask the man to put his arm around the boy's shoulders and you can suggest a strong, family bond.

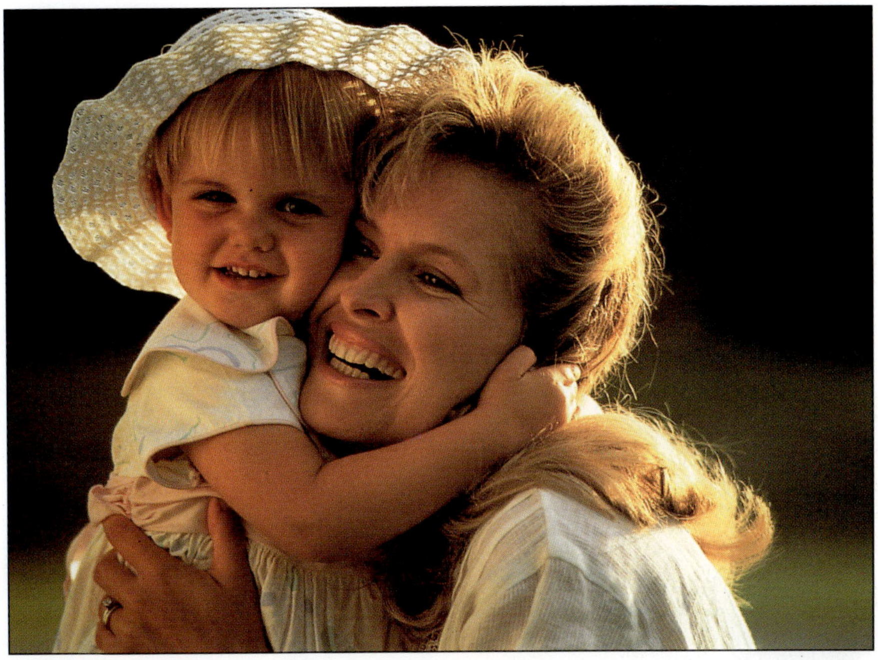

▲ **FAMILY JOY**
This double portrait successfully conveys the warm, loving relationship between mother and child. The photographer chose backlighting to put a highlight in the mother's hair, then lit both faces with a reflector.

8 Create environmental portraits

Concentrating solely on the facial expression of the sitter is only one way of communicating the character of an individual. An equally effective approach is to take a photo which includes the subject's environment. This can both enhance the composition and giving the viewer clues to the subject's personality and occupation.

Shoot people at their place of work. A mechanic in dirty overalls posed in front of a car or an architect with the tools of his trade in front of him tells you much more than a simple head and shoulders shot.

The additional advantage of taking environmental portraits is that you can often capture the subject preoccupied with an activity. A sculptor chiselling at a chunk of stone or a gymnast warming up in a sports hall may be fully aware of the camera. But as they are absorbed in their work, they are unlikely to be concerned about the presence of the photographer.

▶ **DESIGNING THE FUTURE**
Visual clues such as the drawing board and model in the background immediately tell the viewer that the sitters are architects. A high viewpoint creates an unusual and striking portrait.

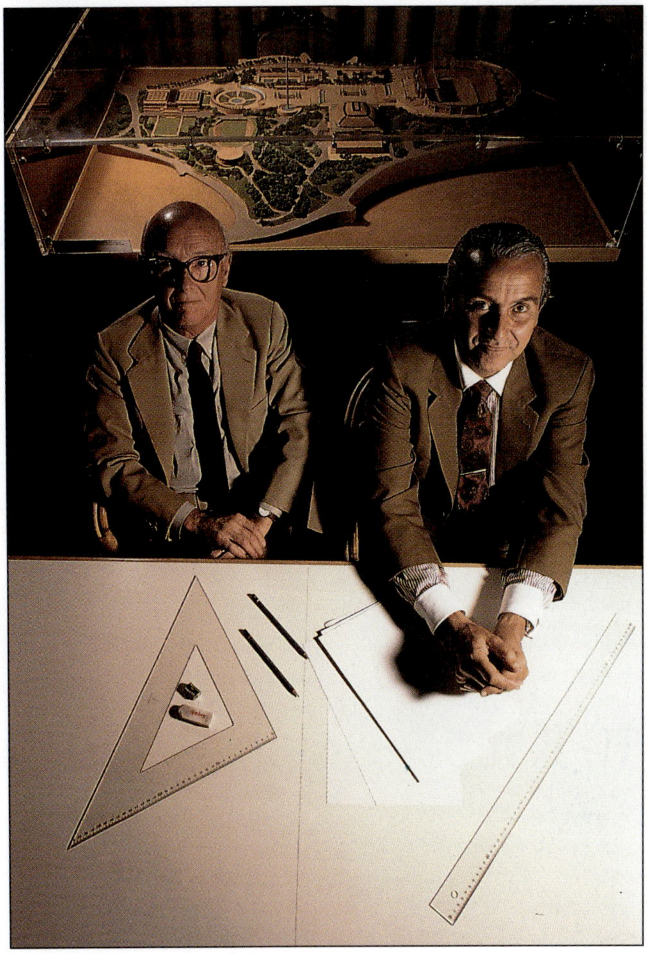

9 Make a self-portrait

Photographing yourself can be highly rewarding. Not only is it fun, but it also gives you the chance to experiment with portraiture without the problem of a reluctant or self-conscious subject.

The simplest way to take your own picture is to hold the camera out at arm's length, point the lens towards you, and press the shutter. Focus on your outstretched hand beforehand so that you can set the right focal distance and stop the lens down to ensure a sharp image.

More handy is a self-timer, which gives you about ten seconds to position yourself once you've set it. Use a tripod and pre-focus on the point where you will be. With an autofocus camera, make sure you will be in the centre of the viewfinder.

For maximum control over a self-portrait you'll need a long cable release or infra-red trigger. Why not use a relatively long exposure and incorporate movements such as jumping in the air for atmospheric, blurred results? Take care to hold the cable release or infra-red trigger in a position where it can't be seen in the final picture.

▼DOUBLE SELF-PORTRAIT
A concealed cable release allowed complete control over this self-portrait. Composition and background were carefully checked beforehand.

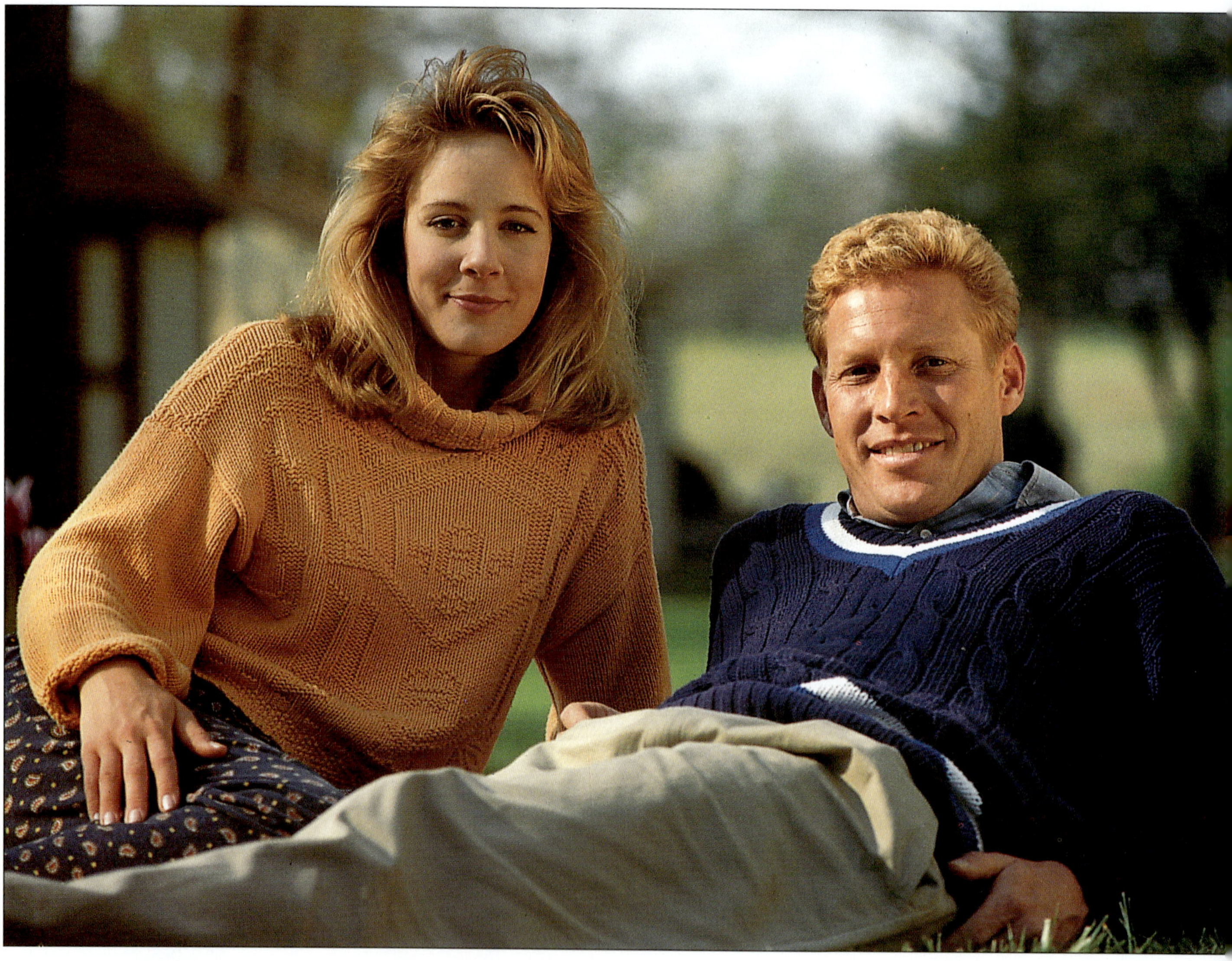

10 Keep sessions short

People can easily become bored and restless so try to keep photo sessions short. If you sense that there are any problems it's always best to take a break and rethink your approach.

Always remain patient with the sitter and try to make them feel involved in the creation of the portrait. Explain to them what you are trying to achieve and ask them for suggestions. You can even encourage them to look through the viewfinder so that they feel more of an active participant in the process.

Using reflectors

One of the simplest and most effective ways of controlling light to get the pictures you want is to use a reflector. You can buy reflectors, or you can make your own quite cheaply and easily.

Whether you are utilizing a single artificial light source, or sunlight streaming through a window, deep shadows are a common problem. Sometimes these add dramatic interest and mood, but more often they obscure details and look unattractive, especially on portraits.

The problem lies in the wide brightness range (high contrast) between the highlight and shadow areas. Film can only record a limited amount of contrast.

An easy way to check the contrast is to look at your subject through half closed eyes. What you see in terms of light and dark is what the camera records. If you can't make out details in the shadow areas, you won't see them in the pictures.

Reducing contrast

One way of dealing with high contrast is to add even more light. By directing light into the shadows, you can reduce the contrast to a point where the film can record detail in both the highlight and shadow areas.

You could tackle contrasty light by moving your subject to a shaded area. Or you can use fill-in flash to lighten the shadow areas without affecting the overall exposure.

Another option is to make use of a reflector. This is a sheet of reflective material that's used to bounce light back on to the subject.

A reflector's usefulness is not limited to outdoor portrait shots. You can use it to equally good effect indoors or in the studio and on a wide range of subjects – anything from a vase of flowers to an articulated lorry.

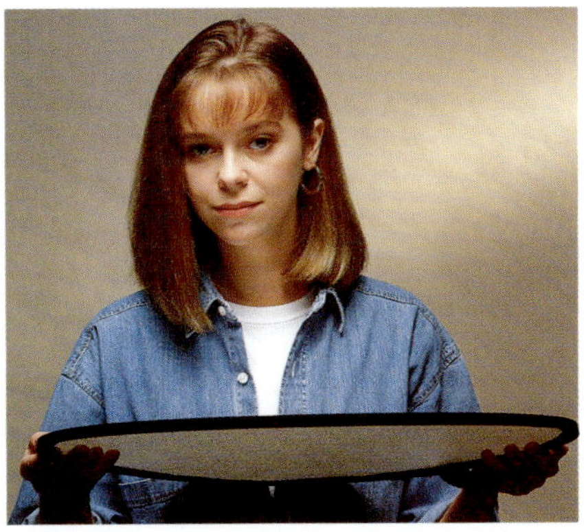

▲ Holding a reflector under the chin bounces light back up into the subject's face – your model can do this herself.

▼ The reflector lightens the shadow areas and produces a more flattering portrait of the model.

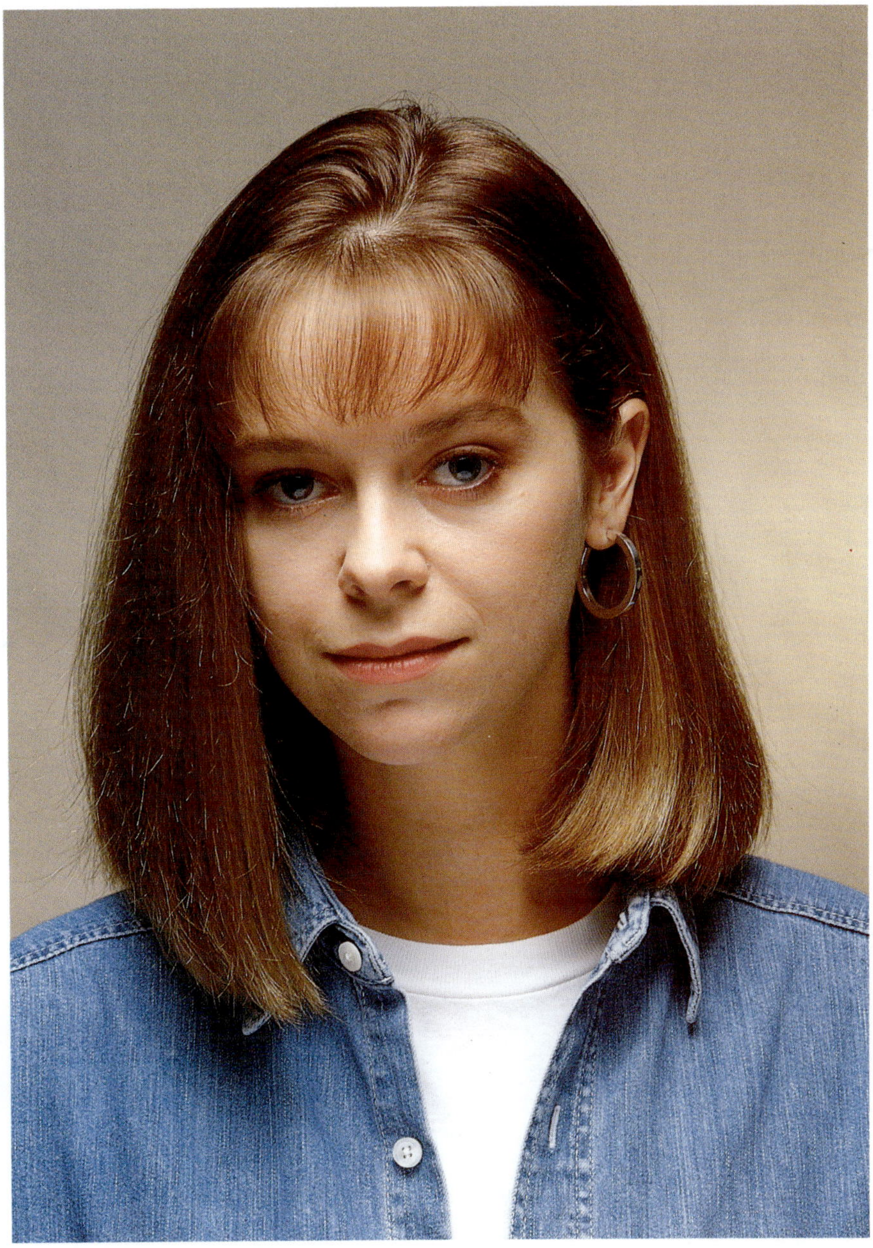

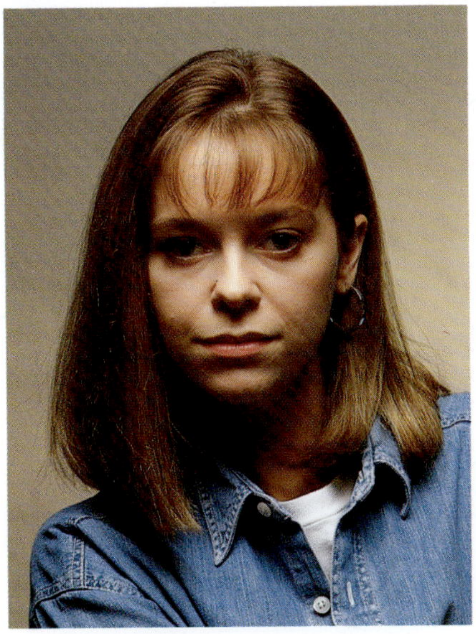

▲ Harsh shadow under the model's eyes, nose and chin obscures facial details and ruins what is otherwise an attractive portrait.

Controlling brightness

A reflector's efficiency – the brightness of the light which it reflects – depends upon a variety of factors.

❏ **Surface finish** Shiny surfaces reflect more light than matt surfaces. Mirrors are perfect reflectors – they reflect all of the light that's falling on them.

❏ **Distance from subject** The closer a reflector is to the subject, the more light it reflects on to the subject. The brightness of reflected light drops off sharply as you move a reflector away from a subject.

For portrait shots, begin by positioning a reflector about one metre away from your subject and then move it closer and further away until you get the effect you want.

❏ **Size** Big reflectors reflect more light than small reflectors.

❏ **Available light** The brighter the available light, the brighter the light that's reflected. The light falling on a subject from a reflector is always weaker than the light from the main source – unless you're using a mirror, in which case the brightness of the reflected lights is equal to the brightness of the main light.

Types of reflector

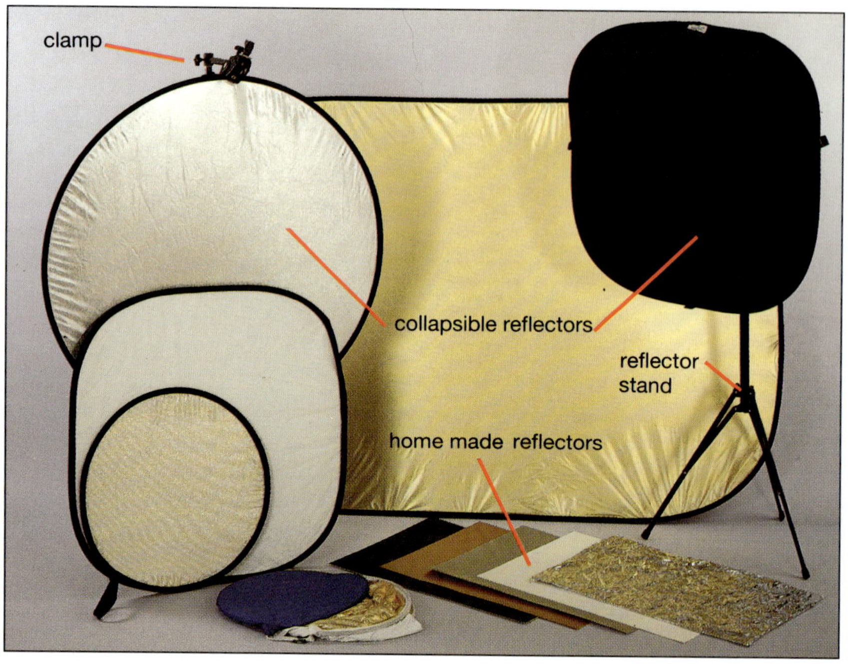

Reflectors come in a variety of shapes, sizes and materials. You can buy specially designed reflectors from camera shops – collapsible versions pack down small and are easy to carry around. You can also buy reflective material from professional photographic retailers if you want to make your own reflectors.

To save money, you can use a wide range of reflective materials found around the house. Stick kitchen foil to a backing card (crumple it to produce a softer reflection), stretch white bed sheets over a home made frame or paint plywood white, gold or silver.

If you have gone out unprepared, you can use a newspaper, white towel or white T-shirt as an emergency reflector.

Do it yourself

Home made reflectors are quick, easy and cheap to make. The simplest and most versatile design requires:

❏ A length of ¾in diameter plastic water pipe.
❏ Four right angle joints.
❏ A dozen bulldog clips.
❏ A white bed sheet.

You can alter the size of this reflector to suit the subject you're photographing.

1 MATERIALS
Cut the pipe into four pieces – the lengths are dictated by the size and shape of reflector you want. 90cm x 60cm is an ideal size for head and shoulder portraits – so you'll need two 90cm lengths and two 60cm lengths. Cut more pieces if you want extra large reflectors or a variety of shapes and sizes.

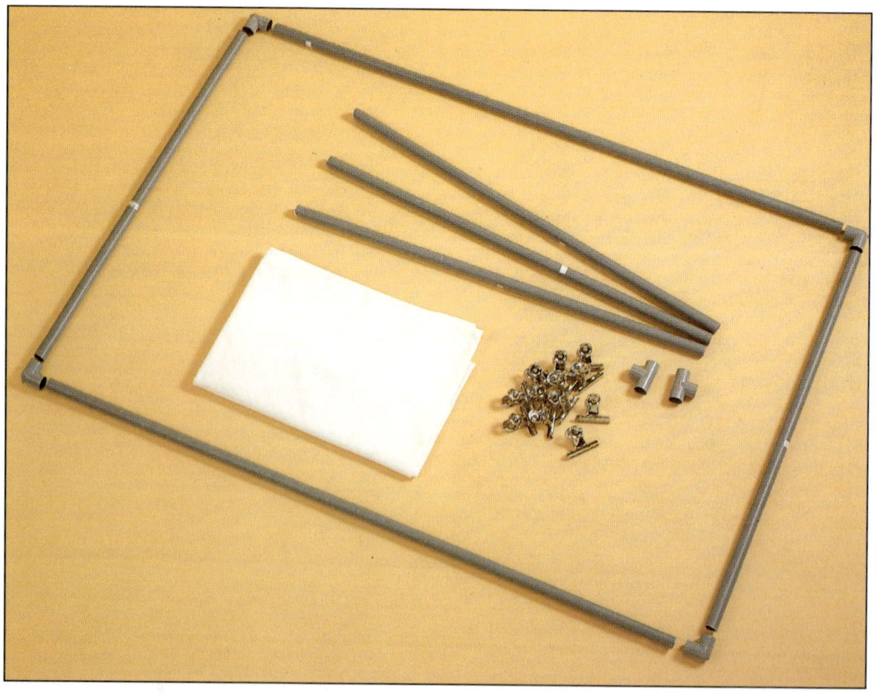

The quality of reflected light

As well as controlling the brightness of reflected light, you can also control its quality – how hard or soft it is – and its colour. Several factors determine the quality of reflected light.

❏ **Surface finish** Shiny surfaces reflect a harsh, directional light that gives pinpoint highlights and shadows which have well defined edges. Textured surfaces soften the light.

❏ **Size** Reflectors that are large in comparison to the subject reflect a softer light than smaller sizes, which produce a more concentrated and directional beam.

❏ **The shape** of the reflector affects the quality of reflected light. A flat reflector scatters light and produces a soft effect. But if you bend a reflector into a concave shape, it works in the same way as a spotlight, producing a hard, directional reflection.

❏ **Colour** You can add colour to the shadow areas by using a coloured reflector. The intensity of the colour in the shadow areas depends on the brightness of the reflected light – the brighter the reflection, the deeper the colour.

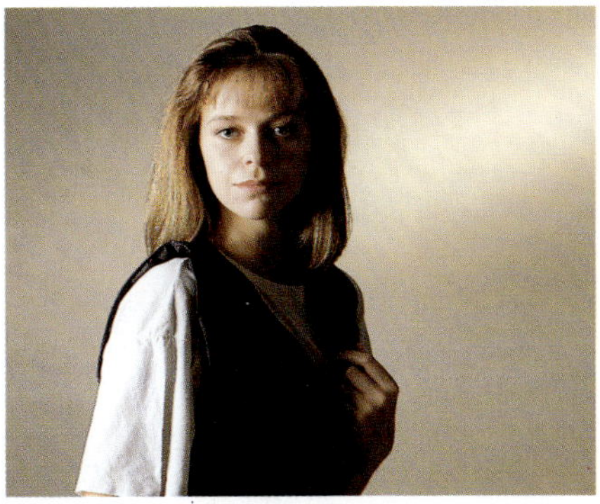

▲ ***With no reflector, sidelighting throws half the model's face into deep shadow.***

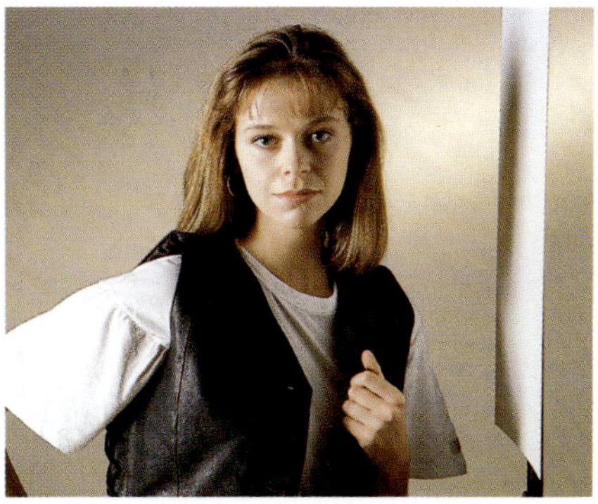

▲ ***A matte white board placed opposite the main light source reflects a soft light into the shadows.***

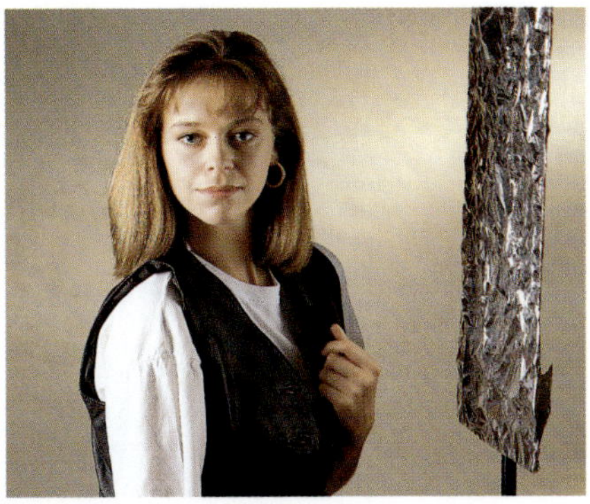

▲ ***Crumpled silver foil gives a hard, cool reflection. Smooth foil would give a harder light still.***

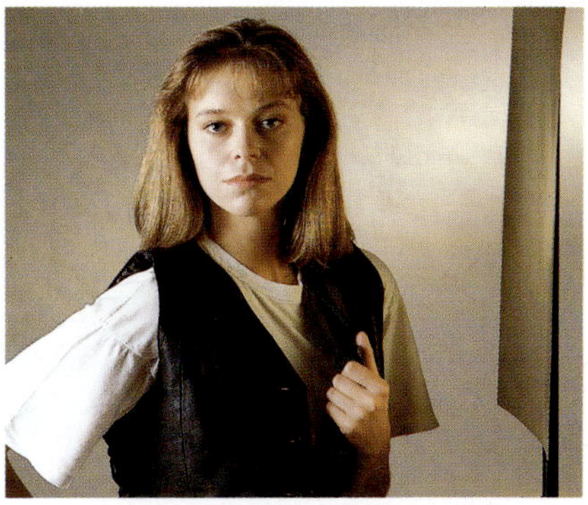

▲ ***Gold board reflects a similar quality of light to the silver board, but introduces a warmer glow.***

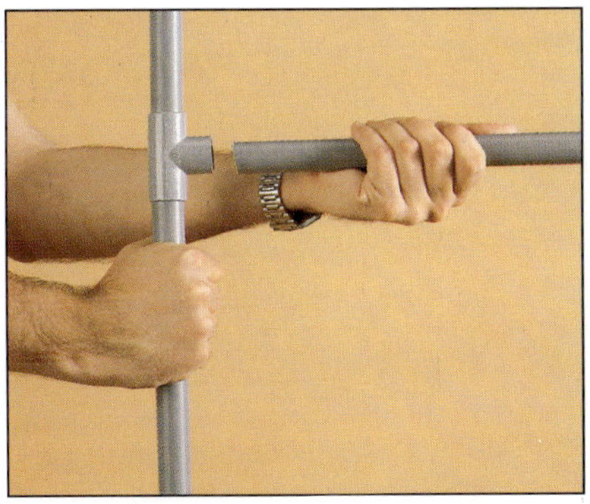

2 CONSTRUCTING THE FRAME
Fix the lengths together using the plastic joints at each corner. If you want to make a large reflector, cut two extra pieces for the sides and join them using three way joints half way down either side. Slot both ends of another piece of pipe into these joints, so it runs across the width of the frame to increase its rigidity.

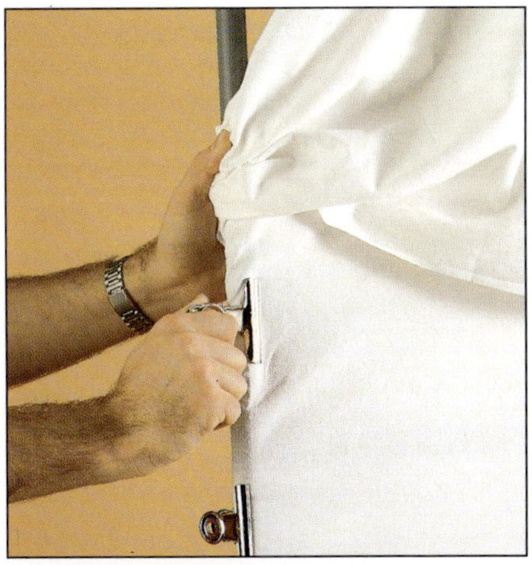

3 ATTACHING THE REFLECTOR
Place the sheet over the frame and secure it using the bulldog clips. When all of the clips are in place, twist them round 90° – this tightens the material and gets rid of any creases. Secure the reflector to a lighting stand.

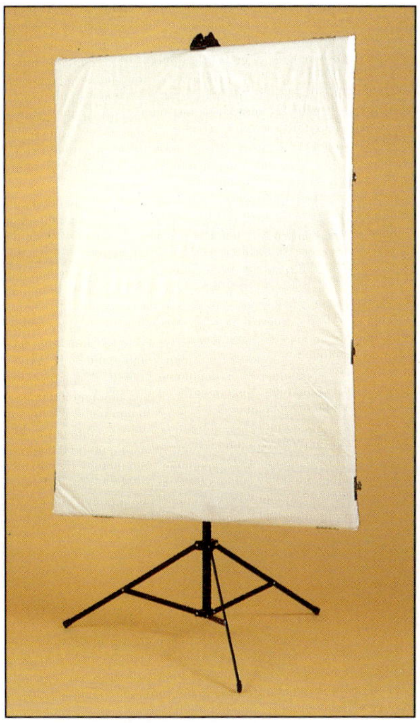

Using a reflector

Getting the best results from your reflector requires patience and a little practice. You need to try positioning it at various angles to find the most pleasing result. Trial and error is the only way to learn how to use a reflector effectively.

Be careful not to lighten the shadow too much as this can spoil the shot by making it too flat.

If possible, get somebody else to hold the reflector and move it around for you. This leaves you free to look through the camera's viewfinder and judge which is the best position for lighting and composition.

Alternatively, you can use a small tripod and tape the reflector to the tripod head or use a lighting stand together with a screw-on clamp attachment. These types of support let you tilt and angle the reflector and lock it into position.

Set ups

The usual reflector position for portrait shots is on the opposite side of the subject to the main light. Any light spilling over from the main light is bounced back into the shadow areas.

When the main light is overhead it tends to throw deep shadows under your subject's eyes, nose and chin. Positioning a reflector just out of shot under your subject's chin bounces light back up into their face and softens the shadows.

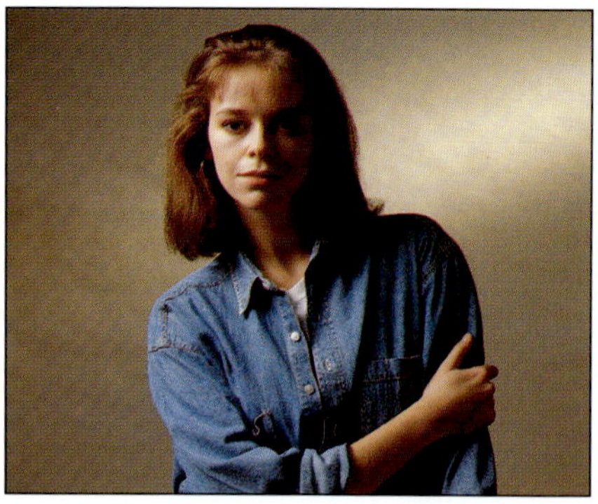

▲ ***Bright light from above and to one side throws too many shadows for one reflector to cope with.***

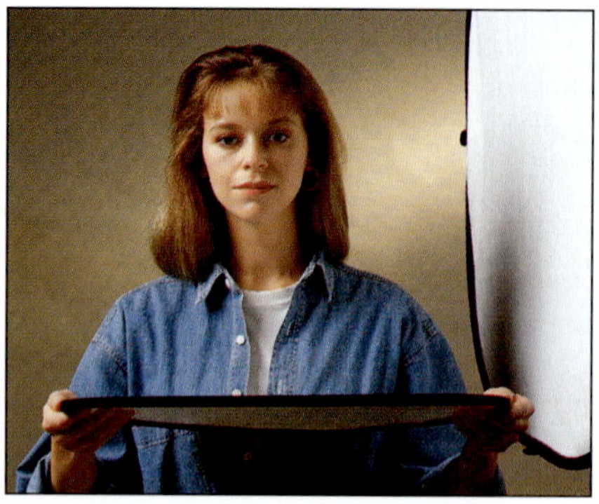

▲ ***Placing a reflector on the shadow side and another under the subject's chin lightens all of the shadows.***

Doubling up

When the main light is high above the subject, but to one side, it throws shadows down one side of a subject's face and under their eyes, nose and chin. A single reflector may not be able to cope with all of the shadows. Position one reflector to the side of your subject and another under their chin.

You can also use your reflector to provide the main frontal light. This is a useful technique if you're shooting at midday, when the light can be harsh and unflattering. Try moving your subject into the shade of a wall, bush, or even a nearby car. Position the reflector in front of your subject so that the sunlight is bounced back on to their face. The result will be a softer, more flattering light.

Watch the bounce

BACK TO BASICS

The most important point to bear in mind is that reflected light bounces off the reflective surface at the same angle as the main light strikes it. For example, if you shine a lamp straight at a reflector, the light is reflected straight back at the light source.

But if you position the lamp so the light strikes the reflector at a 30° angle, the reflected light bounces off the reflector at 30°.

So, before you position the reflector, judge the angle of the main light – this will help you to use the reflector to maximum effect.

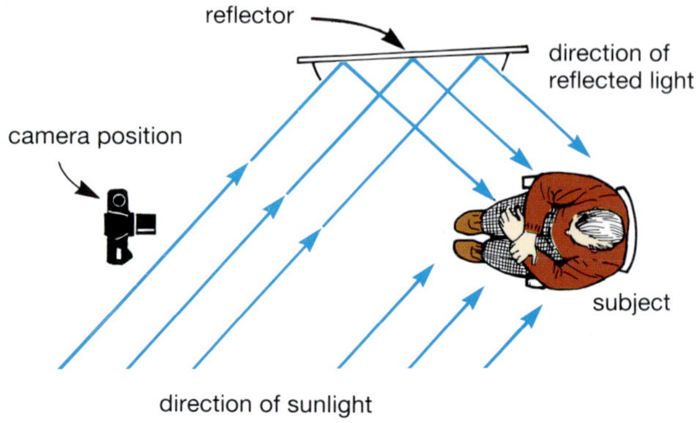

Paint it black

While too much contrast looks unattractive, totally even, flat lighting can look boring. A certain amount of contrast is necessary to emphasize features and form. When the light is very diffused you can increase contrast by using a piece of black card or black velvet to absorb stray light and deepen shadows. Position it in the same way you would position a reflector.

▼ ***No absorbers***

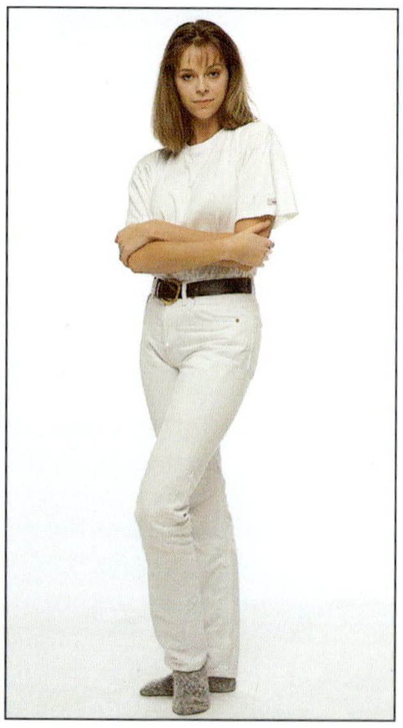

▼ ***Absorbers both sides***

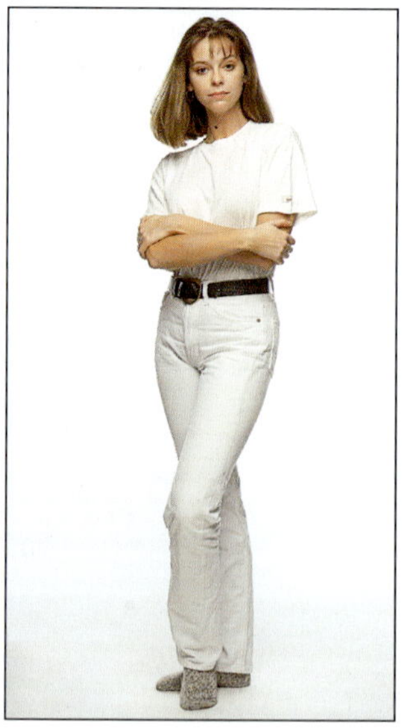

Tungsten studio lighting

Many professionals use both studio flash and tungsten lighting. However, tungsten lights cost quite a bit less than flash to buy and they are perfect for learning the art of creative lighting.

Studio photography affords total control over the way you light your subject. As you are not dependent on the vagaries of sunlight you can use as much – or as little – light as you wish. You position the light source for the exact effect you are after, and you dictate the quality of the light to control mood. In addition, you can repeat lighting set ups day or night for consistent results.

But before you can launch into studio photography you need to equip yourself with a set of lights. The choice is between studio flash and tungsten lighting.

Tungsten advantages

Flash has many advantages over tungsten (the pros of flash are covered separately, later), but it has one major drawback for the newcomer to studio photography – its high price. You can buy a three light tungsten kit, with a selection of accessories, for the same price as a single, middle of the range flash head. The extra lights afford far more versatility, and you can explore many more lighting set ups.

Apart from price, tungsten lighting offers other benefits. For a start, it is a constant light source – like daylight – so you can see the effect of a lighting set up precisely. Flash heads have a tungsten modelling lamp, but this never shows exactly where light from the flash tube will fall.

Another benefit of using a constant light source is that you can use your camera's built-in metering to measure exposures. With flash you have to buy a separate flashmeter.

Tungsten lighting also has a particular quality to it that suits certain subjects. The stunning studio shots of Hollywood stars from the thirties and forties were all taken using tungsten lights.

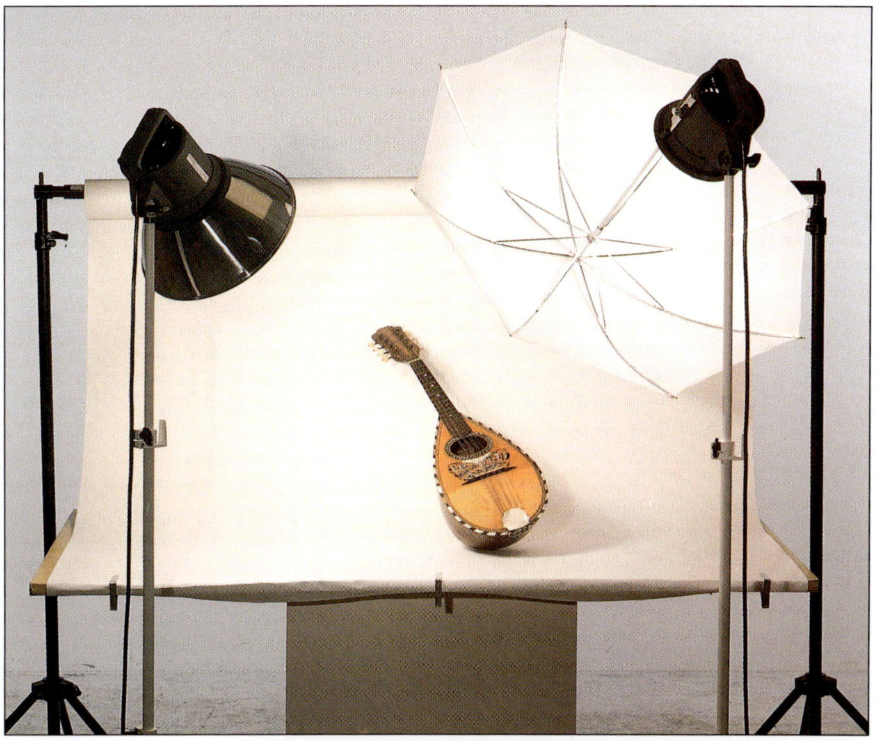

▲ A tungsten lighting kit is relatively inexpensive to buy – it costs about the same as a single flash head. It also offers far more flexibility in use compared with a single flash head.

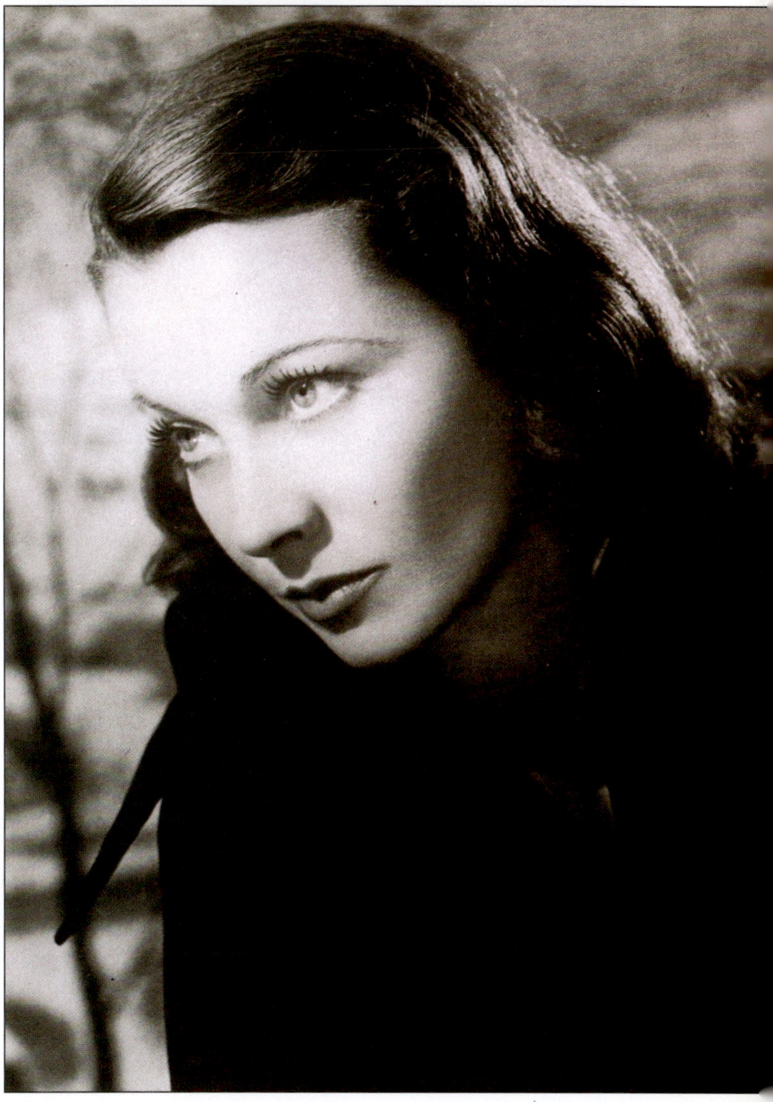

▶ All the famous Hollywood studio portraits from the 1930s and 1940s were taken under tungsten lights,. like this study of Vivien Leigh. The quality of the lighting is still much loved by today's portrait photographers.

Types of tungsten lamps

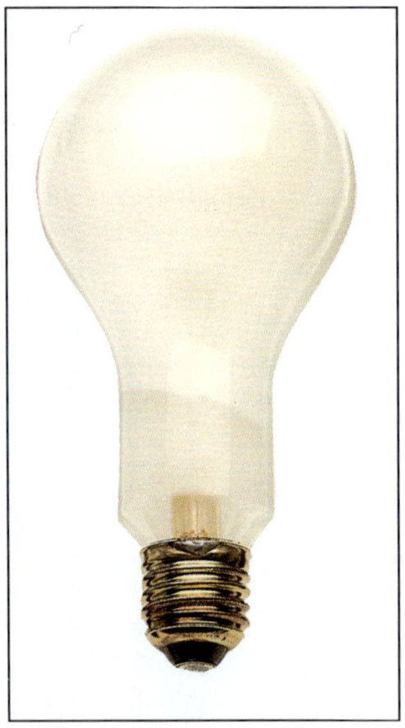

▲ ***'Photopearl' or 'Hundred hour' or 'Nitraphot' lamps burn at 3200K, slightly redder than photofloods. Type B tungsten films are balanced for this colour temperature, while Type A (rare today) is balanced for the 3400K of photofloods.***

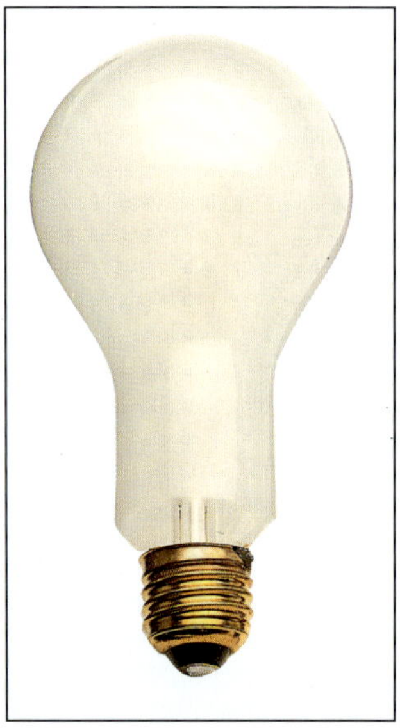

▲ ***Photofloods are cheap to buy, but last only a few hours. The difference in colour temperature can be ignored for most purposes, especially with modern 'warm' films. Alternatively, you can use a weak (81A) warming filter.***

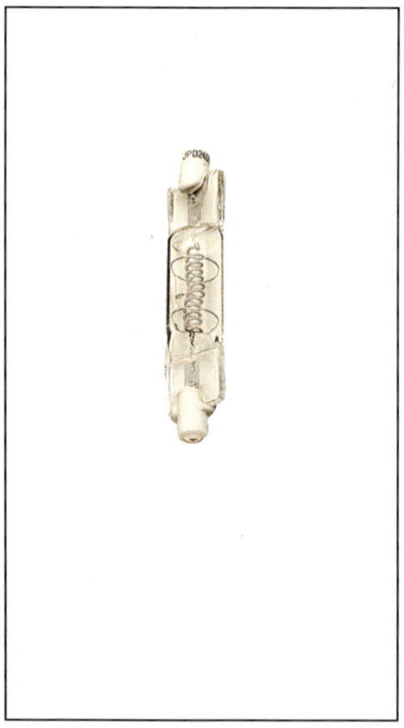

▲ ***Tungsten-halogen lamps burn brighter, for longer and more consistently than other types of tungsten lamp. However, you do need to be extremely careful about handling the quartz bulb, as grease on your hands damages the lamp.***

Pin positions

Tungsten-halogen lamps come in two varieties. You can buy 2-pin single ended lamps and 2-pin double ended lamps.

Single ended types should be fitted in an upright position. Double ended types fit horizontally.

It is very important – for your safety and the long life of the lamps – to ensure that you use them only in the correct position.

There are three types of tungsten lamp, each of which has its own characteristics.

Photopearls are similar to domestic bulbs, but they work at higher wattages, ranging from 275-1000W. They also have a controlled colour temperature of 3,200K and last for up to 100 hours.

You can buy these lamps with a blue coating on the glass, which balances the colour temperature of the light to daylight balanced film. This is useful when you want to mix tungsten light with daylight, without having to filter either the lens or the tungsten light source. However, coated versions are generally more expensive than the standard, uncoated variety.

Photofloods look rather similar to Photopearls and use the same fittings, but they are cheaper and have a slightly higher colour temperature of 3,400K. They also have a shorter working life – sometimes just 2-3 hours of intermittent use.

A disadvantage of both types of lamp is that when the tungsten filament is heated it leaves a black deposit on the inside of the glass bulb. This lowers the brightness and the colour temperature of the lamp's output.

Tungsten-halogen lamps are the smallest, most efficient and most expensive type of tungsten lamp. They use a coiled tungsten filament to give a hard, point source of light. The filament is housed in a quartz bulb, which is filled with halogen gas. This has two advantages over the glass bulbs used in Photopearls and Photofloods.

Filling the bulb with halogen gas prevents the tungsten leaving a black deposit on the inside of the quartz. This means that the lamp maintains a constant output and colour temperature throughout its entire life.

In addition, quartz bulbs are stronger than glass bulbs, so the pressure of the gas inside the bulb can be increased. This extends the life of the lamp. The lifespan of halogen lamps varies widely, but it can be as much as twice the length of Photopearls.

Tungsten halogen lamps are available in wattages ranging from 200-10,000W.

What is a tungsten lamp?

A tungsten lamp is described as an incandescent light source. This means that it glows when it is heated. There are different types of tungsten lamp, but they all work on the same principle.

The lamps comprise a transparent bulb, which houses a fine filament of tungsten metal. The tungsten filament is connected to an electrical fitting. When the lamp is switched on, electricity passes through the electrical fitting and along the tungsten filament, causing it to heat up. When the filament is heated it glows brightly and radiates light.

Some tungsten lamps have a bunched coil of filament, while others have a straight length. The lamps that use a coiled filament give a harder, point source of light.

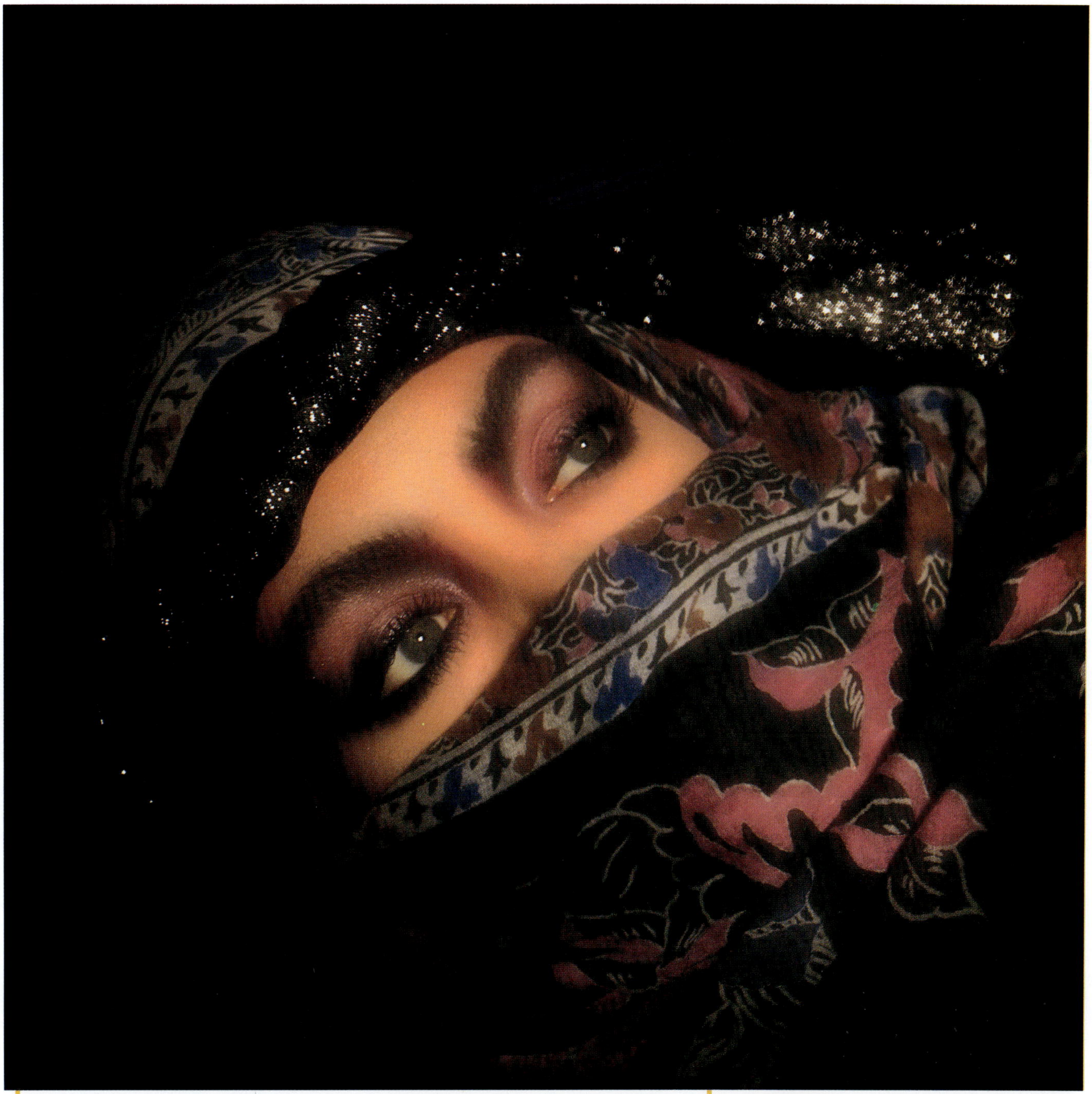

Colour temperature

Tungsten lamps give out a warmer, more orangey coloured light than flash units, or the sun. This is because they are said to have a lower colour temperature. So if you use daylight balanced film, your pictures will show a noticeable orange cast.

The easiest way to gain natural looking results under tungsten lighting is to use Type B tungsten film. This is balanced to the light from Photopearl and tungsten-halogen lamps.

▲ ***Beauty photographers use unfiltered tungsten lighting to give pictures a warm feel. In this shot, the main light came from a studio flash unit, but the photographer added a touch of tungsten fill-in to warm up the skin tones.***

Photofloods give a slightly bluer light. So you'll need to fit an 81A warm up filter over the lens or an equivalent lighting gel over the lamp for neutral results on tungsten balanced film. To shoot daylight film under tungsten light, use an 80A filter for Photopearls or an 80B for Photofloods.

Tip: Skin contact

One drawback of using tungsten-halogen lamps is that quartz is very sensitive to the grease on your hands. Alkalis in the grease attack the quartz and reduce the lifespan of the lamp.

Therefore, you should never touch a tungsten-halogen lamp with your bare hands. Always keep the lamp in its protective plastic wrapper until it is fitted into the light.

Which lighting unit?

There is a reasonable choice of tungsten lights available for both amateur and professional use. However, there are still fewer tungsten lighting units to choose from, compared with the wide range of studio flash heads on the market.

The most basic types of tungsten light are simply a lamp fitting, surrounded by a polished or painted concave reflector. More advanced versions have interchangeable reflectors and let you move the lamp fitting backwards and forwards within the reflectors. The advantage of this system is that you can control precisely the spread of light.

Other units have a lamp fitted inside a spotlight housing. This is made up of a curved reflector behind the lamp, and a simple lens in front. You use the lens to focus the light into a broad or narrow beam.

If you are thinking of buying new tungsten lights, look for units that have a thermoplastic outer casing. Tungsten lights become very hot during use, and it is all too easy to burn yourself on metal casings. Thermoplastic solves the problem, because it doesn't conduct much heat.

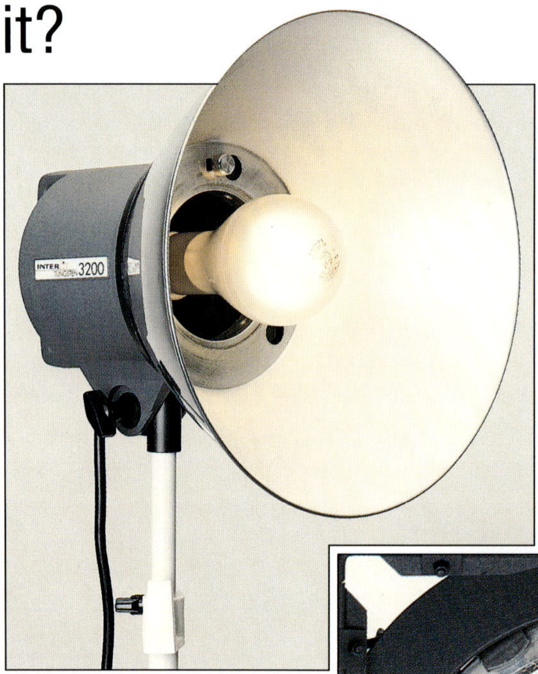

▲ This tungsten light is aimed at amateur photographers. It uses Photoflood lamps up to 500W and accepts a range of reflectors. It is an ideal choice if you are trying studio photography for the first time.

▼ Professional photographers use tungsten lights with tungsten-halogen lamps. This model is more robust than the amateur version, and it has an output of 800W. However, it costs three or four times as much.

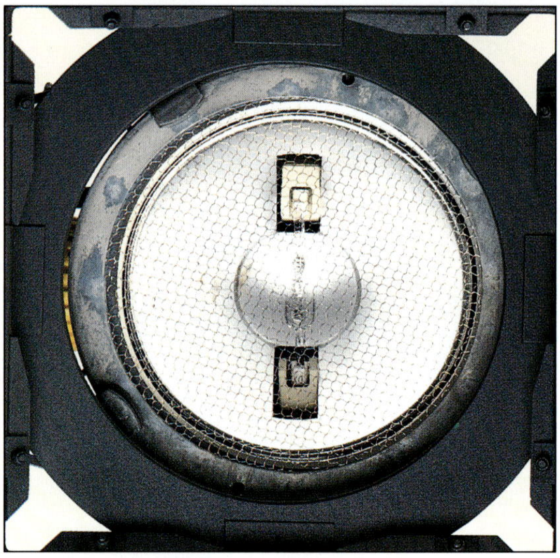

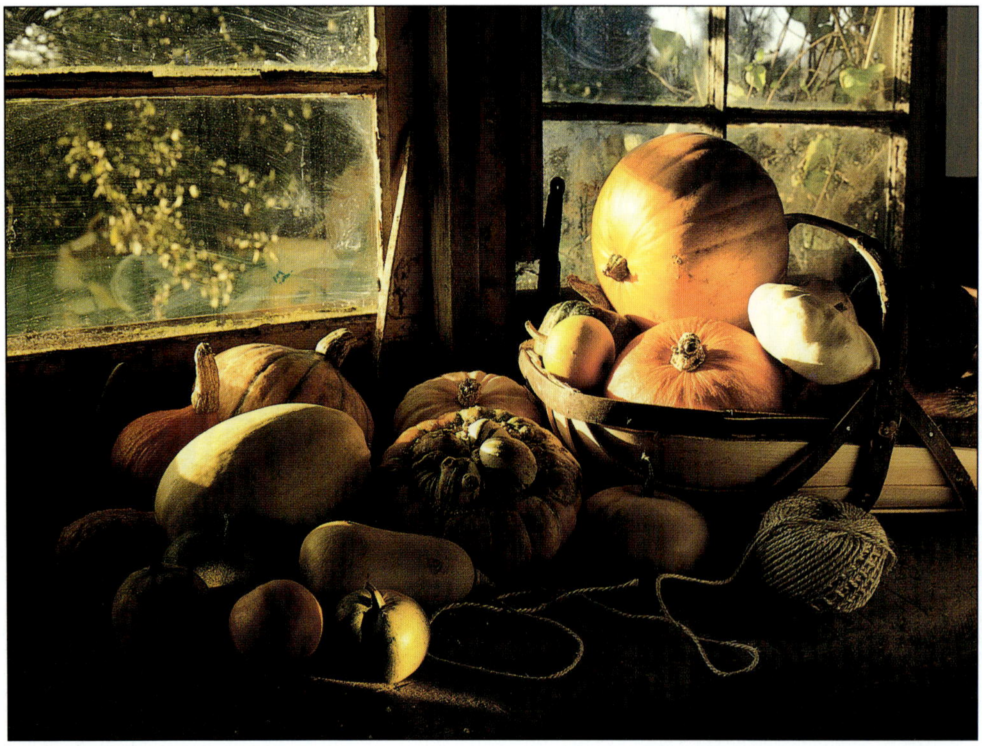

◀ Tungsten lights are ideal for lighting many types of still life. If you load up with slow film and set narrow apertures make sure you use a sturdy tripod. Here, the photographer used a shaft of tungsten light to pick out the fruit in the foreground.

Tip

DIY safety handle

If you own an old tungsten light with a metal rather than a thermoplastic casing, you can avoid burning yourself by fixing a wooden handle to the back of the unit. Wood is a less efficient conductor of heat than metal, so the handle won't get as hot.

Tungsten lighting accessories

Buying a couple of tungsten studio lights lets you explore the basics of studio lighting. Adding a complete range of accessories lets you stretch your creativity to the limits.

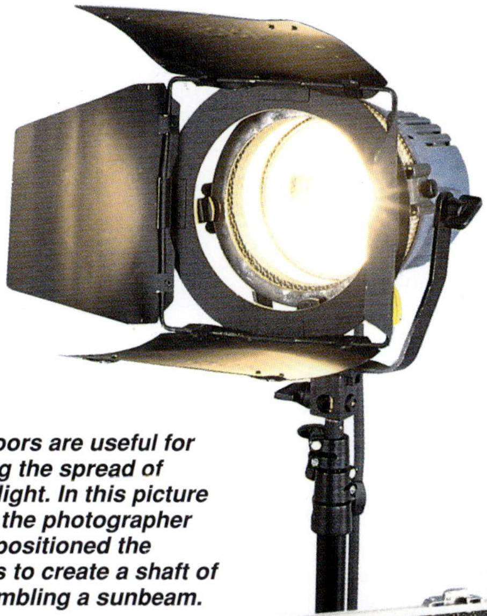

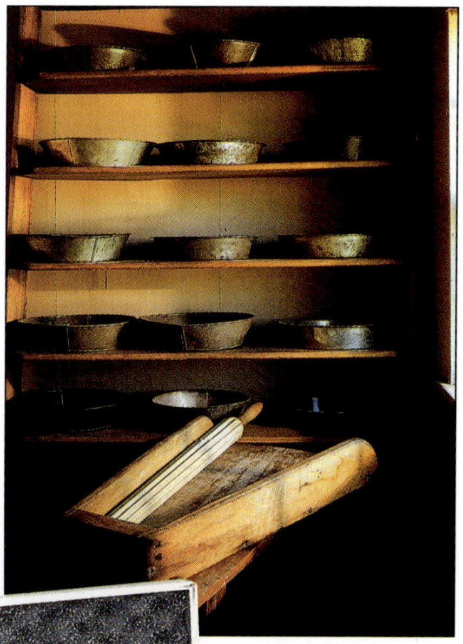

▶ Barndoors are useful for controlling the spread of tungsten light. In this picture (far right) the photographer carefully positioned the barndoors to create a shaft of light resembling a sunbeam.

▼ Some manufacturers offer their tungsten lighting equipment in the form of a kit. Buying a kit makes sense if you can afford it, as it contains all the lights and accessories you need to get started.

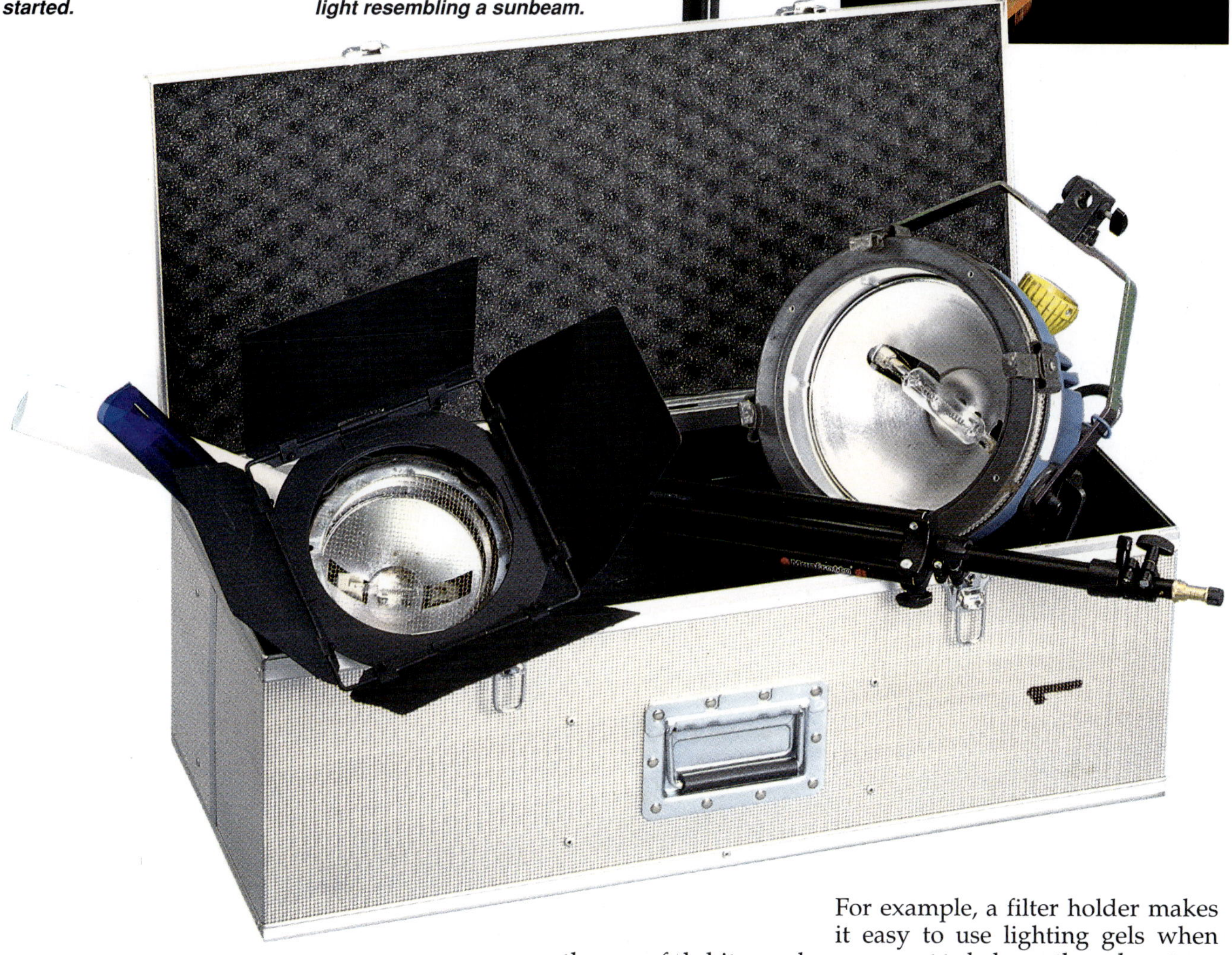

One of the advantages of buying tungsten lights, as opposed to studio flash heads, is that the money you save on the lighting units can be spent on a range of lighting accessories. These may include lighting stands, different sized reflector dishes, filter holders or numerous other useful bits and pieces that make shooting in the studio much easier and far more fun.

While a selection of tungsten lights lets you tackle a wide range of subjects and lighting techniques, your studio photography is seriously restricted if you don't have access to certain key accessories. For example, a filter holder makes it easy to use lighting gels when you want to balance the colour temperature of tungsten lamps to daylight balanced film.

Similarly, having boomstands, barndoors, reflectors, scrims and umbrellas at your disposal lets you control the direction, brightness and quality of the light, for absolute control over the appearance of the final image.

Lighting accessories

When you are choosing a tungsten lighting kit it is a good idea to budget for a few essential accessories – even if money is tight and it means buying one less light. The added flexibility the accessories offer is well worth the sacrifice.

Reflectors come in a range of different shapes, sizes and finishes. They affect the quality of the light. Buying a range of reflectors lets you choose whether to use hard or soft lighting. However, not all tungsten lights will accept interchangeable reflectors.

Umbrellas are useful for softening the harsh light from a tungsten lamp. However, the output of most tungsten lamps is too weak for you to bounce it off the umbrella. Instead, it is more practical to buy translucent (also known as 'shoot-thru') umbrellas, and shine the light through them. This gives a similar effect to flashlight fired through a softbox.

Barndoors are hinged sheets of metal or plastic that fix on to the sides of the reflector, or lamp casing. By opening or closing them you can control the spread of light. But never close them completely when the lamp is switched on (see Safety first).

Filter holders are simply metal frames that you fix on to the lighting stand or reflector and position in front of the lamp to hold lighting gels.

Lighting stands are very important. You must be able to position your lights exactly where you want them for the best results. Boom stands, which have a moveable cross-arm and counterweight, are especially handy.

By attaching a lamp to the fitting on the end of the boom arm you can place the light in almost any position – you can even set up a lamp directly over the top of your camera, for beauty photography.

Scrims are made up from sheets of translucent trace or wire gauze. When you position a scrim in front of a lamp it reduces the brightness of the lamp's output – usually by one stop. However, it doesn't affect the quality or colour temperature of the light.

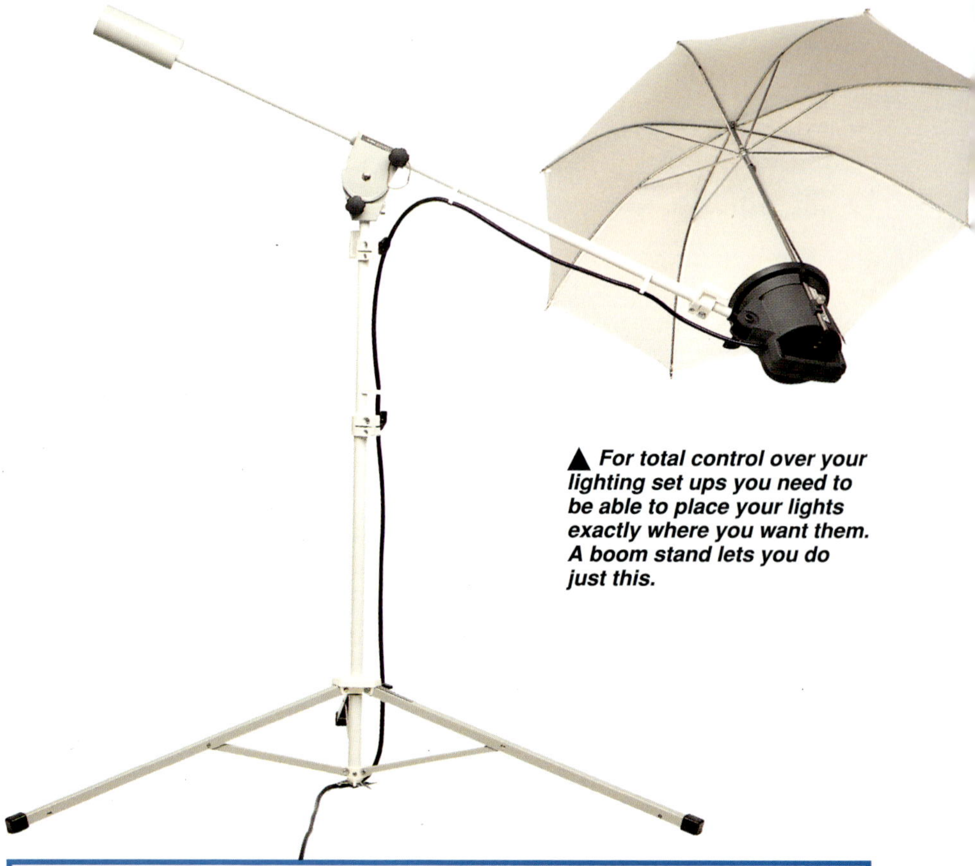

▲ ***For total control over your lighting set ups you need to be able to place your lights exactly where you want them. A boom stand lets you do just this.***

Reflectors

The type of reflector you use affects the quality of the light reaching your subject. Reflectors with a shiny metal finish inside give a brighter, harder light than those that are painted matt white inside.

Deep, narrow reflectors tend to give harder, more directional light than shallow, wide reflectors.

Shallow, wide reflectors with a matt white finish and a direct light shield – a metal disc placed directly over the lamp – give a soft, indirect quality of light. This is an ideal reflector to choose for beauty photography.

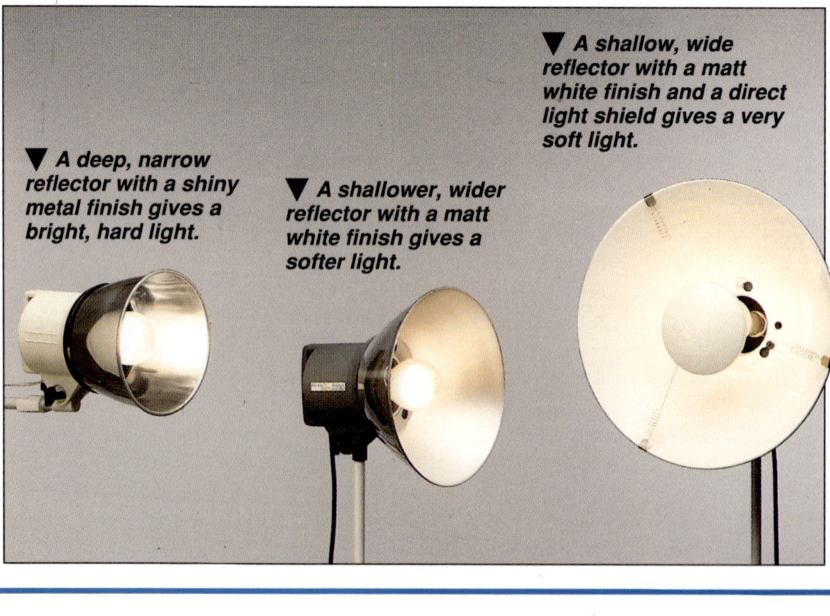

▼ ***A deep, narrow reflector with a shiny metal finish gives a bright, hard light.***

▼ ***A shallower, wider reflector with a matt white finish gives a softer light.***

▼ ***A shallow, wide reflector with a matt white finish and a direct light shield gives a very soft light.***

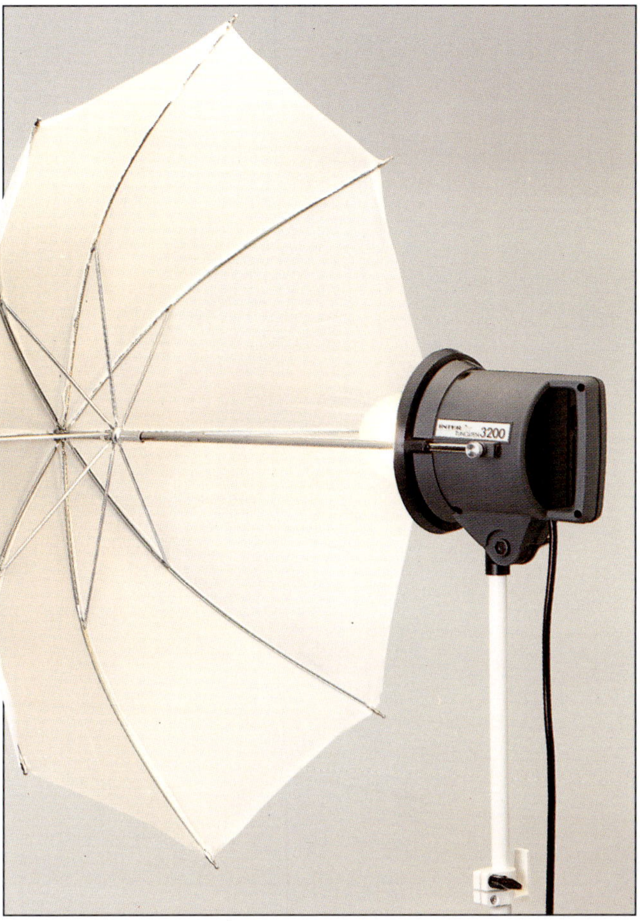

◀ ***A translucent umbrella is useful for softening the harsh light from a tungsten lamp to give flattering portraits and subtle still life shots. Shine the light through the umbrella, rather than bouncing the light off it.***

▼ ***If you want to filter your tungsten lights, buy a filter holder. This holds photographic gels in front of the lamp. Alternatively, use bulldog clips to attach the filter gel to a set of barndoors.***

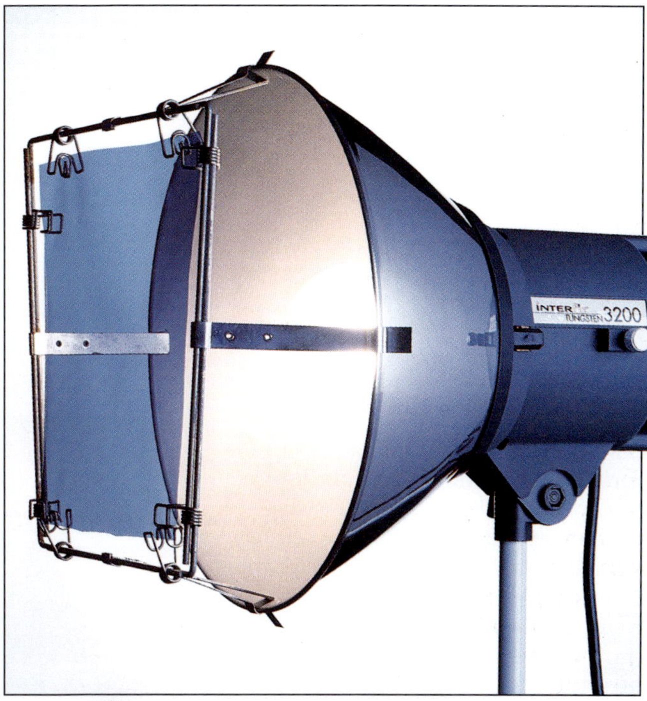

▶ ***The easiest way to control the spread of light from a tungsten lamp is to fit barndoors.***

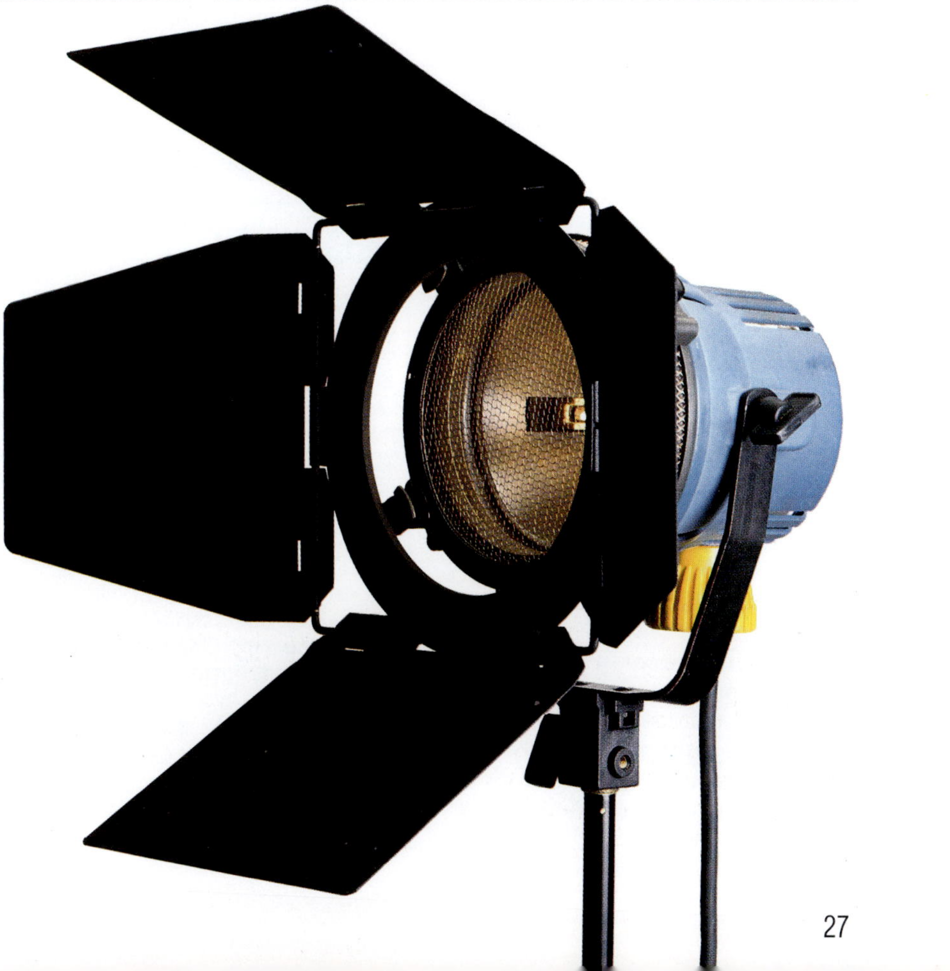

▼ ***A scrim is made up from trace or wire gauze. It blocks about a stop of light, without altering its colour temperature. Fitting diffusion material to the barndoors, as here, produces a softer beam than when the diffusion medium is held in a filter frame, closer to the lamp.***

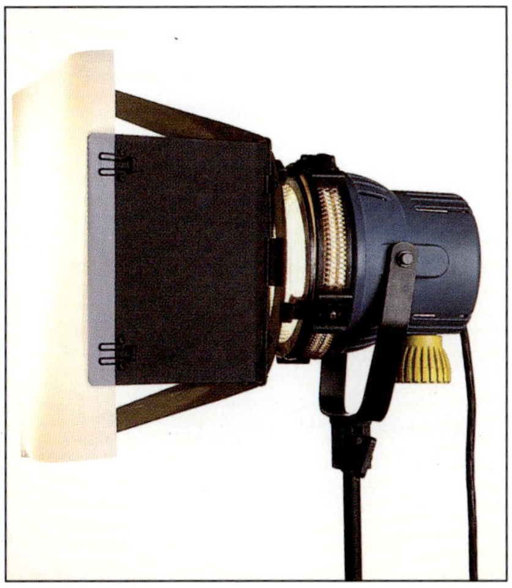

Using tungsten lights

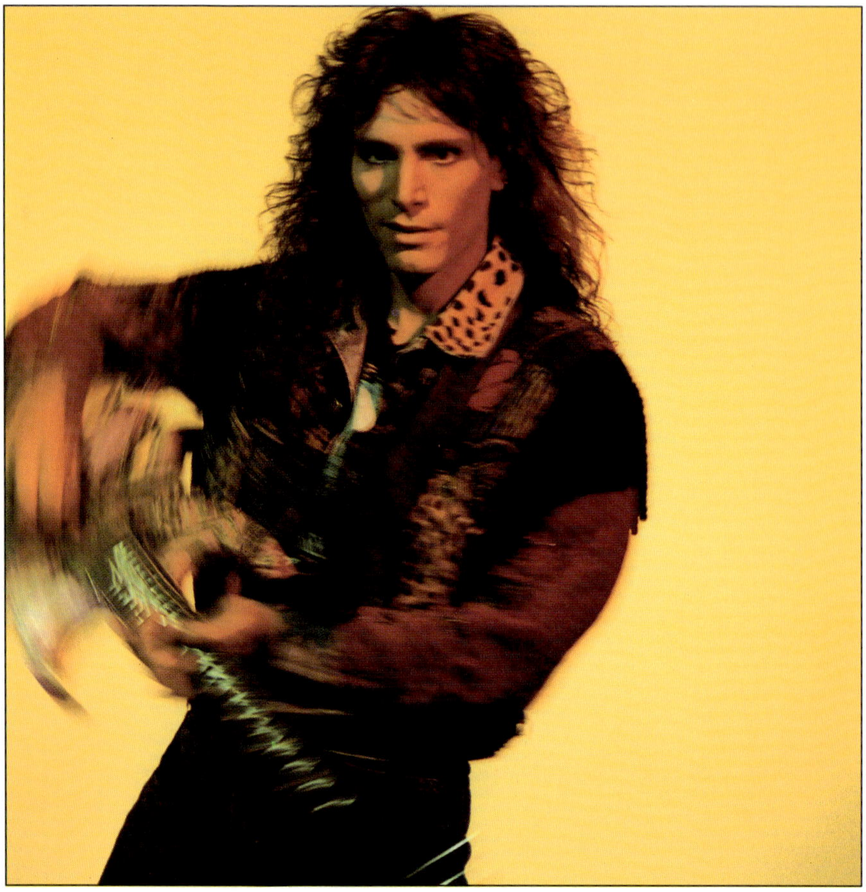

▲ *A filter holder lets you use gels to alter the colour of the light. With a bit of imagination, you can come up with dramatic, multi-coloured images. For this shot, the photographer chose a slow shutter speed to add blur for an even more dynamic picture.*

Before you start using tungsten lighting there are a few points to be aware of. For a start, tungsten lights give off a lot of heat, so they aren't suitable for all subjects – steer clear, for instance, of still life shots containing ice cream!

Measuring exposure isn't much of a problem with tungsten lighting – you can use your camera's meter to take accurate light readings. All modern general-purpose black and white films are rated at the same speed to both tungsten light and daylight, but if you get consistent under-exposure (which can happen with some films, especially Eastern European or Chinese emulsions) you may need to give about half a stop extra exposure.

Exposure pointers

Apart from powerful professional units, most tungsten lights have a fairly weak output, which calls for wide apertures, slow shutter speeds, or both. This can create problems with shallow depth of field, camera shake and subject blur. There are a number of ways to minimize these problems:

❏ Load up with fast film. This lets you set narrower apertures for wider depth of field, and faster shutter speeds for preventing camera shake and subject blur.
❏ Choose tungsten balanced film for colour photography, so you don't need to use colour conversion filters – filters absorb light.
❏ Always use a solid tripod. This lets you use slower shutter speeds, without risking camera shake.

For total control over your images you need to be able to alter the brightness of the light reaching your subject. There are several ways you can do this:

❏ Move the lights closer to, or further away from, your subject. Moving a light twice the distance from your subject as the main light gives a 4:1 fill-in ratio.
❏ Use a control box – a form of dimmer switch – if you are shooting on black and white film. You can't use this type of unit for colour work, as reducing the output of the lamp by as little as 10% gives your pictures an orange cast.
❏ Fit your lights with lamps of different strengths.
❏ Put a scrim in front of the lamp.
❏ Use neutral density filters to reduce the brightness of light reaching the subject.

Safety first

BACK TO BASICS

Tungsten lighting may be cheap to buy and simple to use, but it can also be dangerous if you don't follow a few simple safety rules.

❏ Do keep inflammable materials away from the lights.
❏ Do use a wire scrim in front of your lights for portraits – if a lamp should shatter, the glass won't reach your sitter.
❏ Do use flame-proof umbrellas.
❏ Don't put a tungsten photographic lamp into a domestic light. Even though the lamp fittings are the same as those on tungsten lights, the materials used in domestic lights are not designed to withstand the heat generated by a photographic lamp and may melt.
❏ Don't touch the lamp, casing, or reflector when the lamp is in use – they may be hot enough to burn the skin off your hands. Try to buy lamps with thermoplastic casings. These conduct less heat than metal casings.
❏ Don't move the lamps when they are hot – you may damage the filament.
❏ Don't risk fusing your domestic electrical circuits by using lots of very powerful tungsten lights in your own home. 8000W is the maximum amount of lighting you should consider using.
❏ Don't enclose a tungsten light inside a softbox. The heat from the lamp can build up in the enclosed space and may cause a fire.

A film star portrait

One of the best ways of putting lighting theory into practice is to try to duplicate the effects of portraits from the past – in particular, the 1940s, when the Hollywood glamour portrait was at its height. Steve Parker learns how.

I have always wanted to shoot a portrait of a model and make her look like Lauren Bacall musing dreamily about Bogart. I had my own ideas about composition, but I let professional portrait photographer Tobi Corney give me a few tips about the format and lighting.

I used Tobi's camera, which is a Hasselblad with a 6 x 6cm back, loaded with Agfa APX 100 black and white print film. Most portrait photographers from the Forties and Fifties used a standard lens, so I followed suit – though I drew the line at using the 4x5 inch and 8x10 inch cameras they would have used.

I arranged a canvas director's chair facing away from the camera and asked our model, Jo, to sit in it and turn towards the camera. Tobi suggested we flag off the flash lights to try and imitate the harsh directional tungsten lights fashionable in the Forties. So I placed the light to Jo's right and a reflector to the left to provide a lot of fill-in.

I asked Jo to turn to the camera and run her fingers through her hair, as I suspected a glamorous Hollywood model might. When I saw the moody look I was after, I took a picture.

Tobi's turn

Tobi felt that, attractive though the model was, her clothes, hair and make up were still very 1990s, and this jarred with the period feel. A trip to the props cupboard was rewarded with an old ballgown that could pass for a period costume. Also on hand was make up artist, Stuart Pantrey, who Tobi had hired to add a little Forties glitz.

Tobi was also unhappy with the background, which he felt 'should be made moodier or killed altogether'. Thirdly, the lighting was wrong. This, according to Tobi, 'had far too much fill-in' and 'needed to be more dramatic'.

Last but not least, he reckoned that Jo's 'look' was all wrong. I should have cultivated a look of 1940s mystery, not the confidence associated with the 1990s. I decided at this point it was probably time to let Tobi have a go.

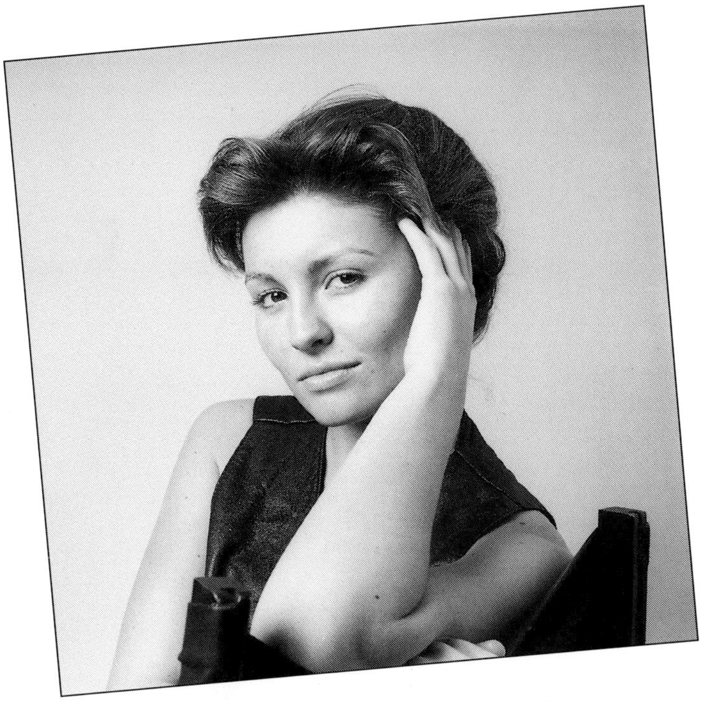

◀ Steve originally thought his shot was quite good. But he had to admit that the make up and hair style were not very 1940s. He took Tobi's point about the background, which was too bright and didn't really add anything to the overall image. He was also striving for a moody look to the portrait, and agreed that the light was far too even and bright to give the dramatic results he was after.

A FORTIES LOOK

1 ▼ MAKE UP THE MODEL
Tobi asked make up artist, Stuart Pantrey, to give our model a 1940s look. This meant heavy make up and loosening Jo's hair. Tobi moved the reflector back to create more modelling on the side of her face, and spotlit the background to create a shaft of light behind her.

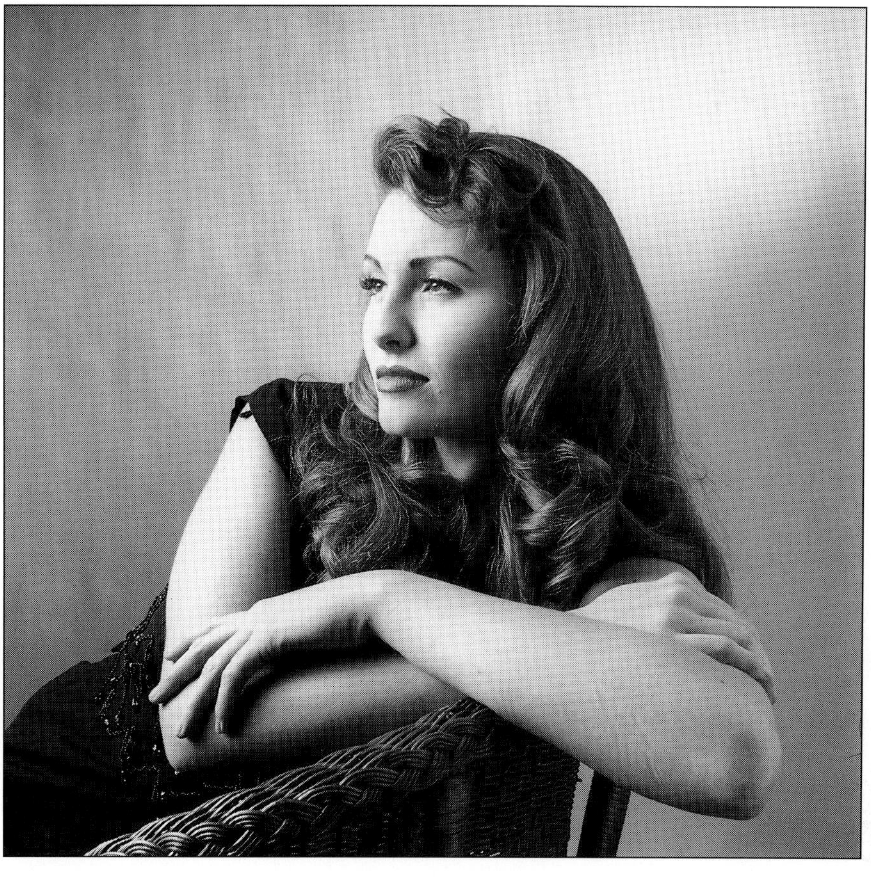

2 ▶ SOFTEN THE BACKGROUND

Tobi tried a really dramatic approach next. The shaft of light on the background hadn't entirely worked, as it showed up the mottled texture of the backdrop. He abandoned the background spotlight and replaced it with a light shining through a gobo. To make a feature of the background, he moved the camera back slightly, and to add even more modelling to Jo's face, he moved the reflector even further away from her. To inject a bit more glamour into the shot, Tobi found a pair of elegant gloves for Jo to wear.

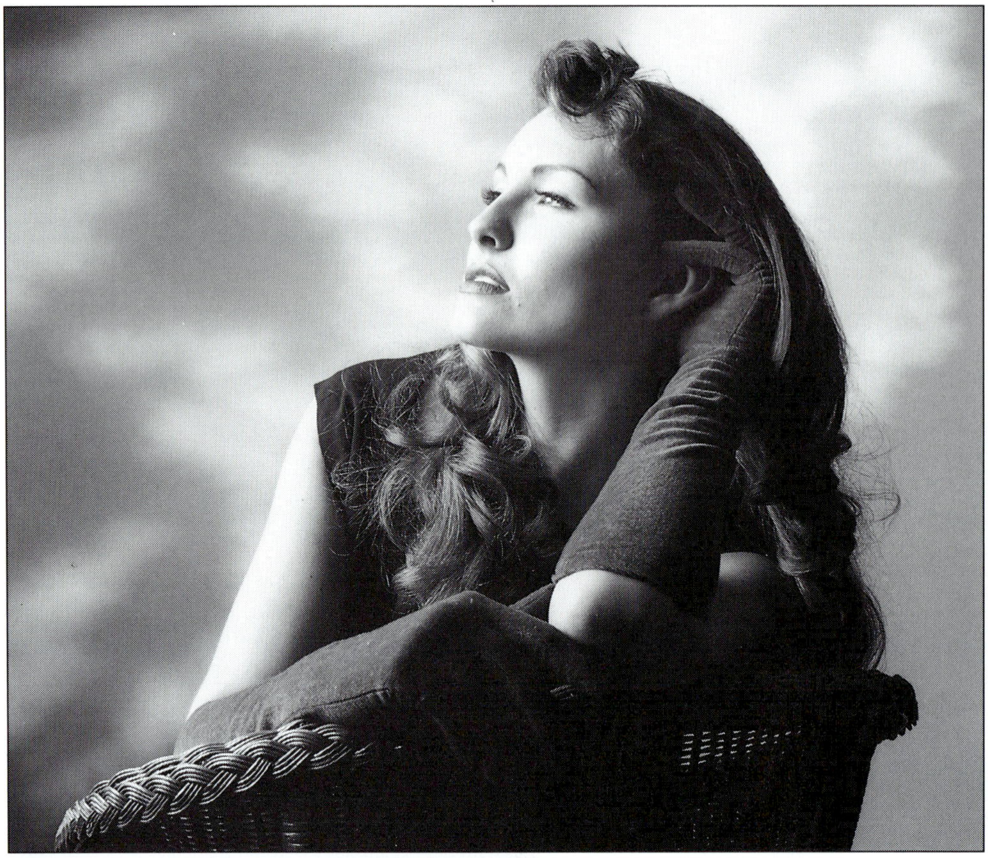

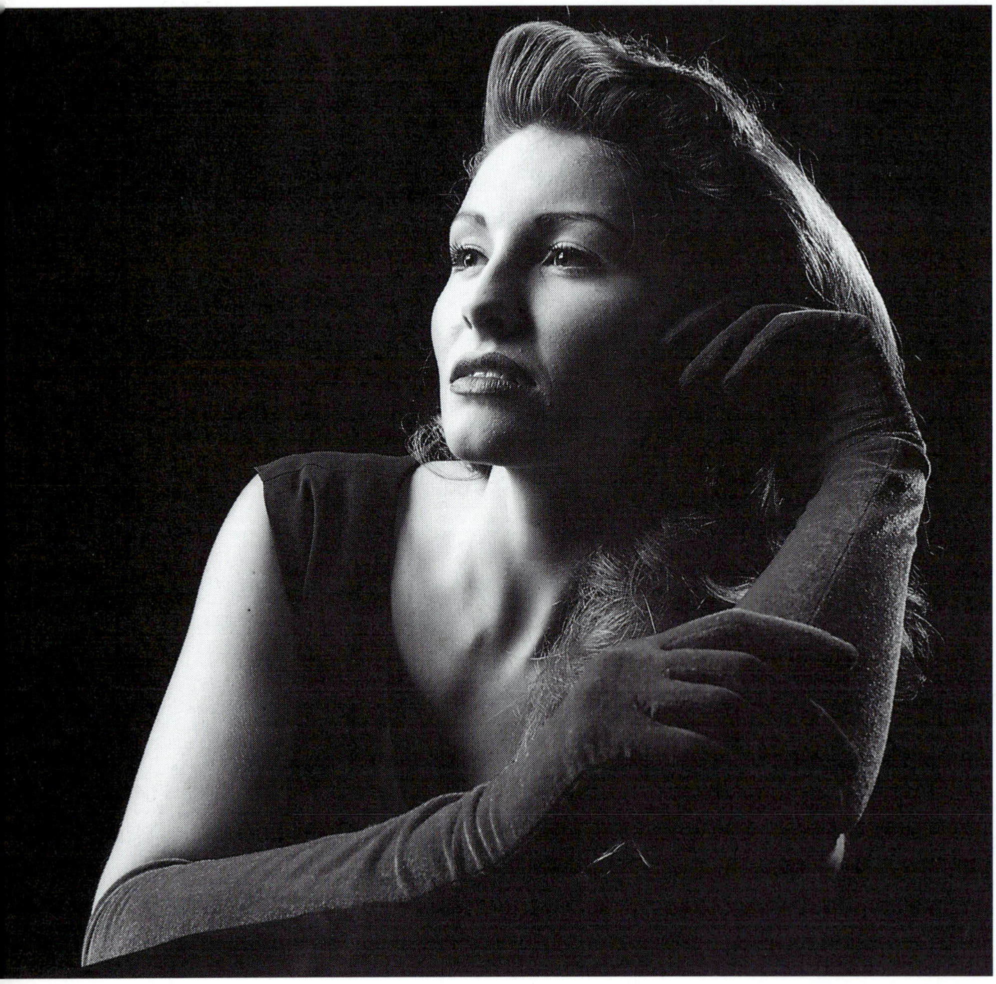

3 ◀ HARSH LIGHTING

Time to become a little more daring. Tobi decided to kill the background completely and replace it with a backlight shining directly on the model. He also took away the reflector. A lot of Hollywood shots took this approach – using a single soft sidelight for primary illumination and a very strong spot as a backlight – creating an attractive halo around the model. To emphasize this further, Tobi got Stuart to flow Jo's hair back to make it look more striking.

The final set up

After the first few shots, Tobi removed the reflector and background light completely and used only two flash lights – a 2000W sidelight and a 3000W for the backlight.

The sidelight was softened by a softbox, but it was heavily flagged off so that no illumination fell on the background. Tobi chose an aperture of f22 to keep all of the model sharp.

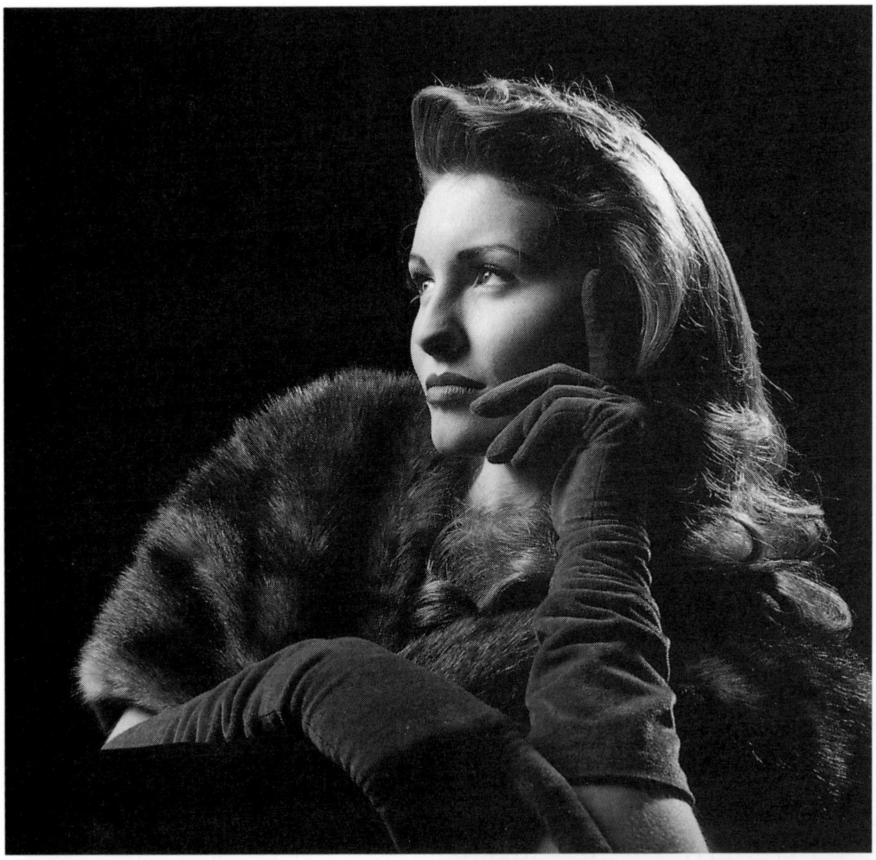

SLR tip

For a dreamy feel, soften the image by stretching a stocking over the lens. Unlike diffusion filters, with a stocking, some of the light reaches the lens without being diffused, and only some of the light rays are diverted. You may have to experiment first to see which colour and thickness of stocking gives the best results. Remember also that it will reduce the exposure by about a stop.

Compact tip

This shot is impossible to take with a compact, but you may want to try another photo featuring cigarette smoke. With a thin column of smoke coming from a cigarette, make sure nobody in the room moves and that all windows and doors are shut. The slightest movement of air currents means the smoke will not rise more than a few centimetres without breaking up.

4 ▲ ADDING A FUR
After the glamour of the gloves was added, Jo began to look a little under dressed in the simple ball gown top, and another trip to the props cupboard was in order. Tobi came back with a fur shawl, which absorbed far more light than Jo's skin. In the previous shot, the right arm was as bright as the face, and was in danger of drawing the eye too much. To help concentrate attention on the face further, Tobi made the sidelight even more directional, so that less light fell on the gloves than in the previous shot. He also had Jo adopt a more relaxed pose, telling her to imagine she was 'dreaming of Bogart'. This is reinforced by the coy position of the left hand, which now covers part of her face.

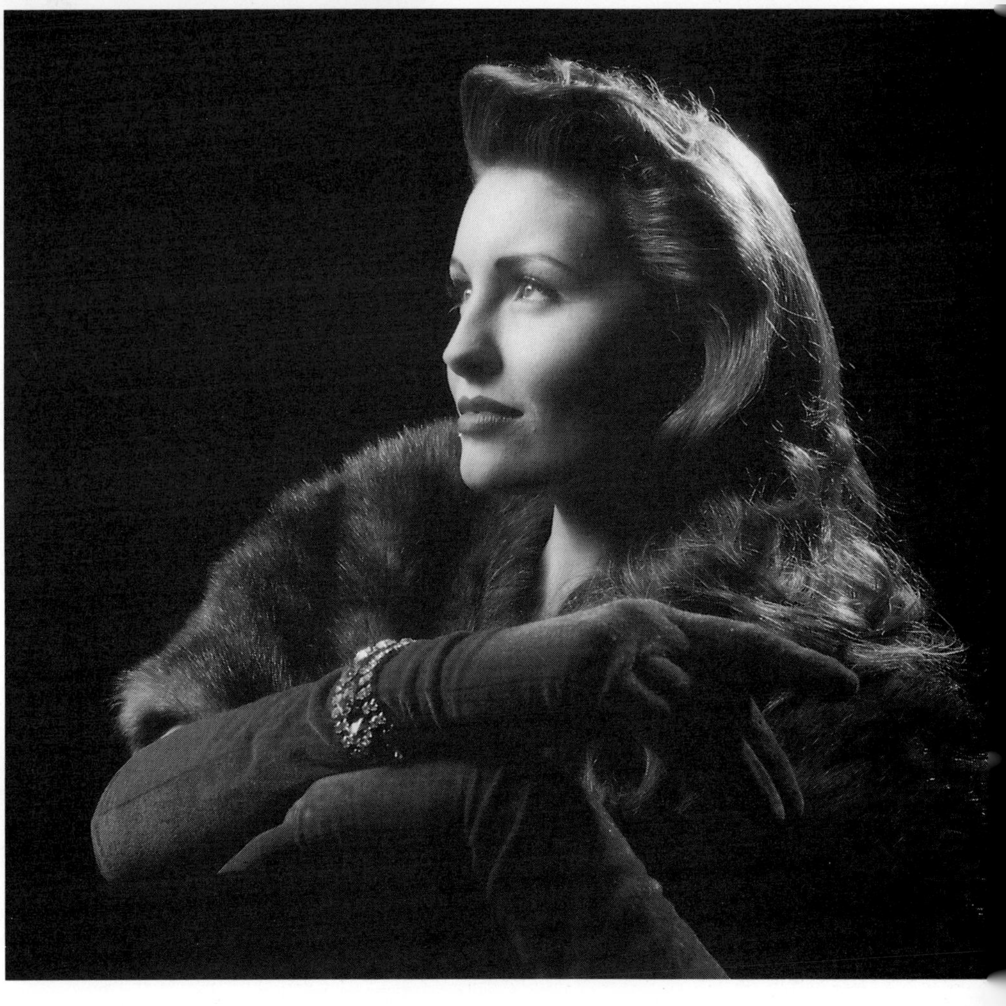

5 ▶ HARDENING THE LIGHT
To boost the drama of the shot still further, Tobi concentrated the sidelight by narrowing the barn-doors. He also moved the backlight further to his right, and placed a stocking over the lens for a soft focus effect. As a cosmetic touch, he boosted the glamour slightly by adding a bracelet from his prop cupboard.

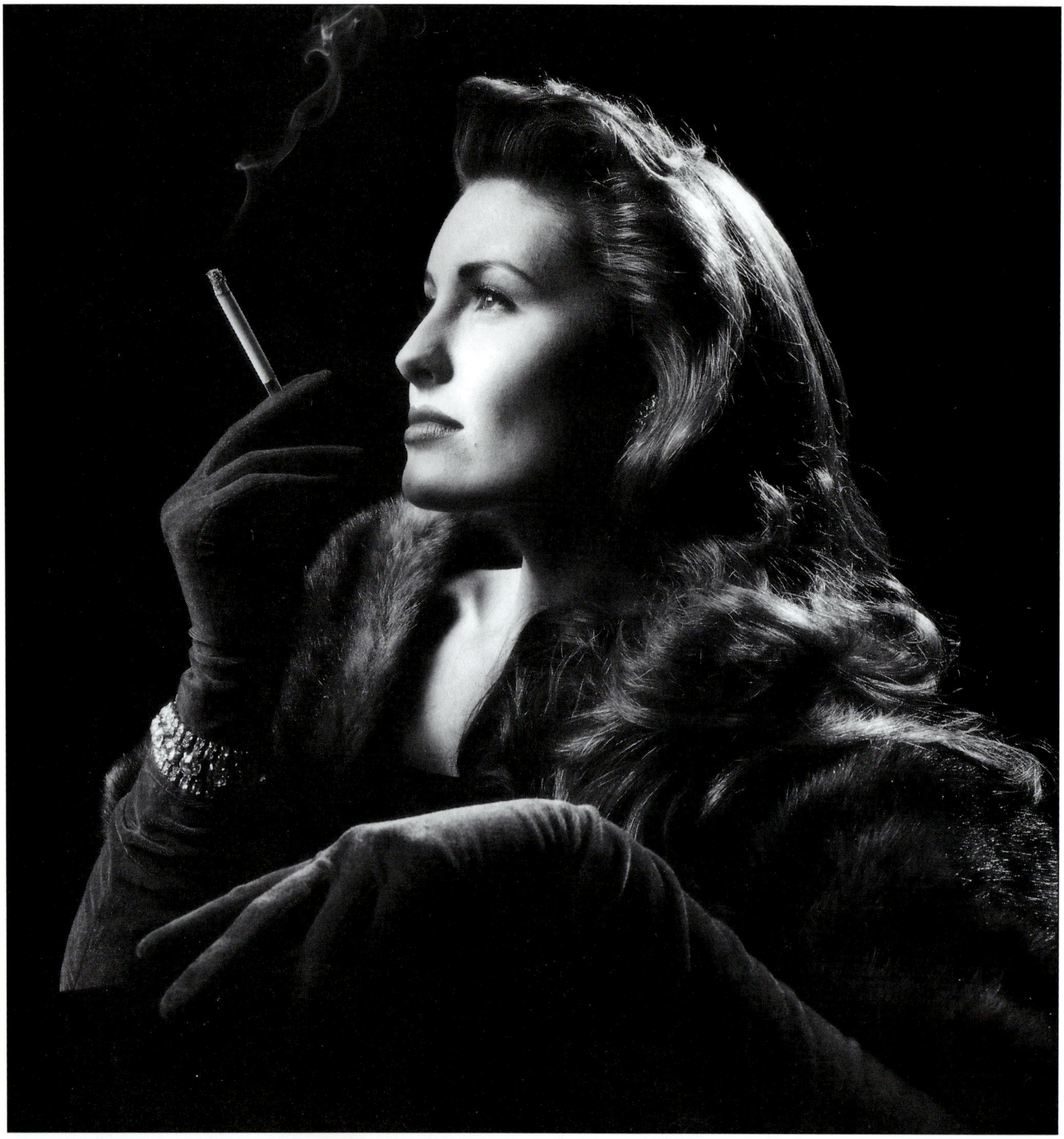

6 ▲ THE FINAL TOUCH Though not accepted in every social circle today, in the 1940s smoking cigarettes was considered glamorous. For his final shot, Tobi had the model look up dreamily, and close her lips. The position of her arms and the dramatic profile of her head makes Jo look totally relaxed.

Tip

Make up

When imitating Forties make up, copy the very distinct eye and lip line. False eyelashes, too, are essential. Eyebrows are tricky, as Forties women tended to pluck theirs narrower than women today. Apply foundation very evenly, for an even tone. With flat lighting, use make up to emphasize cheekbones, but this is unnecessary with sidelighting.

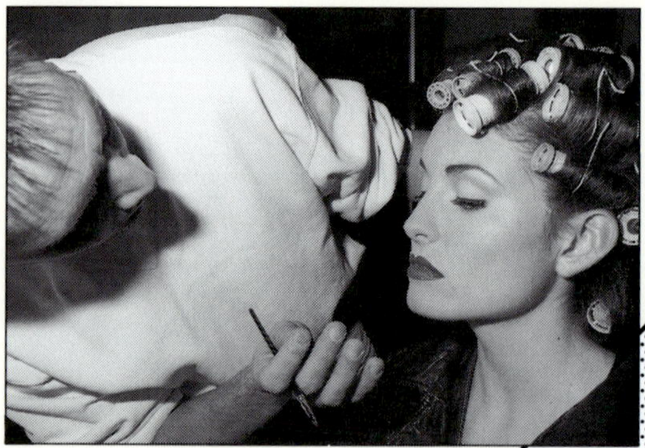

Incident lightmetering

If it's accurate exposures you're after, take a tip from the pros – forget about your camera's lightmeter and try out a hand held incident lightmeter instead.

Before the introduction of built-in metering systems, all light readings were taken using hand held meters. Nowadays – despite the sophistication of modern TTL metering systems – hand held meters still play an important part in accurate light measurement.

Hand held meters come in many types and designs and are capable of measuring light in a variety of ways. You can use them in the same way as your camera meter – to measure light reflected from your subject. They are often more sensitive than built-in meters and give more accurate readings – some give exposure readings to the nearest 1/10th f stop.

The main advantage of hand held meters, however, is that you can use them to take incident light readings. This involves measuring the brightness of the light falling on to the subject rather than the brightness of the reflected light.

Incident lightmetering is very accurate because the readings are not influenced by your subject's tones. Under even lighting conditions dark, light and mid tones are all recorded faithfully.

Fitting the diffuser

Most hand held meters can be used to measure both reflected and incident light. In the reflected metering mode, light from the subject enters a small window on the front or side of the meter and strikes a photo sensitive cell. In incident mode the window is covered by a translucent white plastic diffuser dome. Light passing through the dome enters the window and strikes the photo sensitive cell underneath. On some meters the dome just slides over the window, while on others you have to screw or snap it into place.

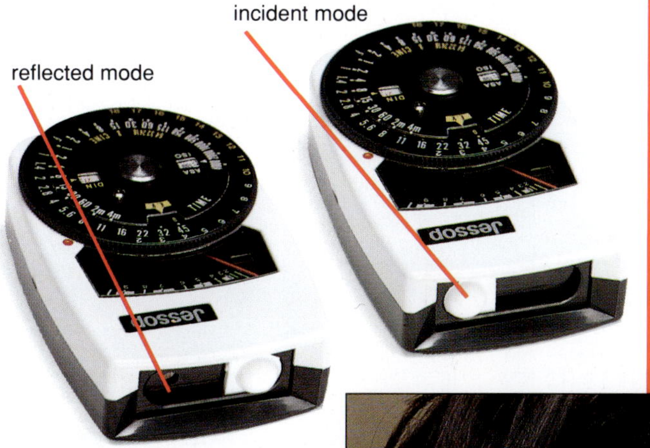

▲ ***This meter uses a permanently attached plastic diffuser dome. In reflected mode you slide the dome across the top of the meter so the metering window is uncovered. In incident metering mode you slide the dome so the metering window is covered.***

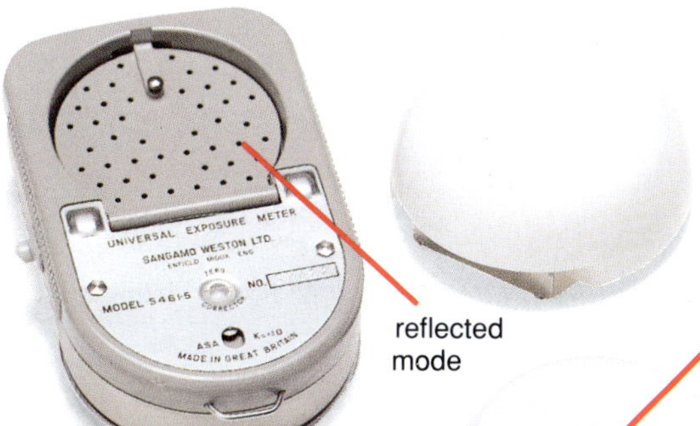

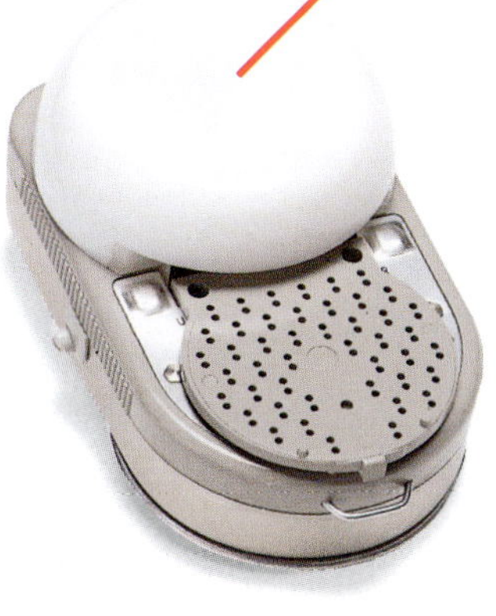

▲▶ ***This version uses a separate snap-on diffuser dome for measuring incident light. To take a reflected light reading you leave the photo sensitive cell uncovered. For an incident light reading you just attach the diffuser over the cell, using a metal clip on the back of the dome.***

▼ ***Hand held lightmeters are an essential part of most professional photographers' kits. They're versatile, very accurate and easy to use. In the incident metering mode they measure the light falling on to the subject so they're not fooled by light or dark subject tones.***

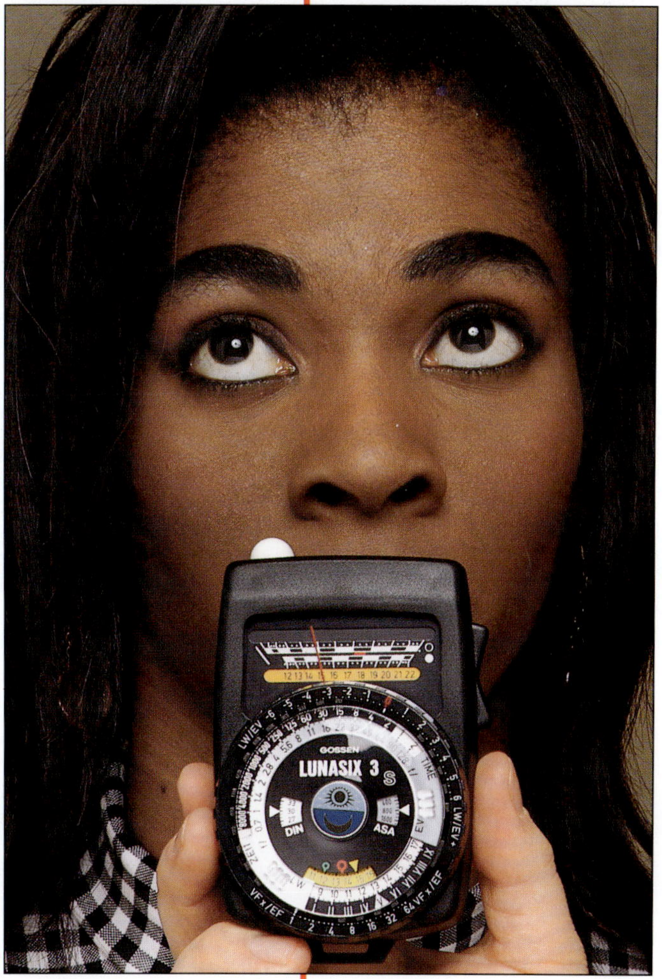

How it works

A reflected lightmeter assumes a subject is mid toned and reflects 18% of the light falling on it. So a reading is only correct if you meter from a mid tone – light and dark subjects reflect different amounts of light and can fool the meter into under and overexposure.

Incident lightmeters measure the light that's falling on to the subject. This means the subject's tone doesn't affect the reading.

The diffuser dome that covers the metering window on your hand held meter substitutes for a three dimensional subject and transmits 18% of the light falling on to it. So the brightness of light reaching the photo sensitive cell is the same as the brightness of light reflected from a mid toned subject.

If you set the exposure suggested by an incident light meter and shoot a dark toned subject, the subject reflects less than 18% of the light falling on it and is recorded as darker than average. So it's correctly exposed. The reverse is true for light toned subjects.

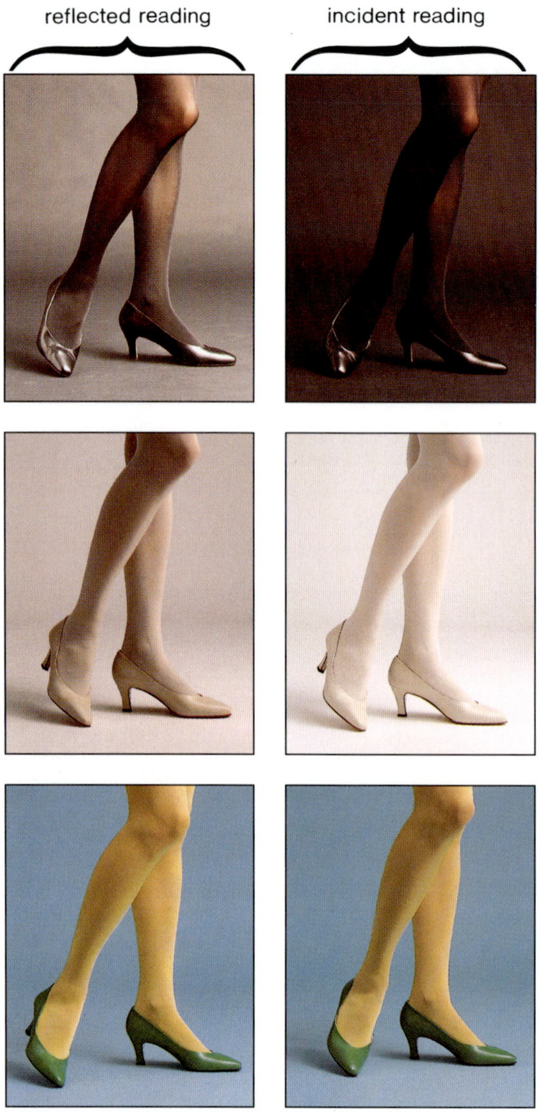

◀ A reflected lightmeter assumes all subjects are mid toned. If you meter from a dark toned subject the picture looks overexposed (far left). By measuring the light that's falling on a subject, an incident meter gives a correct exposure reading (left).

◀ If you set the exposure suggested by a reflected light reading taken from a light toned subject, the picture is underexposed (far left). An incident light meter ignores a subject's tones, so light toned subjects are correctly exposed (left).

◀ If you take a reflected reading from a mid toned subject the result is a correctly exposed picture (far left). An average toned subject poses no problems for an incident meter either, which is set up to record mid tones faithfully (left).

When to use it

There are many occasions when an incident light reading is preferable to a reflected light reading. For instance, if you're taking portraits of a dark skinned model an incident light reading will give an accurate indication of exposure, whereas a reflected meter reading would lead to overexposure.

Similarly, if you shoot a lightly coloured scene with high key lighting, a reflected reading is likely to underexpose the shot. Once again, an incident reading will be more accurate.

Spot on for slides

If you're using slide film your exposures have to be exact. If you're taking a reflected light reading you have to be certain that the area of the scene you are metering from is a mid tone. If it isn't, you must be able to judge the tone precisely, if you are to decide how much exposure compensation is needed. This ability comes with time and practice, but the technique is prone to error.

An incident light reading is likely to be more accurate because it doesn't matter whether your subject is light, dark or average toned – you still get an accurate exposure.

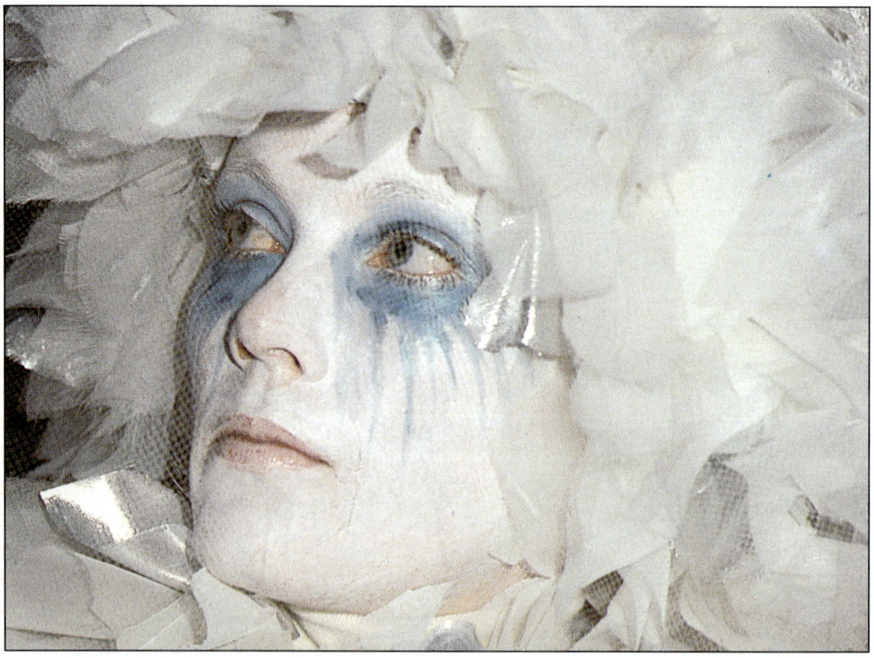

▲ The tones in this shot are lighter than average and would have fooled a reflected lightmeter into underexposing the picture. Instead, the photographer took an incident light reading, which was not influenced by the pale subject tones and gave a correct exposure reading.

How to do it

Using a hand held meter to take incident light readings is simple, as long as you follow a few basic procedures. To begin with you need to set the film speed. You do this using push buttons or a dial on the front of the meter. (Detailed instructions on how to operate individual meters' controls are covered in a later chapter.)

The most important thing to get right is the positioning of the meter. Place it near to your subject and point it at the camera – not at the light source. The light striking the meter must be of the same brightness as the light hitting your subject. Be careful to avoid casting shadows on to the diffuser dome as this can fool the meter into overexposing the shot.

If the lighting is very contrasty, you'll need to check that the film can cope with the difference in brightness between the highlights and shadows. To do this, take one reading from an area of shadow and another from an area of highlight. Some meters have a function that averages the two readings to give a combined exposure.

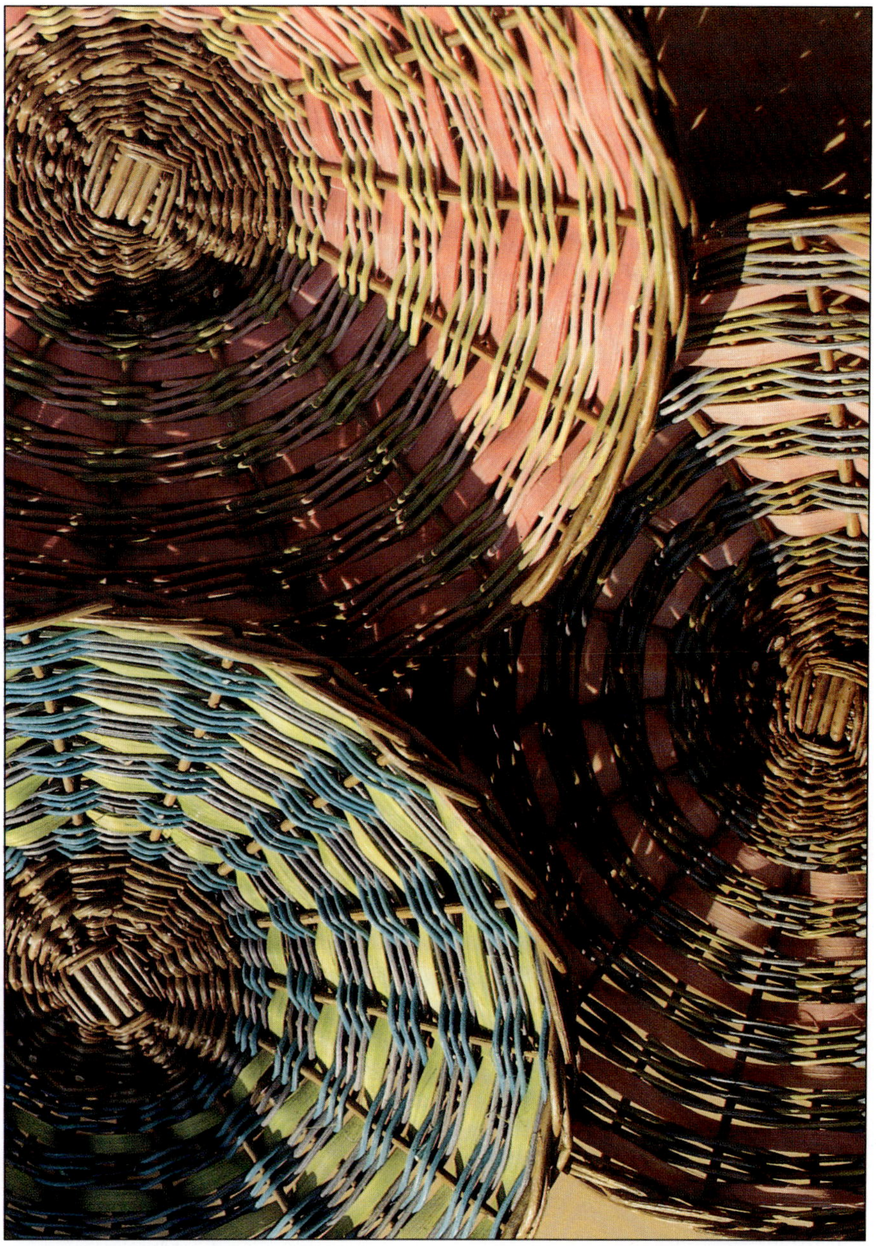

▲ For contrasty lighting you'll need to take two readings – one from the highlights and one from the shadows. This lets you check the brightness contrast in the scene. In this case the photographer set an exposure midway between the two readings which meant that the film was able to record details in both the highlight and the shadow areas. If the contrast had been too great for the film, the photographer could have reduced it by bouncing light into the shadows.

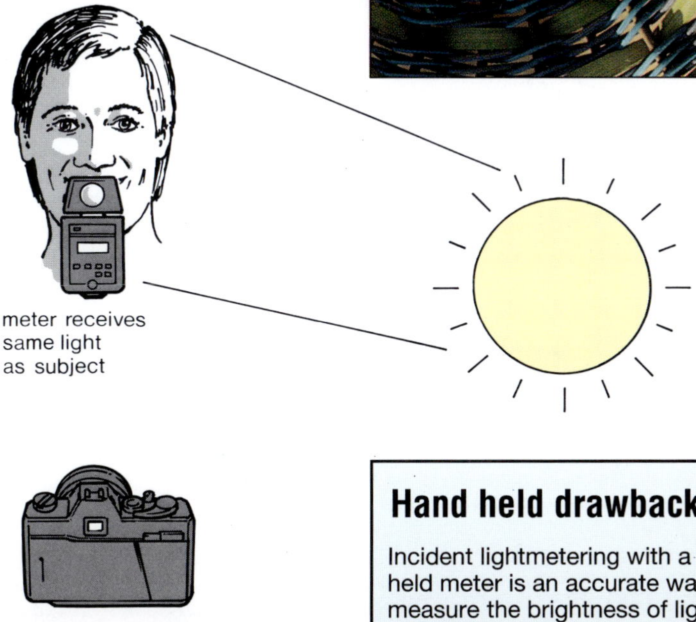

▲ When the boldness contrast is fairly low, point the meter at the camera, take a reading and set the suggested exposure on your camera. Position the meter so that it receives the same brightness of light as your subject.

Hand held drawbacks

Incident lightmetering with a hand held meter is an accurate way to measure the brightness of light, and is preferable to camera meter readings if you're using slide film. But hand held meters do have a few shortcomings:

❏ You have to carry another piece of equipment around with you.
❏ They don't take filter factors into consideration.
❏ They're difficult to use if your subject is a long distance away.
❏ They make no allowance for extra extension in extreme close-ups.

A hand meter should complement, rather than replace, your camera meter.

Cheap and cheerful

If you've spent a lot of money on a modern SLR with advanced metering modes a hand held meter may seem like an unnecessary expense. Fortunately, there are some cheaper alternatives to hand held meters if you want to take advantage of incident lightmetering techniques.

A photographers' grey card is not expensive, has a mid tone finish and is available from most photographic shops. You place it in the same position as an incident lightmeter, and take a reflected light reading from it using your camera's meter. The reading will be the same as from an incident lightmeter.

You must fill the frame with the card, so the camera isn't fooled by other tones around the edges. Avoid casting shadows on the card and angle it so that there is no glare – this can fool the camera's meter.

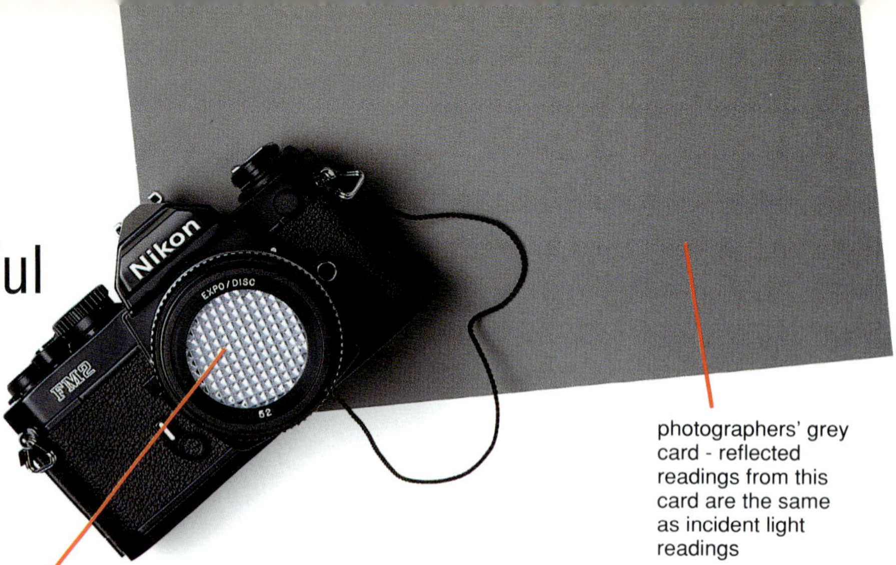

photographers' grey card - reflected readings from this card are the same as incident light readings

screw-in translucent disc - lets you take incident readings with your camera meter

You can also buy a translucent disc, which looks like a filter, that you screw into the lens. This acts like a diffuser dome and turns your camera's reflected lightmeter into an incident meter. You can then use your camera in the same way as a hand held meter for taking incident readings.

Tip

Palmistry

Take a reading off the palm of your hand if you do not have a grey card handy, then increase exposure by up to ½ stop depending on your own skin tone. Take care not to shade your hand with the meter and make sure the light falling on your hand is the same as the light falling on your subject.

Hold the highlights

BACK TO BASICS

Sometimes the light is so contrasty that taking an average reading gives overexposed highlights *and* underexposed shadows. So you have to bias exposure towards one area or the other. This depends on the film you're using.

If you're shooting on slide film try to hold detail in the highlights – correctly exposed bright areas and dark shadows appear more natural than washed out bright areas and correctly exposed shadows. This is because our eyes are drawn to bright areas of a picture or scene and are used to seeing fine detail in these parts. Similarly, our eyes are used to seeing deep shadows that reveal very little detail.

If you're using print film, it's best to expose for the shadows. This is not because our eyes view prints differently to slides. Rather, it's because print film has more latitude for overexposure – up to three and a half stops – as the highlight areas can usually be 'burnt in' at the printing stage.

If you do expose for the highlights on print film, the shadows tend to look muddy and colour shifts can occur. It's next to impossible to correct this at the printing stage.

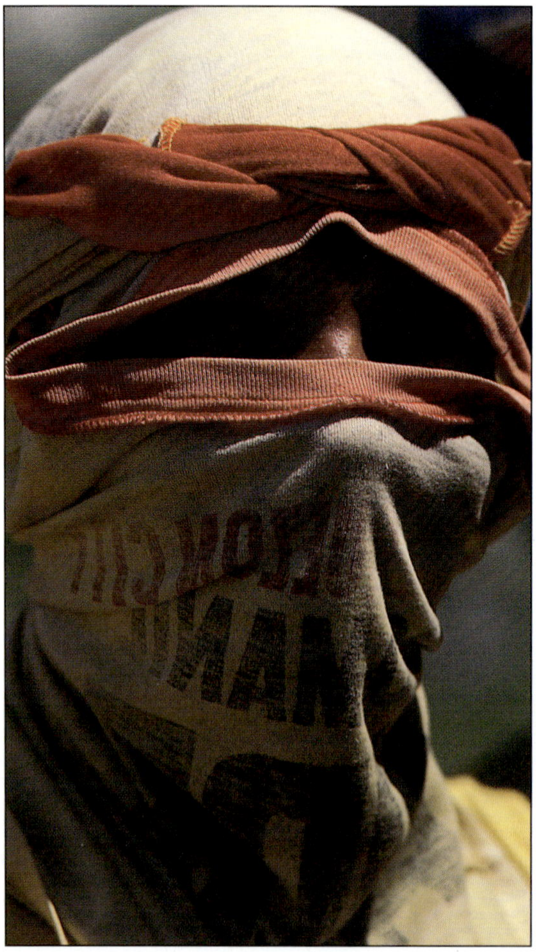

◀ In this shot, the brightness contrast between the highlight on the man's head and the shadow on his face was so high the slide film couldn't record detail in both areas. So the photographer had to decide which area to expose for.

He chose to expose for the highlight area, which gave a rich, powerful and natural looking shot even though the man's eyes – the usual focal point for a portrait – are in deep shadow.

Exposing for the shadow area, to reveal the man's eyes, would have overexposed the rest of the shot. The top of his head would have lacked any detail and the colours in the picture would have looked completely washed out.

Choosing a lightmeter

If you decide that you would like more metering control than your camera is able to provide, you can choose from a wide variety of meters. This guide should help you decide which one best meets your needs.

A major consideration when choosing any piece of photographic equipment is price. Fortunately the wide range of lightmeters on the market means there's one to suit every budget.

At the bottom of the range you can pick up a basic model for as little as the cost of half a dozen films. Alternatively you can opt for a top of the range, multi-function meter that measures ambient light and flash. These cost as much as an advanced SLR camera and lens.

Price is determined by the range of meter functions. Some meters are only capable of taking, and displaying, a single brightness reading. Others have more advanced features, such as a memory function. This lets you take several readings and store them, so you can compare brightness contrast within a scene.

The most advanced meters are described as exposure analyzers. You can use them to measure both flash and ambient light, and they can display the proportion of flash and ambient light in mixed lighting situations.

When you buy a meter you must decide which functions you need and which you can do without. It is pointless spending a small fortune on a 'do it all' meter if you only need to take a single brightness reading from the main light source. Similarly, you may find a basic model restrictive if you frequently mix ambient light and flash or make multiple flash exposures.

Metering attachments

All hand held meters do basically the same job – they measure the brightness of light falling on a subject. But the range of metering functions found on different lightmeters varies widely. So does the range of attachments and accessories that fit individual meters. This means you can choose a model that exactly matches your metering requirements.

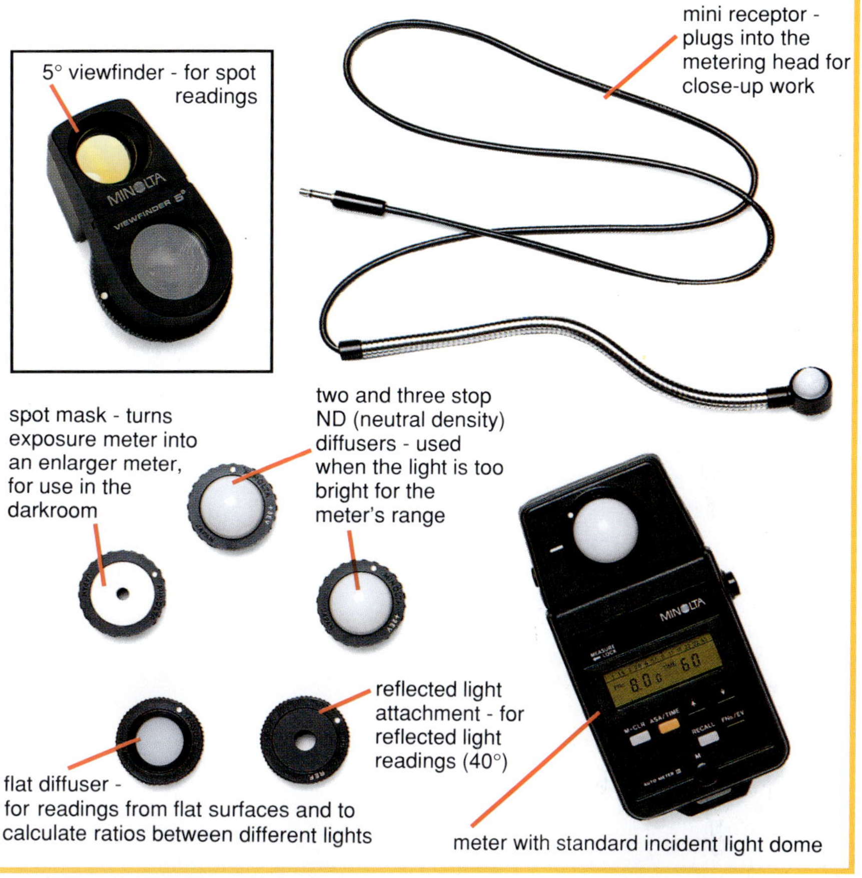

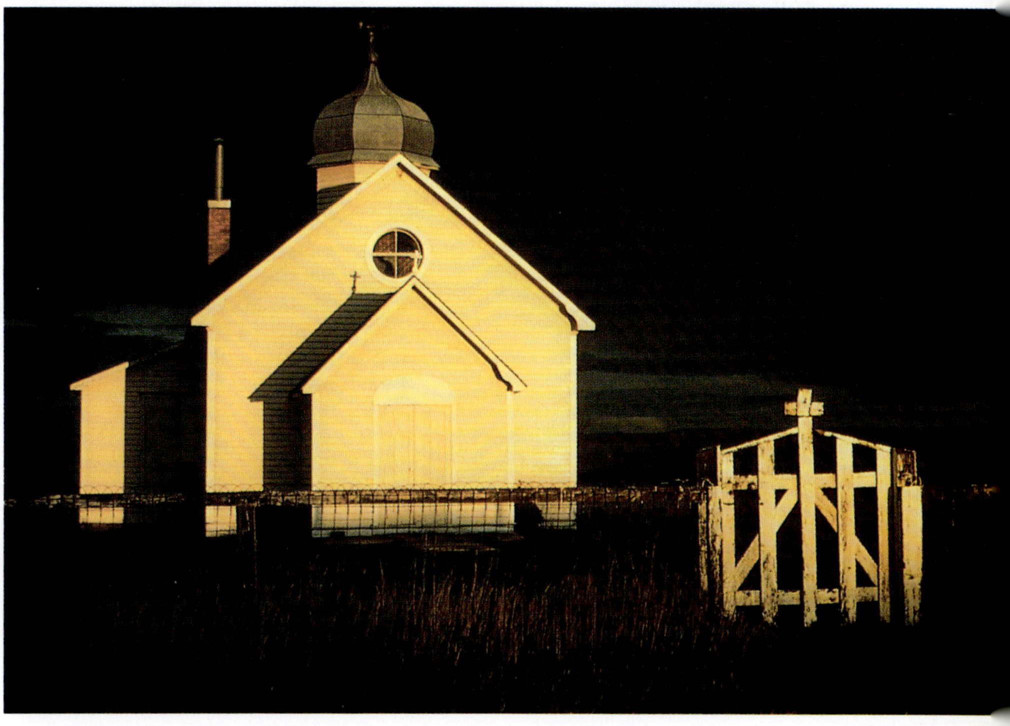

▶ ***Modern hand held incident lightmeters are incredibly sensitive and give accurate exposure readings under the dimmest lighting conditions. Their accuracy makes them ideal when you're shooting slide film, which is less tolerant of exposure errors than print film.***

Swinging needle meters

Different meters use different types of displays. All the early meters, and many of today's modern versions, use a swinging needle.

To use these meters you first set the film speed on a dial on the front of the meter. You then position the meter in front of your subject and press the metering button. The brightness of the light falling on the photo sensitive cell behind the diffuser dome, is indicated by a needle which swings across a printed EV scale in the meter's window. Some meters use two scales showing different EV ranges for measuring low light and bright light. You select the appropriate scale using a button or dial.

To translate the reading into exposure settings just turn the EV dial on the front of the meter until the EV setting shown in the meter window is alongside the arrow. You can then simply read off the range of appropriate aperture and shutter speed combinations for the metered brightness of light.

On some meters, the EV scale is replaced by a zero setting and under and overexposure markings. When the needle is pointed at zero, the aperture and shutter speed combinations shown on the dials on the front of the meter give correct exposure.

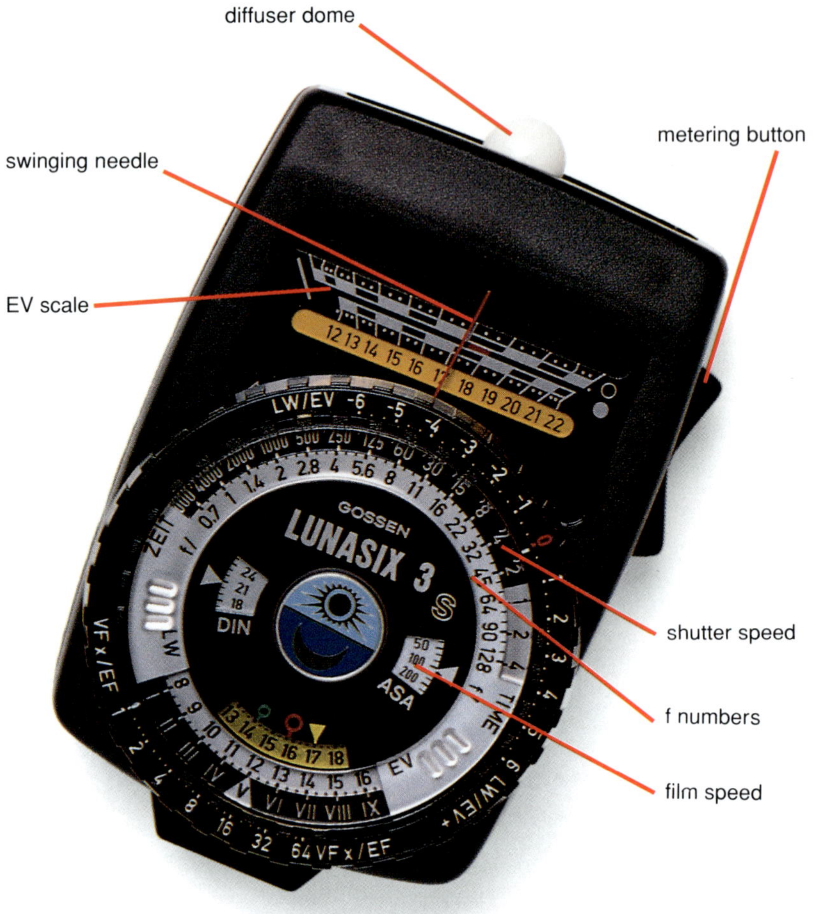

Meter features

Although the specifications of different lightmeters vary widely, there are several important features you need to look at carefully – whatever meter you're considering buying.

The lightmetering range is the range of brightness levels the meter can measure. A good metering range would stretch from EV-2 to EV20 at ISO 100. Some meters have separate ND (neutral density) diffuser domes that extend the top of the metering range by several stops. A 4X diffuser extends the range by two stops and an 8X diffuser extends it by three stops. This is useful when you're working in very bright available light or using powerful studio flash.

The accuracy of the readout Some basic meters give readings in half f stop intervals. They are accurate enough if you shoot on print film, but are not accurate enough for slide film users. Most models give readings to the nearest 1/3rd f stop and many digital meters show aperture settings to the nearest 1/10th f stop. This degree of accuracy is unnecessary for most types of photography – you can only set camera controls to the nearest half or third stop, in any case. However, it does come in useful when you're using advanced, computer controlled studio flash packs, because you can adjust the strength of their output in 1/10th f stops for incredibly precise exposures.

The shutter speed range The fastest shutter speed on your meter should match the top speed on your camera as closely as possible. Many digital meters have a top shutter speed of 1/8000th sec to match the fastest shutter speed found on most advanced AF SLRs. At the other end of the scale, a long exposure time of 30 mins is more than adequate, though some meters measure exposures up to eight hours.

ISO scale Make sure the meter can handle the fastest and slowest film speeds you're likely to use. Most meters let you use films as slow as ISO 12 and as fast as ISO 6400.

Digital meters

These modern lightmeters use a microcomputer to analyse brightness readings and an LCD panel to show exposure readings. Some people find them easier to use than earlier, swinging needle versions.

Using push buttons or dials, you set the appropriate film speed and then set an aperture value or a shutter speed setting – depending on the meter. Some meters let you set either, in the same way that certain SLRs give you a choice between aperture and shutter priority exposure programmes.

To take a reading just press the metering button. This is usually positioned on the side of the meter. The meter shows the correct aperture or shutter speed setting – depending on whether you used the meter in aperture or shutter priority mode – for the measured brightness.

Many digital meters have a memory function so you can take several readings and store them for later comparison. This is useful if you want to calculate the brightness contrast in a scene.

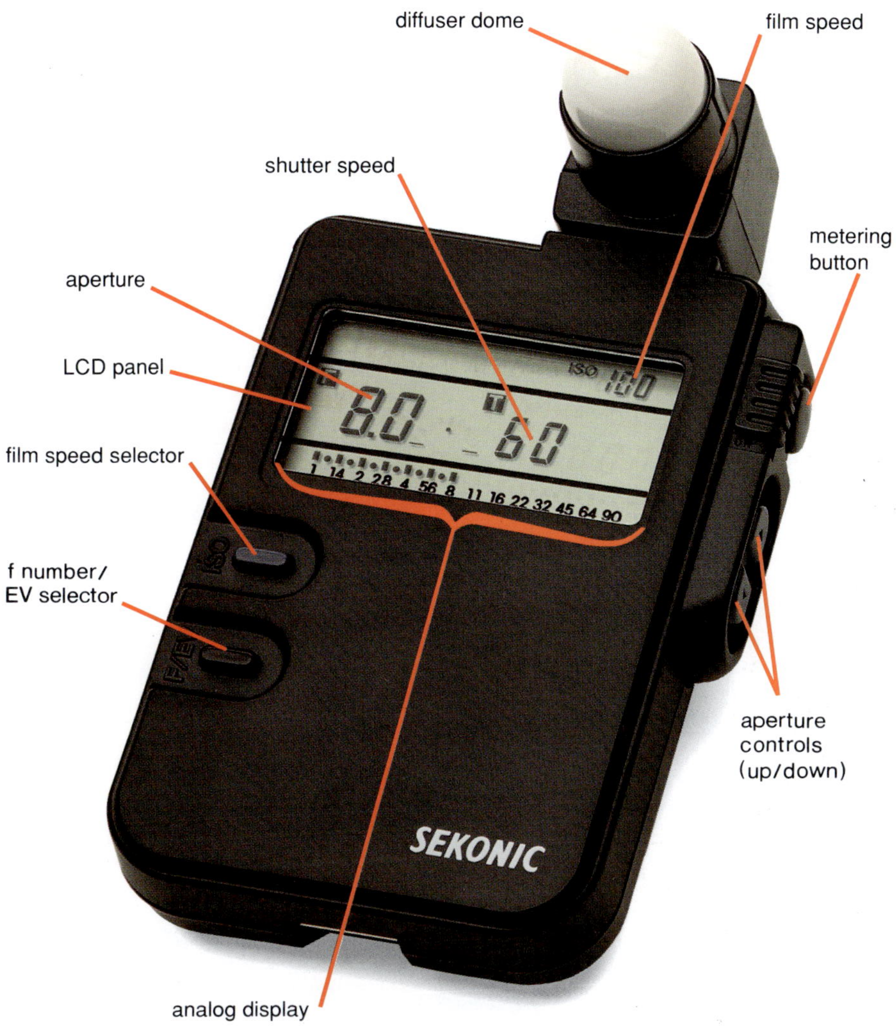

▼ ***Hand held meters give accurate exposure readings for backlit subjects. They measure the brightness of the light falling on your subject's face and ignore the light from the background.***

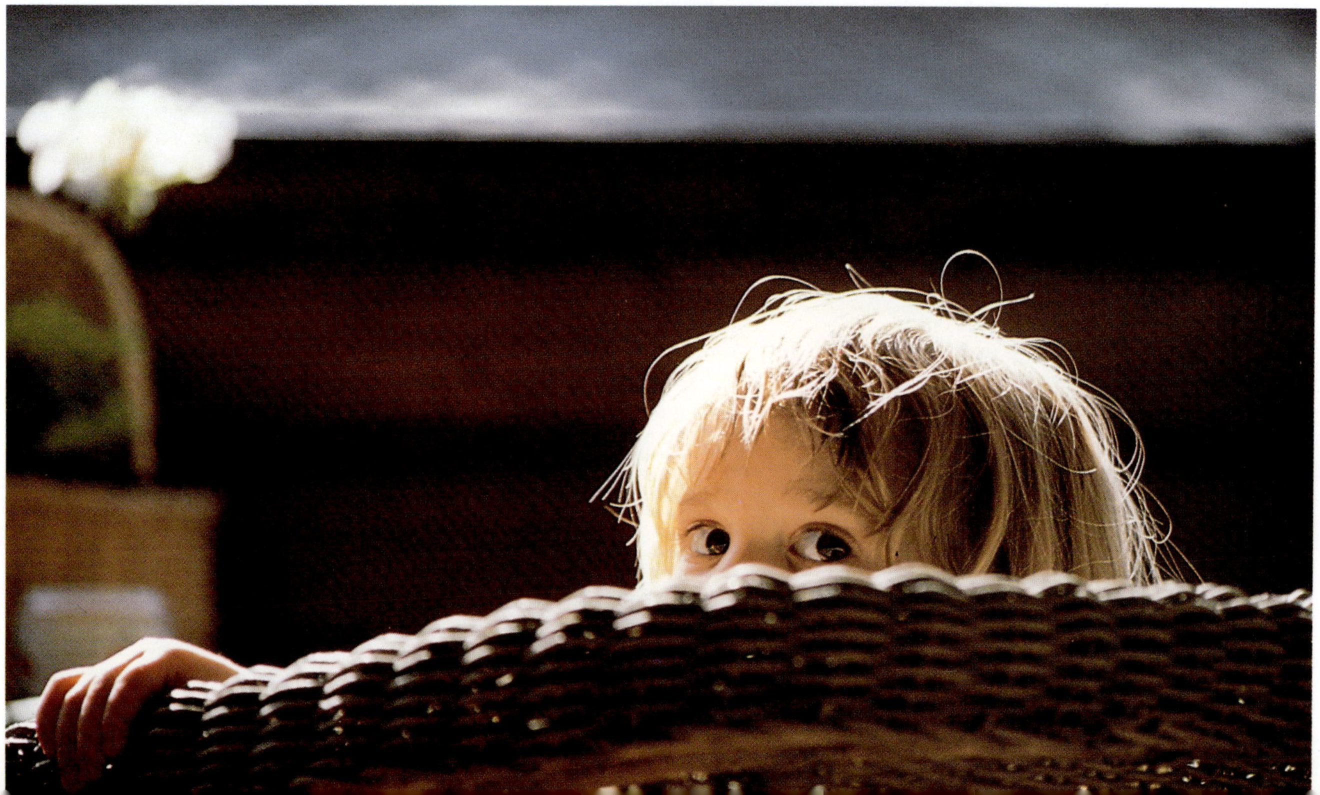

Ambient light/ flash meters

If you take flashlit studio shots, as well as pictures outdoors using available light, it makes sense to buy a meter that measures both types of lighting.

The advantages of this type of meter go beyond space and weight saving considerations. For example, they are able to measure available and flash light simultaneously for mixed lighting set ups and are able to display the proportion of each type of light. Exposure can then be adjusted to make either light source dominant.

These meters can also calculate multi-flash exposures. You can set the meter to give the correct f number for the combined exposure from several flashes, or set it to tell you how many times you need to fire your flashgun to use a certain f number. This is useful when you want to control depth of field.

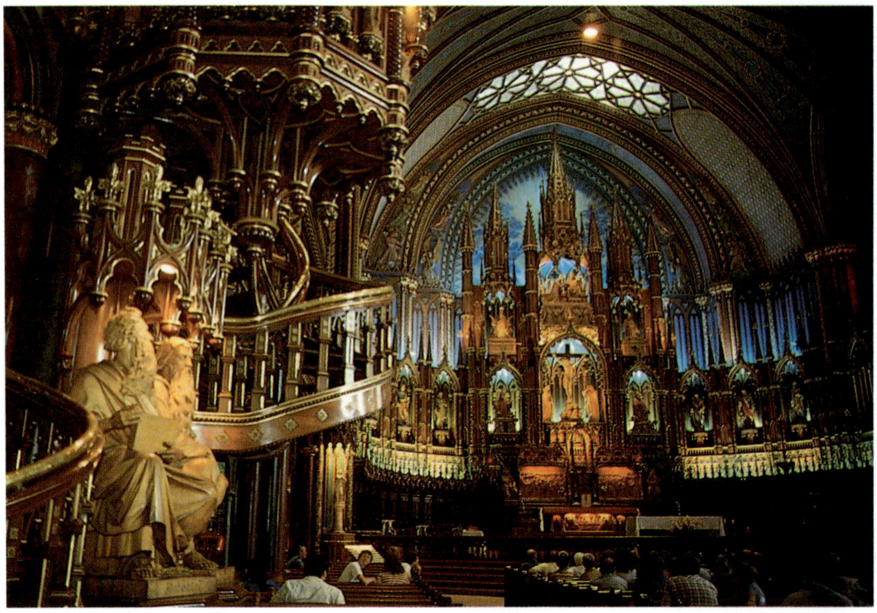

▲ ***Advanced ambient light/flash meters are able to measure both natural and flashlight simultaneously, to give spot on exposures under mixed lighting conditions.***

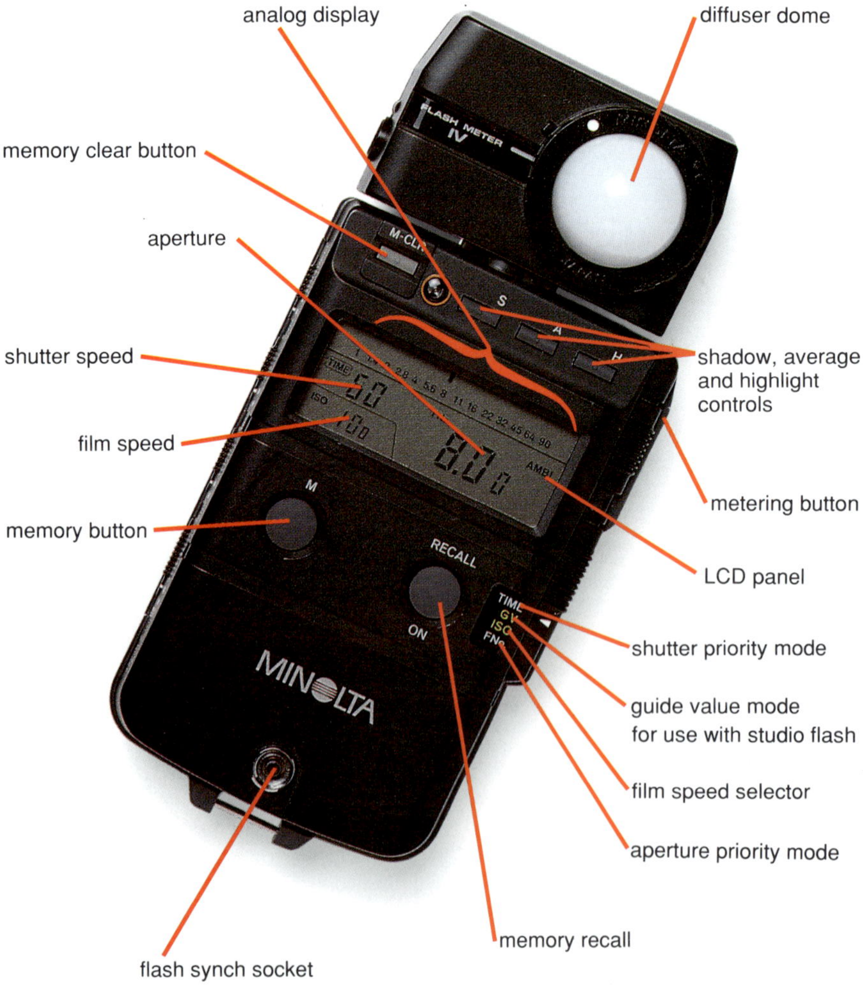

Which cell

BACK TO BASICS

When you buy a meter, your choice will depend on many factors, one of which is the type of photosensitive cell the meter uses.

Selenium cells are solar powered – you don't need batteries – and perform well in bright light. They aren't sensitive enough to take readings under dim lighting, but they are a good choice for cold weather work – they're not affected by low temperatures, unlike battery powered cells.

CdS (cadmium sulphide) cells are extremely sensitive, but they have an exposure memory. So if you meter from a bright area and then immediately take a reading from a dim area, the reading from the bright area can influence the second reading. CdS meters also react fairly slowly in dim and quickly changing light.

Silicon cells don't suffer from exposure memory, have wide metering ranges, react quickly to changing light and give very accurate readings. However, meters using these cells are usually more expensive than CdS equivalents.

Flashgun attachments

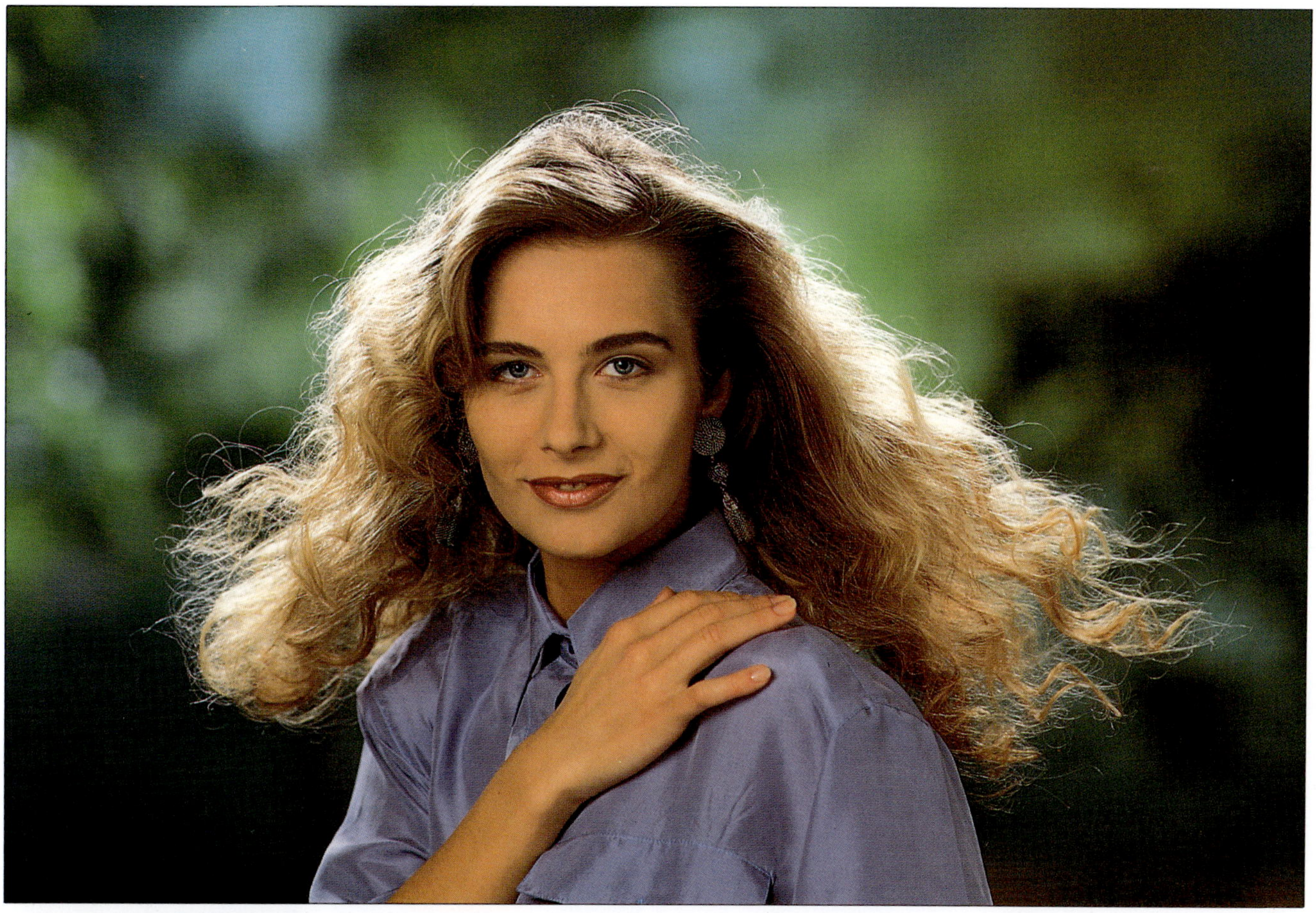

If you want to get more out of your hotshoe mounted flashgun, take a look at the range of flashgun attachments on the market. For the price of half a dozen films, you can alter the quality, direction and even the colour of the flash light.

▲ *The whole point of using fill-in flash is to gain a natural looking picture. But the harsh quality of light from a hotshoe mounted flashgun can have the opposite effect. Fitting a diffuser or reflector produces a softer light for a more flattering result.*

Hotshoe mounted flashguns have a place in most photographers' bags. For portraits or nature close-ups, sports or still lifes, a flashgun provides a reliable, repeatable and controllable light source that you can carry with you wherever you go.

However, there is a drawback – the light is very harsh and direct. This emphasizes skin imperfections, risks red eye, creates hot spots and casts heavy shadows.

Often, it is possible to soften the flashlight by bouncing it off a ceiling or a wall. But there are many occasions when this just isn't possible – for example, when you use your flashgun for fill-in lighting outdoors.

A more practical alternative is to use a clip-on attachment to spread and soften the light. There is a wide range of reflectors and diffusers available – most are inexpensive and all types produce a noticeable improvement in the quality of the flash light.

Portable reflectors and diffusers have the advantage that you can carry them with you, so wherever you are you can take advantage of soft lighting. Also, they produce a more controllable and repeatable effect than bounced flash from ceilings or walls.

As well as the attachments for altering the quality of the light from your flash, you can also buy a range of accessories to alter the direction, coverage and even the colour of the light. Used creatively, these items help you to take flashlit pictures that you wouldn't have believed possible.

▼ *There are many different types of flashgun attachment to choose from. Most of them are inexpensive, simple to use and very effective. Simply by choosing the appropriate attachment, you can change the quality of the flashlight, its direction and even its colour. This will give you far more control over the look of the final image.*

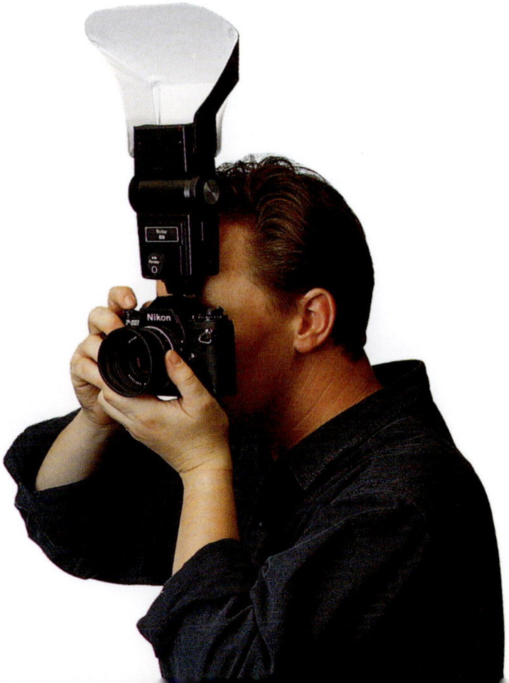

Reflectors

A much used technique for spreading and softening flash light is to bounce it off a reflective surface. But there are problems with using this method. For example, the surface finish of the reflective material has a marked effect on the quality of the light. Also, if the reflective surface is coloured, the light reaching the subject will be tinted the same colour. In addition, there is always the possibility that you won't have a reflective surface to hand when you need it.

Clip-on reflectors solve these problems. They are simple to attach and easy to use. You choose the surface finish of the reflector, so you can control the quality of the light, as well as its colour. In addition, they are so compact and lightweight you can keep one permanently in your camera bag.

Most importantly, clip-on reflectors let you produce spot-on results time and time again. For example, when you bounce light off a ceiling, you have to consider the height of the ceiling and the effect it has on exposure.

Similarly, if you are bouncing light from a wall, you have to take into account the effect of the wallpaper, or the type of paint, on the quality of the light. With a custom made reflector all of these factors are fixed, so your lighting will look the same every time.

▼ CLIP-ON REFLECTOR
This reflector clips over the front of your flashgun. A panel flips up to act as a reflective surface and direct light towards your subject. But light loss is high – you lose about 2 stops of light. However, this is much less than you normally lose if you bounce light from a wall or ceiling. The panel is translucent, so you can fasten it over the flash head and shoot through it.

Using it in this way gives a harsher, more direct quality of light, but there is less light loss. This is useful if you have a low powered flashgun, or you need to illuminate a subject farther from the camera than usual.

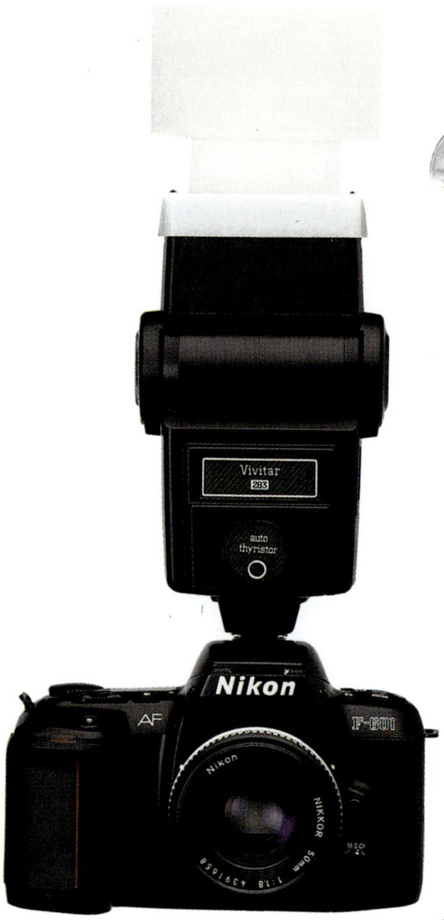

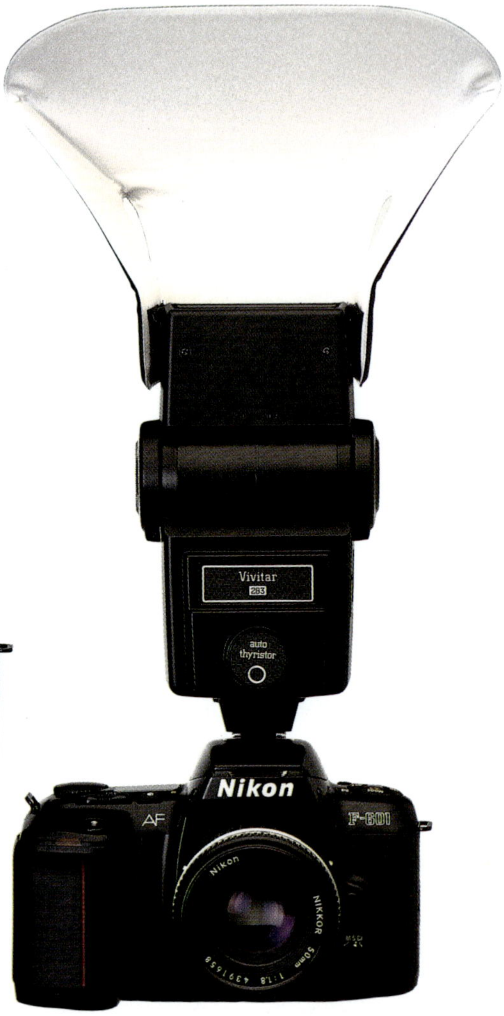

Tip: Improvized reflectors

You don't have to spend a fortune on a reflector – most cost about the same as half a dozen rolls of film. However, you can save money by making one yourself.

Stick a piece of 125 x 75mm white card on to the back of your flash head using strong sticky tape. Then bend the top over at an angle of 45° and tilt your flash head through 90°, so it points straight up. When the flash fires, the light is bounced off the card and on to your subject.

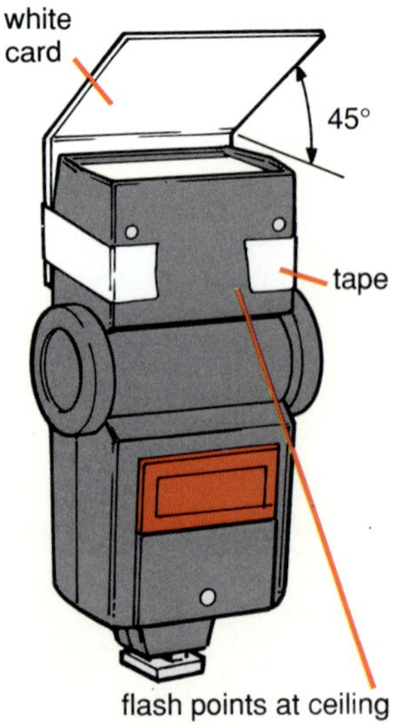

▲ STICK-ON REFLECTOR
The model above right is one of the most useful, efficient and practical reflectors on the market. You attach it to your flashgun using three adhesive tabs. This means it fits many sizes and shapes of flashgun.

It gives bright, soft lighting that does away with dark, obtrusive shadows, and light loss is low – you only lose 1$^{1}/_{3}$ stops of light. The major advantage of this reflector over others is that you can fit inserts for full control over the lighting.

Fitting a silver insert increases the brightness of the light reaching your subject and gives a slightly harder quality of light. A gold insert, on the other hand, adds warmth. Some flashguns output light with a slightly blue cast. Fitting a gold insert into the reflector not only softens the light, it also removes the unattractive blueness.

Diffusers

An alternative method of softening flashlight is to diffuse it. Instead of bouncing the light off a reflective surface, you fire it through a piece of translucent material. This scatters the light, which softens it, to give a similar effect to bounced flash. However, because the light is fired towards the subject, the lighting is more direct and has a slightly harder quality than reflected light.

There are numerous flash diffusers on the market, though they can be split into two types – those with rigid plastic diffusion screens and those which have soft material screens. The rigid versions tend to give a softer, flatter effect, but they also absorb more light, which reduces the brightness of the flash's output.

Correct exposures

BACK TO BASICS

Bouncing light off any surface – other than a mirror – leads to a fall-off in the brightness of the light reaching your subject.

If you use your reflector with a TTL flashgun, your camera will automatically compensate for the light loss. Similarly, an automatic gun can increase the duration of its output to compensate for the light loss automatically.

If you are using a manual flashgun, however, you need to compensate manually by setting a larger aperture. To calculate the amount of extra exposure needed, take a test roll of slide film and try out several aperture settings.

Start with the correct aperture for direct flash, then take a series of pictures – opening up the aperture an extra half stop on each consecutive frame. Make sure you keep notes of the aperture setting for each frame.

When you get the film back, check to see which exposure is correct. This will tell you how much wider the aperture needs to be compared to the aperture setting for direct flash. Because the reflector is a fixed distance from the flash head you can open up the aperture by the same amount each time you use it – irrespective of how far you are from your subject.

▼ INFLATABLE DIFFUSER
This is a convenient alternative to a fold-up diffuser. It works in the same way – the flash is positioned inside the diffuser and the light is fired through the translucent front screen – but instead of using metal braces to hold a cover in place, the diffuser is inflated. This makes it easier to use and carry.

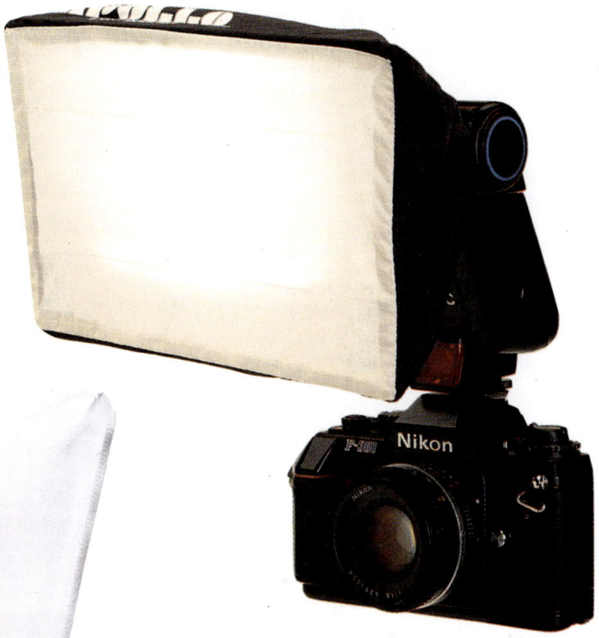

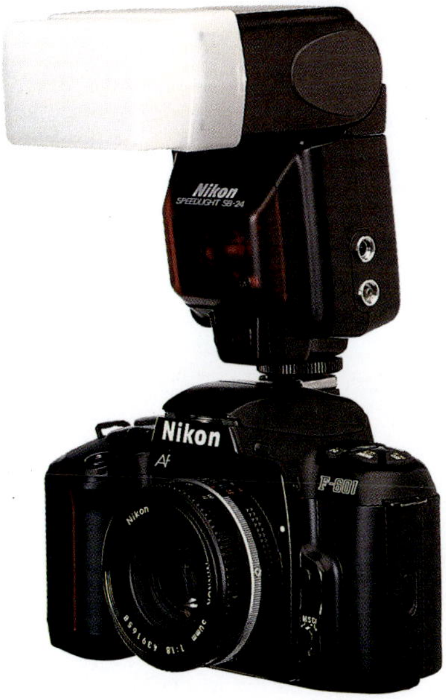

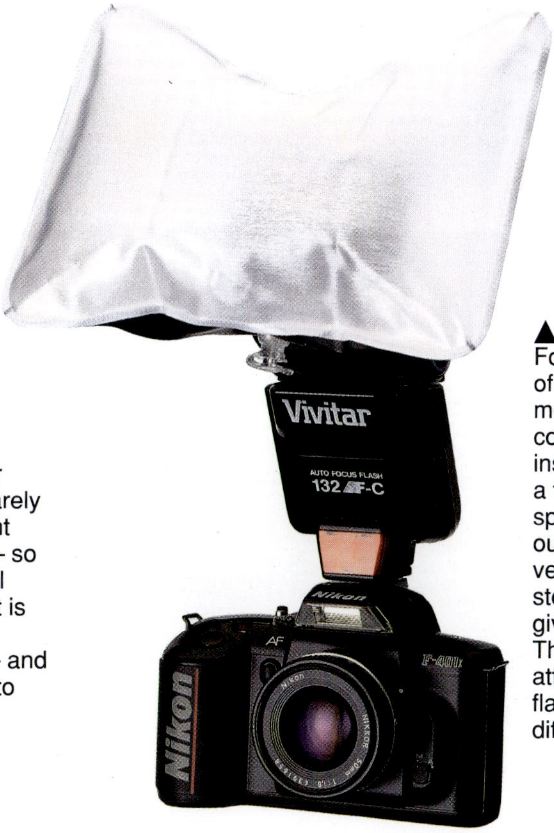

▲ CLIP-OVER DIFFUSER
This rigid, plastic clip-over diffuser gives very soft, flat lighting and barely any modelling on the subject. Light loss is relatively high – $2\frac{1}{2}$ stops – so this unit is best used with powerful flashguns, or at close distances. It is easily attached to the flash – you simply clip it over the flash head – and it is available in a variety of sizes to match different sized flashguns.

▲ FOLD-UP DIFFUSER
Fold-up diffusers are smaller versions of studio softboxes. They comprise metal braces, which support a fabric cover. The flashgun is positioned inside the diffuser and is fired through a translucent screen at the front. This spreads and softens the light. The light output through the diffusing screen is very bright – light loss is a mere $1\frac{1}{3}$ stops – but the light is still soft and gives good modelling on the subject. The drawback with this type of attachment is that you have to take the flashgun off the hotshoe to fit the diffuser.

Spreaders and splitters

Flashgun attachments don't only improve the quality of flashlight to give more flattering pictures. You can also buy attachments which allow you to alter the direction of the light.

Spreader attachments Many modern flashguns have a zoom facility, which lets you match the coverage of the flash to the field of view of your lens. This avoids the problem of vignetting – when the corners of the frame receive less light and come out too dark.

If your flashgun doesn't have a zoom facility, or the shortest setting on the zoom doesn't match the widest lens you use, you may experience problems with vignetting when you use wide angle lenses.

Fortunately, there is a solution to the problem – you can fit an inexpensive spreader attachment. This faceted piece of plastic clips over the flash head and spreads the light, so that it reaches the corners of the frame.

There are limits to how wide the attachment can spread the light, but you should be able to use a 24mm lens with most flashguns.

Splitter attachments For close-up photographs it is best to keep lighting fairly flat and even, so that you do not obscure any fine details. Mounting your flashgun on the hotshoe is far from ideal as this gives a definite top lighting effect, throwing parts of the subject into deep shadow.

For the best results you should use a ringflash. This type of flash fits around the end of the lens and has four flash heads to give an all-round even light. The drawback is the high price of these units.

An inexpensive alternative is to buy a splitter unit. This strange looking device fits over the end of your hotshoe mounted flashgun and splits the flash beam in two. The beams are then passed through two translucent screens positioned close to the lens – one on either side. This gives flat, even lighting that is just perfect for close-up photography.

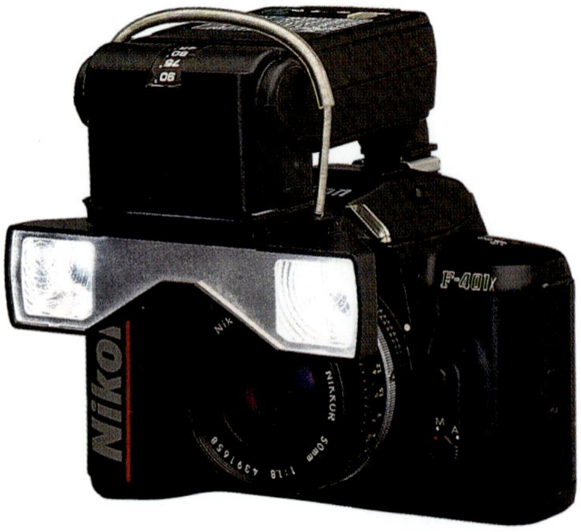

▲ ***A splitter unit is an inexpensive alternative to a ringflash unit. It gives flat, even lighting for close-ups and photomacrography.***

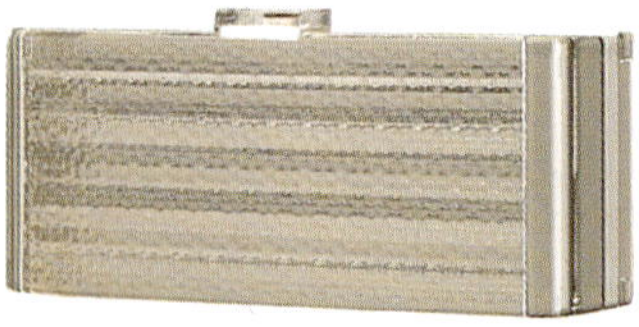

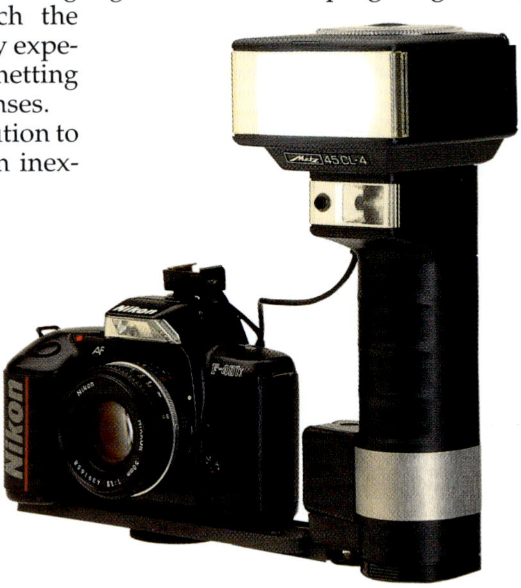

▲▶ ***The limited coverage of this hammerhead flashgun (right) causes obvious vignetting when you use a 24mm lens. Fitting a plastic spreader attachment (above) over the flash head spreads the flashlight, so the entire frame is evenly lit.***

Filters for flash

One of the most effective ways of altering the look of a flashlit picture is to fit a coloured filter over the flash head. This technique opens up a world of weird and wonderful flashlit effects.

Rigid plastic flash filters are usually sold in sets, comprising a range of different colours. Several of the 'system' filter manufacturers sell cheaper sets of flexible acetate filters which you can simply cut to match the shape of the flash head.

Some flashguns have a custom designed filter holder, which snaps over the end of the flash. Often, though, a couple of pieces of sticky tape or Blu-tac will work just as well.

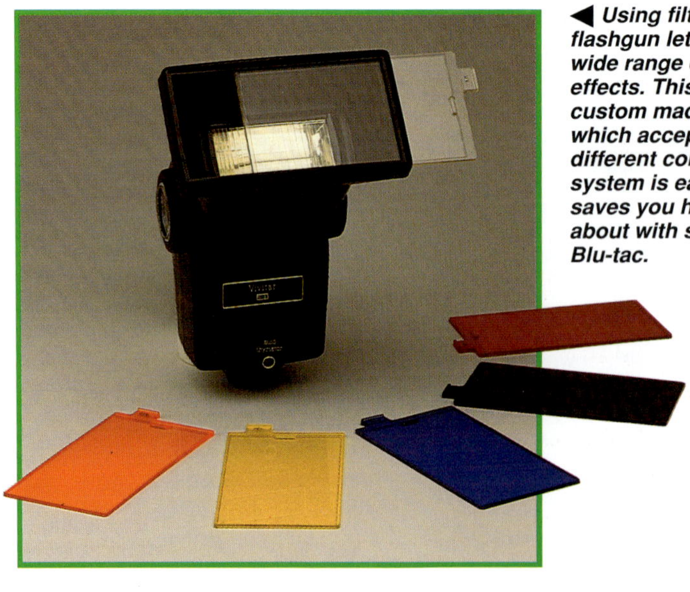

◀ ***Using filters over your flashgun lets you explore a wide range of creative effects. This flashgun has a custom made filter holder, which accepts a range of different coloured filters. This system is easy to use and saves you having to fiddle about with sticky tape or Blu-tac.***

Portable flash in the studio

When you take pictures with flash in a studio, it is vital to control the lighting. By moving the flash away from the camera and modifying its output, you gain far greater subtlety and creative control.

Most modern cameras have either a built-in flash unit or a hotshoe mounted flash. This saves both time and trouble but it doesn't make for good photography. The light source is within a few centimetres of the lens, giving you very little control over the lighting. The result is a flat, harsh light and shots with no modelling.

The answer is to take the flash off the camera. This option gives you more creative control – you can move the flash around your subject to create backlighting or sidelighting; you can use diffusing material or reflectors to soften its beam; you can create advanced lighting set-ups by adding more flash units.

Off camera flash

The simplest way to move a flash unit off the camera is to use a separate synchronization cord. Just take the flash off the camera and plug one end of the synch chord into the flash and the other end into your camera's synch socket.

Bounced and diffused flash

The problem with off-camera flash is that it casts long, harsh shadows. There are two ways to make the beam softer:

❑ Bounce the light from a reflector. You can place the reflector exactly where you want it, to create the desired effect.

❑ Diffuse the beam with a semi-transparent material such as tracing paper. Set up the diffuser in front of the flash – separate the flash and diffuser by between 30cm and 1m for best results.

Whether reflecting or diffusing the light, it's easier to understand

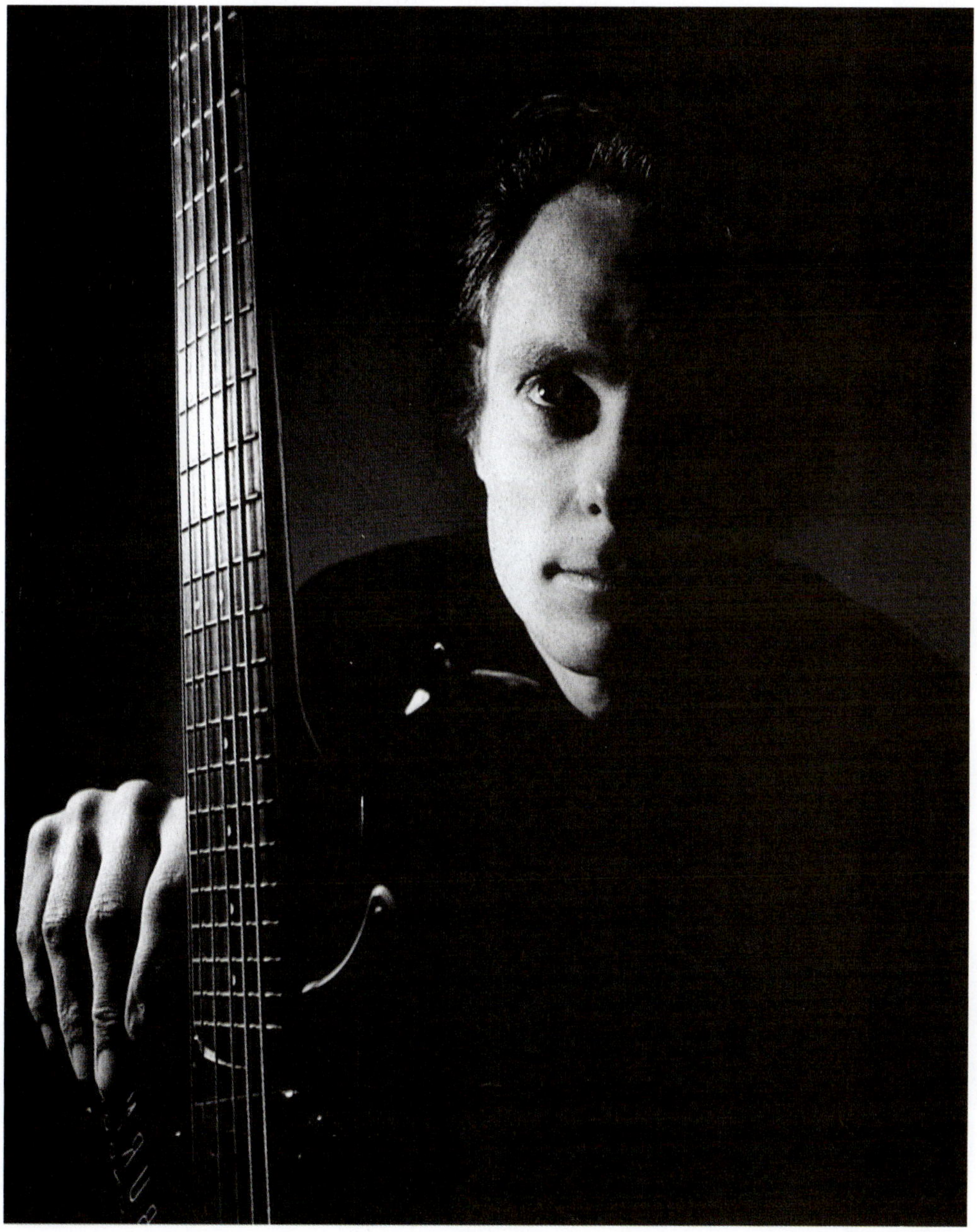

◀ *Off-camera flash gives a direct light which creates strong highlights and deep shadows. Here the photographer has used these effects to advantage, making a dramatic and contrasty portrait, appropriate to the subject.*

Tip: Slave cell

If your flash unit is built in to the camera, you must buy another flash. You can synchronize the flash and the camera using a cable. Again, you'll need an adapter if the camera lacks a synch socket.

Better still, use an inexpensive cordless synch device called a slave cell. It incorporates a photo-electric cell which detects when the on-camera flash fires.

At that instant the slave cell triggers any flash units plugged into it.

On and off camera flash

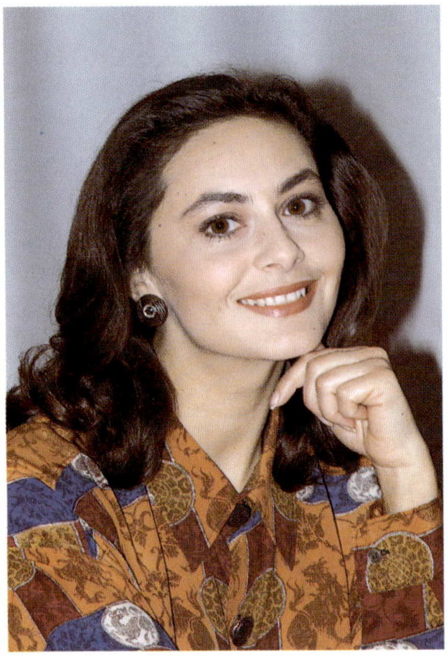

On camera

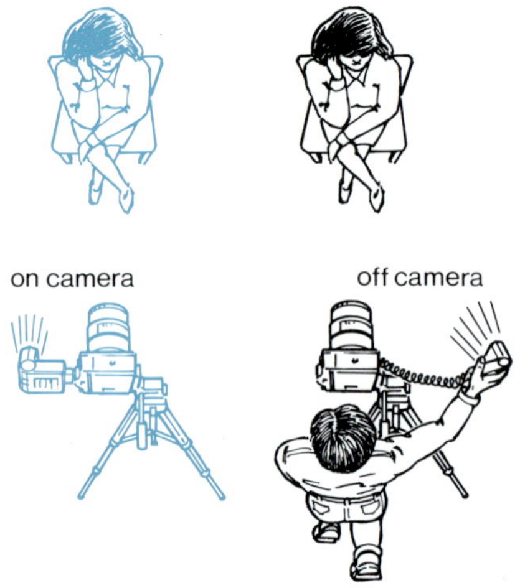

A portrait lit by on-camera flash has very little modelling: the face looks flattened by the frontal lighting. A heavy shadow is cast behind the head. Move the flash away from the camera and the facial features spring to life – and the shadow vanishes.

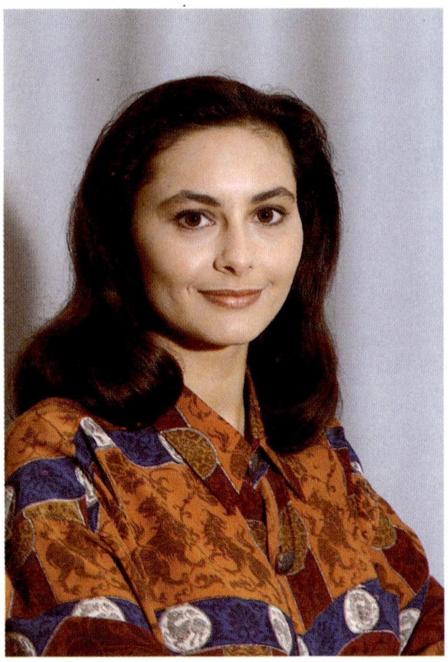

Off camera

Bounced flash

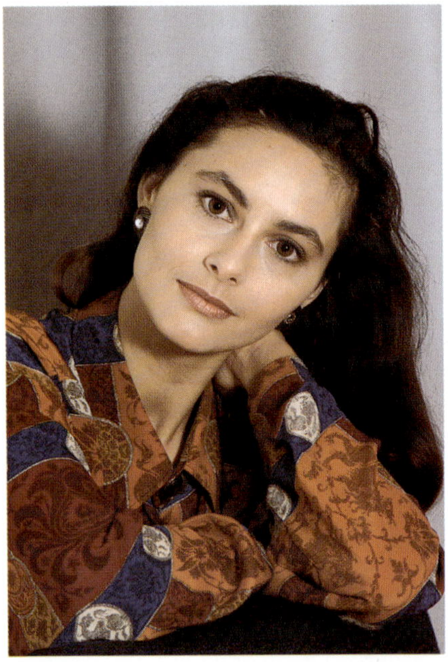

Position 1

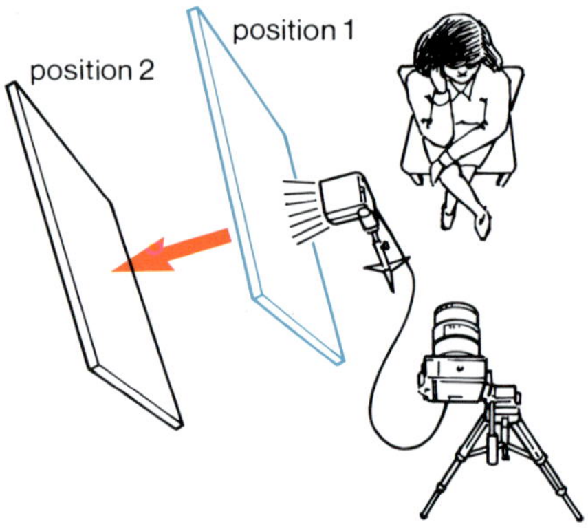

Placing a reflector close to the flash increases the size of the pool of light, but the light falling on the subject is still fairly hard and directional (Position 1). Greater separation between flash and reflector creates a bigger pool of light – so a softer beam falls on the subject (Position 2).

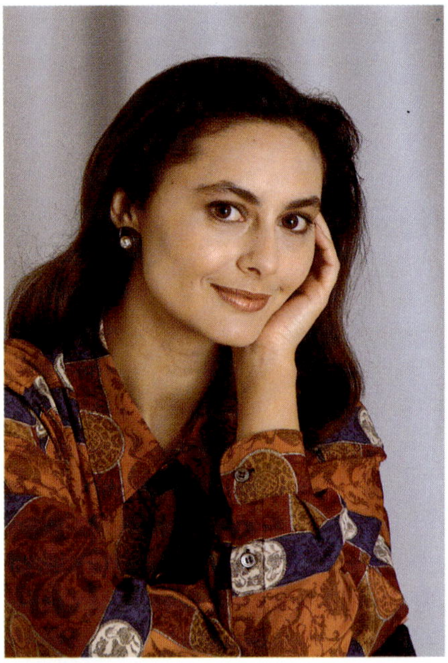

Position 2

and use studio flash lighting if you try to forget that the flashgun itself is the true light source. Instead, think of the pool of light that the flash casts on the reflector or diffuser as a new, bigger light source.

Setting exposure

Moving the flash off the camera and diffusing or reflecting the beam complicates exposure settings. The key point to remember is that almost anything you do reduces the amount of light reaching the subject.

You'll probably need to set an aperture at least two stops wider when you bounce or diffuse the light from the flash. So a flash that gives you an aperture of f8 when it points directly at a subject 3m away will only permit a setting of about f4 when you bounce or diffuse its light. TTL (through the lens) flash guns connected with an appropriate cord compensate for this automatically.

The surest way to get exposure right is to use a flashmeter. Otherwise, you need to bracket widely.

Diffused flash

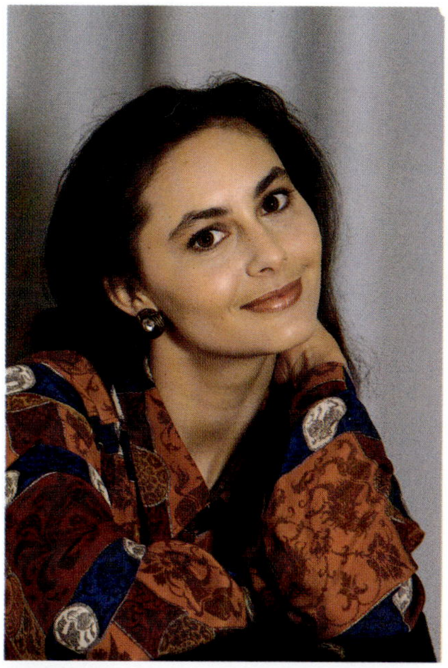

Position 1

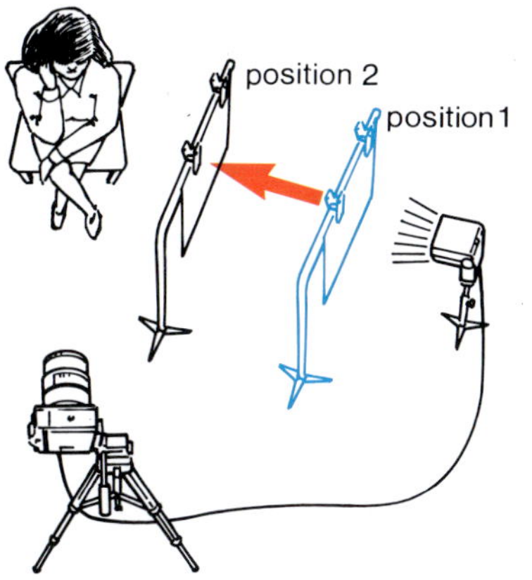

A diffuser has a similar effect to a reflector – which you use is really a matter of preference. Place the diffuser close to the flash and far from the subject for hard, directional light (Position 1). Move the diffuser further away from the flash and closer to the subject for a softer look (Position 2).

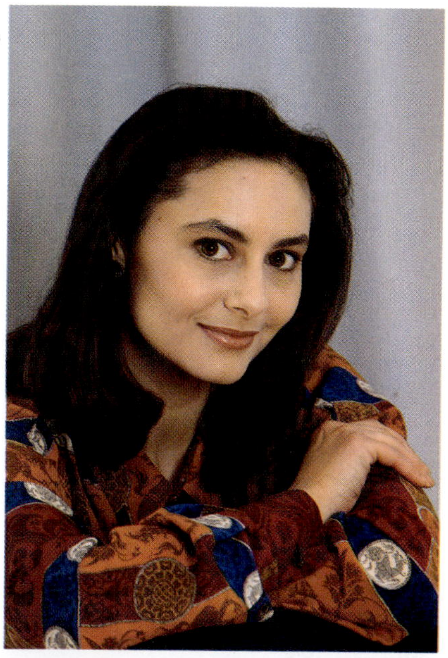

Position 2

Adding an extra unit

By adding an extra flash unit you can achieve a much greater range of effects. A simple 'Y' connector enables you to fire two flashguns from a single synch socket. Try out different positions until you achieve the lighting you want. For example, an extra flash positioned behind your model's head gives an attractive glow to the hair.

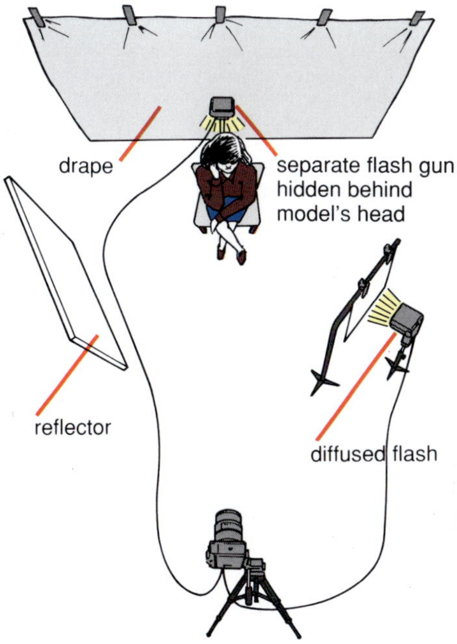

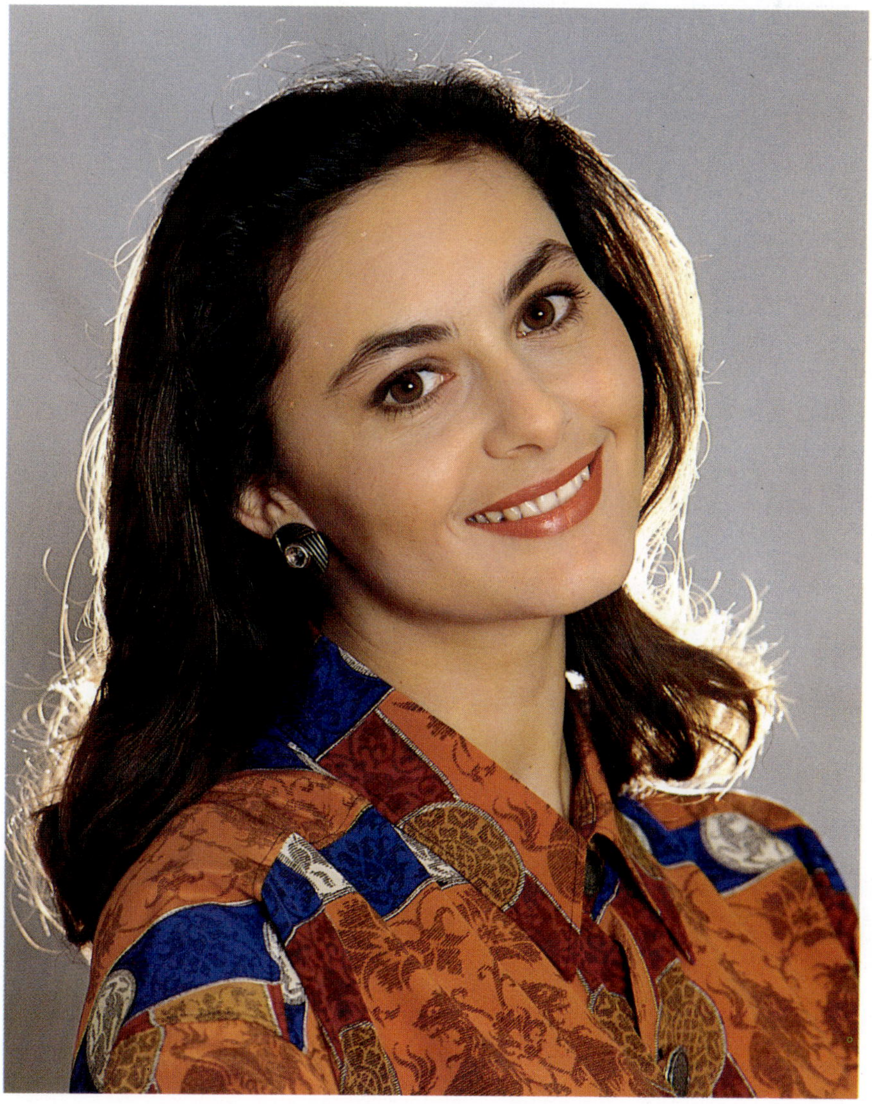

Softer lighting

An extra flash unit gives you the option of softening the lighting even further. You can add a diffuser in front of your main flash to soften the light and bounce a second flash off a reflector to further fill in the shadows. A synch cord triggers the second flash.

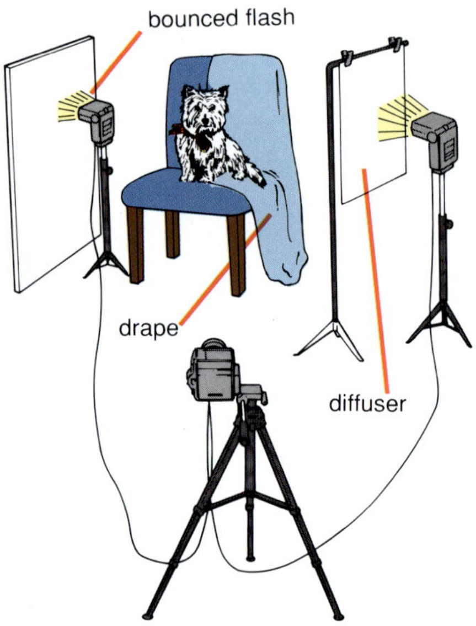

▶ ***Here, diffused flash is used to light the dog while the bounced flash provides fill-in lighting which lightens the shadows to reveal detail. When photographing dogs, it's a good idea to have someone stand behind you to distract the animal's attention and keep its eyeline away from the flash.***

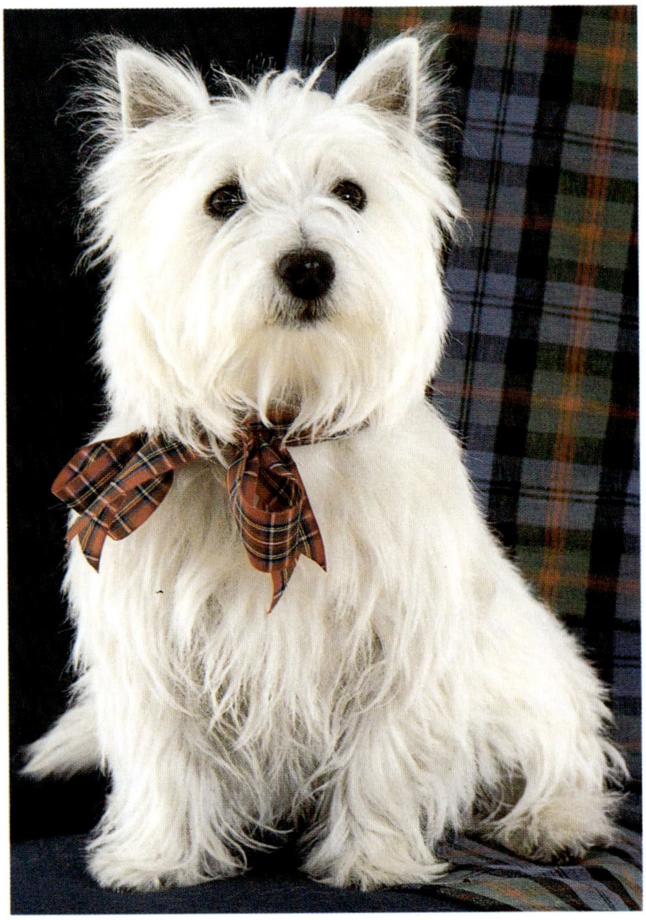

Still life

The same set up of two off-camera flash heads is useful for still lifes, too. Because you can take time to compose each shot carefully, still life photography gives you plenty of opportunity to experiment with more unusual, dramatic lighting. For example, you can illuminate the background to emphasize the shape of your still life objects. This gives your shots added interest.

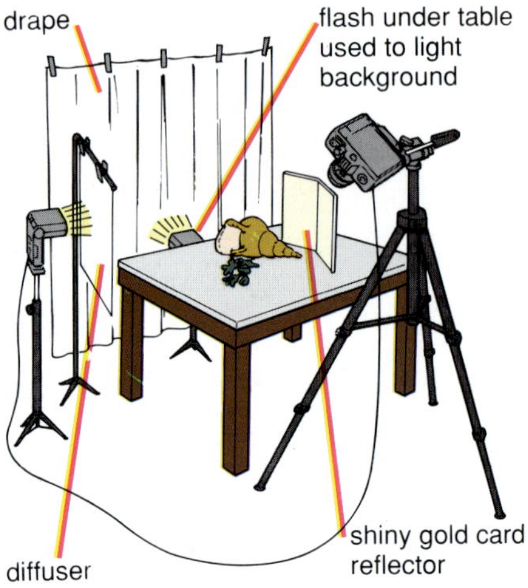

▶ ***In this still life set up, the photographer placed the second light under the table, pointed at the background. This created a halo effect on the background which emphasized the shape of the shell.***

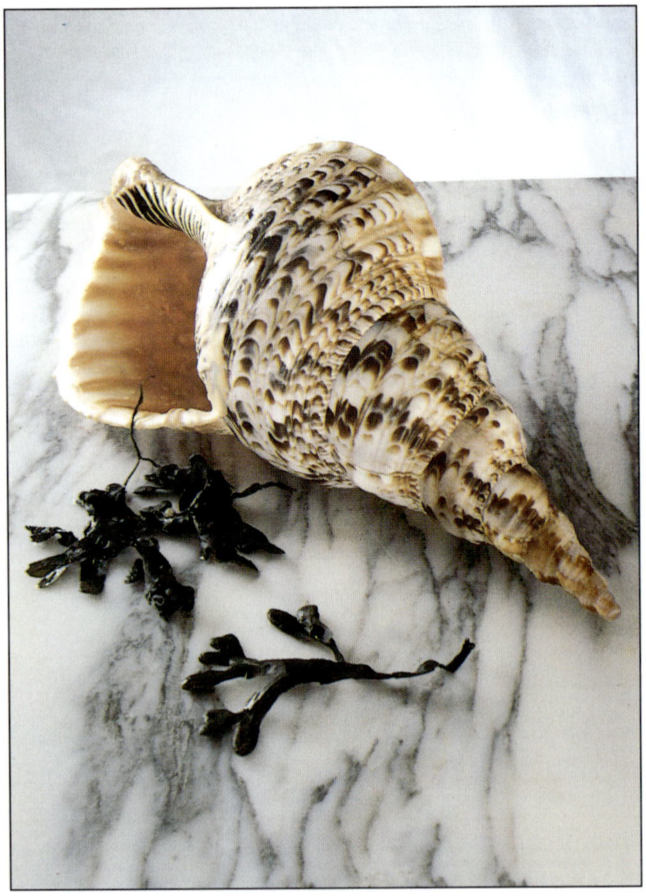

Fill-in flash

The studio is not the only place where it is useful to be able to control the light. Have a go at using fill-in flash to supplement daylight, for shots that are effective but still natural looking.

Fill-in flash comes into its own when you want to reduce contrast in a scene, so that you can retain detail in both the shadows and the highlights. It is especially useful when your subject is backlit – that is, the sun is behind them and facing towards the photographer.

If you use automatic exposure without flash, your camera's meter is fooled by the amount of light around the subject and is certain to underexpose the shot. A burst of flash allows you to remove shadows on your subject while keeping the background correctly exposed.

On an overcast day, on the other hand, you won't see hard shadows but you may wish to 'perk up' your subject. Adding flash puts a catchlight in your subject's eyes, and brightens up the shot a little.

The technique is also very useful when you want to convey action. Flash allows you to record a sharp image while daylight records the movement as a blur, creating an eye catching picture.

Banish red eye

Using a built-in or hotshoe mounted flash for portraits normally causes problems with red eye. However, this is unlikely to be a problem with fill-in flash, for two reasons. Firstly, the natural lighting level is relatively high so your subject's pupils won't be dilated. Secondly, the flash burst is at a lower strength than normal.

What you need:

For fill-in flash, you probably have the equipment you need already. Most advanced compacts and some SLRs with built-in flash have a fill-in flash button. This makes it easy to try the technique.

On SLRs without built-in flash, the method is a little more complicated. In any case, it's best to have manual control over your flash so that you have maximum control over the balance of flash and daylight.

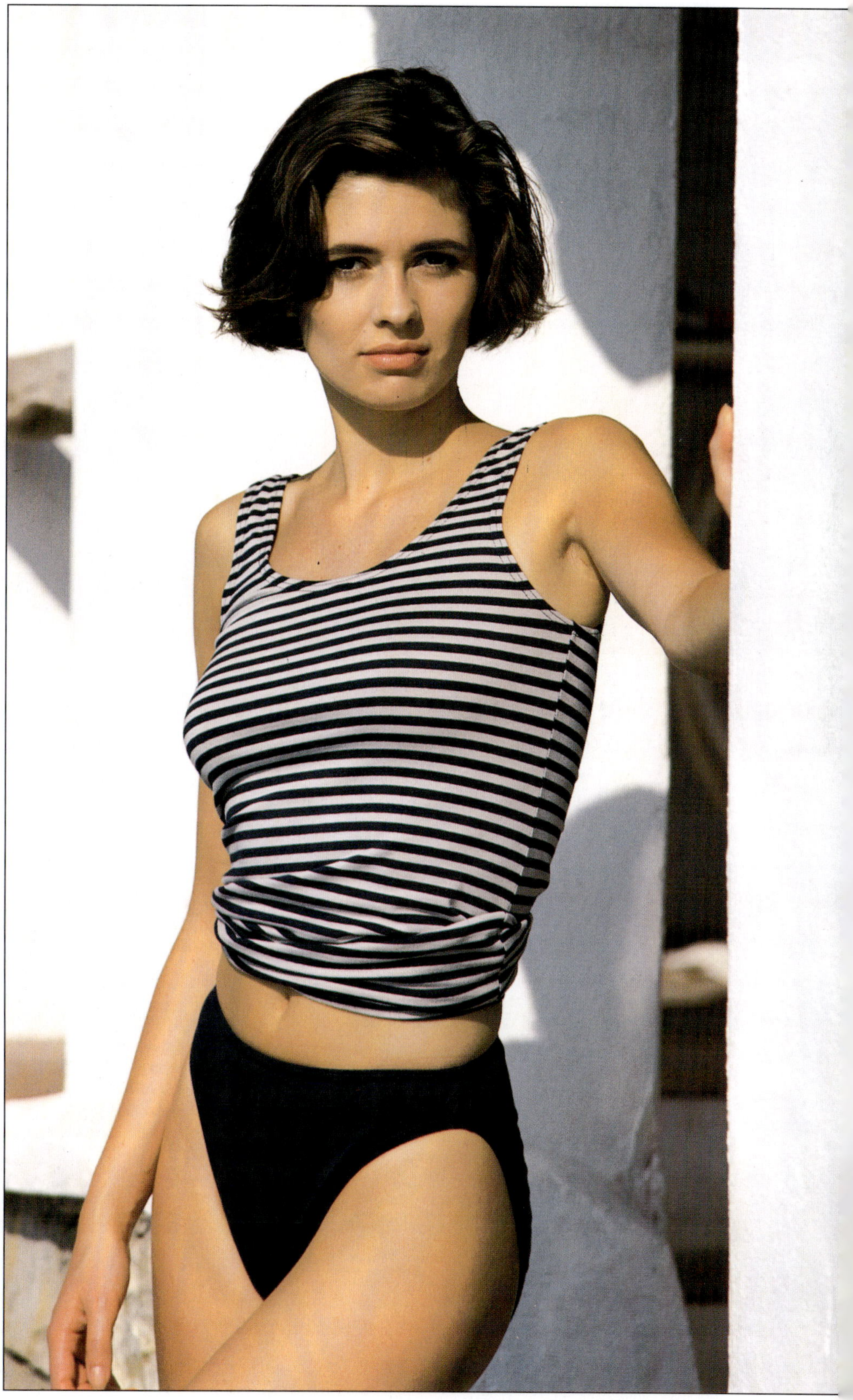

▼ ***Here the photographer applied a burst of low power fill-in flash, using a gun mounted on the camera's hotshoe. The extra illumination from the flash brightens up the girl's face but in a subtle way – she still looks as if she's lit by daylight.***

Fill-in strength

The right proportions of flash and daylight vary according to the situation and the effect you want to achieve. Remember that the aim is to supplement daylight, not overpower it. To start with, take a series of shots with different ratios and see which work and which don't. It's best to bracket your shots to be on the safe side, or use print film, because this has a wider exposure latitude than slide film.

The fill-in flash ratio is expressed as two numbers: the first figure refers to the flash, and the second stands for the amount of natural light. For example, a ratio of 1:1 means that flash and daylight contribute equal amounts to the scene. A ratio of 1:2 means that the flash is half the value of daylight, and 1:4 indicates a quarter – that is, the flash is 2 stops dimmer. So the higher the second number, the lower the flash power and the more subtle the effect.

Often, a ratio of 1:2 or 1:4 is about right. If, for example, your subject is backlit, or strongly sidelit so that one side is in shadow, and you're unsure of the correct ratio, begin by using a 1:2 ratio. With practice, you'll get to know which combination is right for different situations.

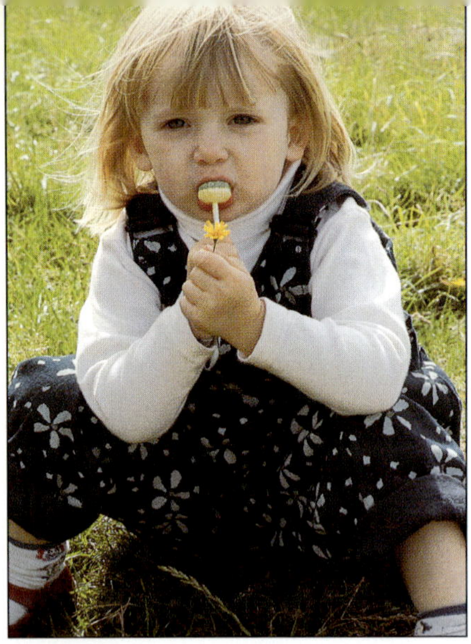

▲ ***No flash – lens at f22.***

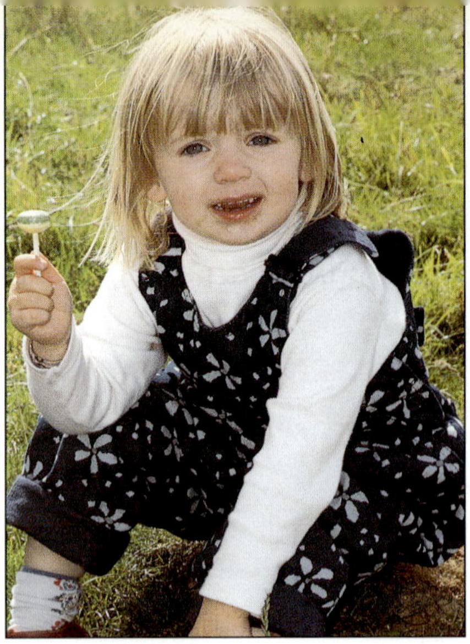

▲ ***1:8 ratio – flash at f8.***

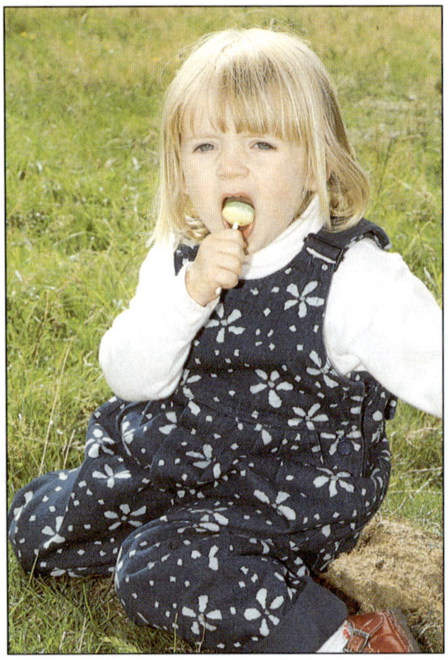

▲ ***1:2 ratio – flash at f16.***

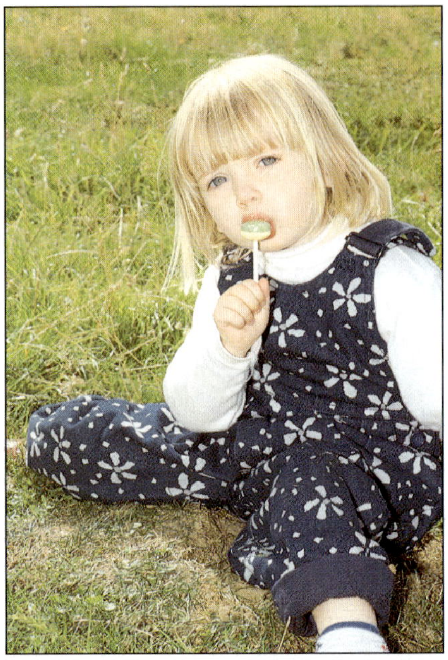

▲ ***1:1 ratio – flash at f22.***

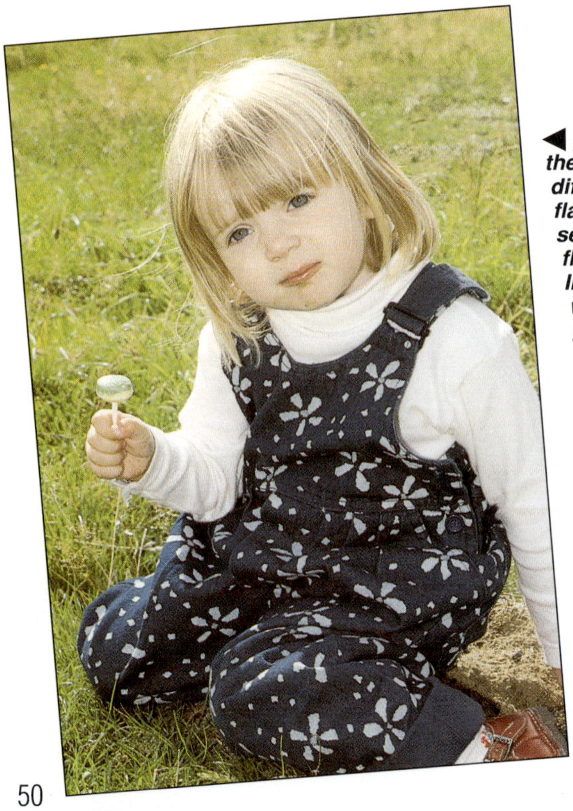

◀ ▲ ***In this series of pictures, the photographer used 5 different ratios to provide fill-in flash. The lens aperture was set to f22 each time and the flash aperture was changed. In this case, a ratio of 1:4, with the flash set to f11, gives the best result (left). The girl is backlit by sunlight but the flash removes shadows from her face.***

Tip

Easy flash

To make using fill-in flash easier, choose a camera with either a high synch speed (found on newer SLRs) or a leaf shutter (found on some medium format cameras). A leaf shutter lets you use whatever shutter speed you want with the flash.

With a faster synch speed, you can use flash even when light levels are high. Pictures are less prone to a ghost image formed by daylight (unless this is the effect you're after), but just as important is the fact that you can use a wider aperture. This means that with a flashgun in the same position you can use fill-in flash on more distant subjects or, alternatively, use a less powerful flash.

Technique 2: Reset film speed

This is also for automatic flashguns.

1 Set the correct film speed on the camera.
2 Set a faster film speed on the auto flash. For a ratio of 1:2, set double the true film speed on the flashgun – for example, from ISO 100 to ISO 200. This fools the flashgun into giving a shorter output of flash.
3 Choose an aperture from the flash scale. The setting you choose depends on the brightness of the natural light level, the power of your flash and how far away you are from the subject. However, it's likely to be a fairly small aperture because the lighting level is probably quite high.
4 Set the same aperture on the camera, then use the camera's meter to find the correct shutter speed.
5 Is shutter speed faster than synch speed? If so, take another meter reading and keep setting a smaller aperture until shutter speed is the same or slower than the flash synch speed. Also re-set the flash aperture.

How to do it

With a compact, simply press the fill-in flash button. With an SLR, there's more than one way to create fill-in flash. Try all the techniques and see which you find easiest – you'll find it becomes easier after you've had some practice.

This is one technique where you should keep the flash mounted on the camera's hotshoe, or (if you are moving the flash further back) on the same level as the camera – that is, normally at eye level. The most expensive flashguns let you set the ratio you want just by moving a switch on the gun.

Technique 1: Reset aperture

This method is suitable for automatic flashguns which have several aperture settings. You need to know your camera's synch speed first – this will be stated in the manual, but typical synch speeds are 1/60th or 1/125th second.

1 Take a meter reading of the subject.
2 Using this reading, set a combination of aperture and shutter speed on the camera that will give the correct exposure, making sure that the shutter speed is the same as or slower than the camera's synch speed. For example, with a synch speed of 1/125th second, a setting of 1/125th at f11 is acceptable.
3 Now set the auto flash to a larger f stop than that set on the camera. For example, for a fill-in flash ratio of 1:2, if the camera's meter gives a reading of f11 at 1/125th second, set the flash to f8.

Technique 3: Move flash from subject

This is a very simple method. Because the flash is used off-camera, you must have an extension lead that links the flash to the camera. (Otherwise, if you keep the flash on the hotshoe, you'll have to change to a longer focal length lens as you move away from the subject.)

1 Set the flash and camera to the correct film speed.
2 Now assume that each is being used separately, and adjust both to give the correct exposure.
3 Move the flash away from the subject (on manual) to reduce its contribution to the light.

For a 1:2 ratio, find out the camera to subject distance and then move the flash away by one and a half times this amount. If you are 1m from your subject, the flash should be 1.5m away from it.

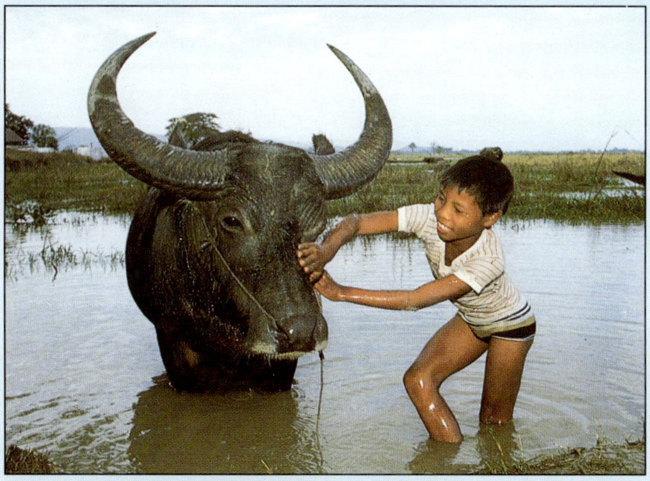

Technique 4: Vario power flash

1 Set this type of flash to manual. With the flash switched to full power, work out the correct aperture setting for the subject to camera distance.
2 Set this aperture and the correct shutter speed on the camera.
3 Then set the flash to half, a quarter or an eighth of its power, depending on the ratio you want. For a ratio of 1:2, for example, set the flash to half power.

◀ ***Fill-in flash brightens up pictures taken in open shade. You can tell that the technique was used here because of the highlights on the boy's leg, where the water reflects the burst of light from the flash.***

Technique 5: Cover flash

Set your flash to manual and hold a neutral density filter over it to reduce the amount of light coming from the flash. For example, a 2X filter cuts down the flash's power by 1 stop – that is, it halves the illumination.

You can improvize and use a white handkerchief in place of a neutral density filter. The amount of light it cuts out depends on its thickness and how many times it's folded over:

1 Set your flash to manual and set the camera aperture as indicated by the distance scale on the flash, or use the guide number to work out the correct aperture.
2 Set this aperture on the camera, and meter the daylight as normal.
3 Then take a series of shots, folding the hanky over the flash head by an additional thickness each time. Use the most successful combinations in future. For a fill-in flash ratio of 1:2, either use a 2X neutral density filter over the flash, or use the handkerchief thickness that cuts out 1 stop of light.

Creative flash

You can combine flash with a long exposure to produce an attractive blurred effect. The flash freezes the subject but the background is lit by just natural light, and records on film as a blur.

Try to shoot in dim lighting conditions – at dusk or at night. This is because you need a slow shutter speed to blur movement. For good results, use a strong burst of flash – the fill-in flash ratio may need to be as high as 1:1.

For your first subject, choose something that you can have lots of attempts at shooting – for example, children on fairground rides.

Slow synch

The above method can also be used when your subject is stationary and likely to be underexposed without flash. Dusk is the best time for this. The classic use of this technique is when your subject is standing in front of a sunset. It allows you to photograph the sunset in all its glory *and* record details of the subject's face instead of turning them into a silhouette.

Whether you're after creative blur or you want to use slow synch for a stationary subject, take a few shots on different settings to increase your chances of good results: first vary the shutter speed, then the aperture, while keeping the flash constant.

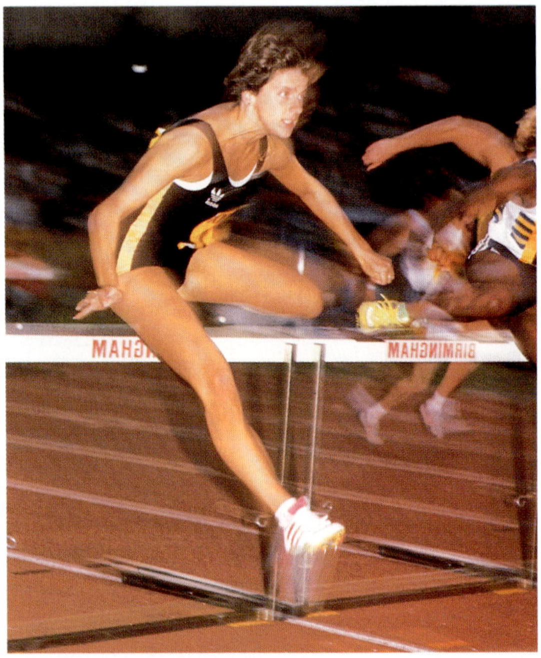

◀ A burst of flash freezes the hurdler in action, while the existing stadium lighting allows a blur of movement to be recorded on the film as well. The result conveys movement more effectively than if flash had been the only light source.

▼ A meter reading was taken from the sky at dusk and a long shutter speed used so that it would be correctly exposed. Flash illuminates the man in the foreground so he is also exposed correctly, while not affecting the exposure for the sky at all.

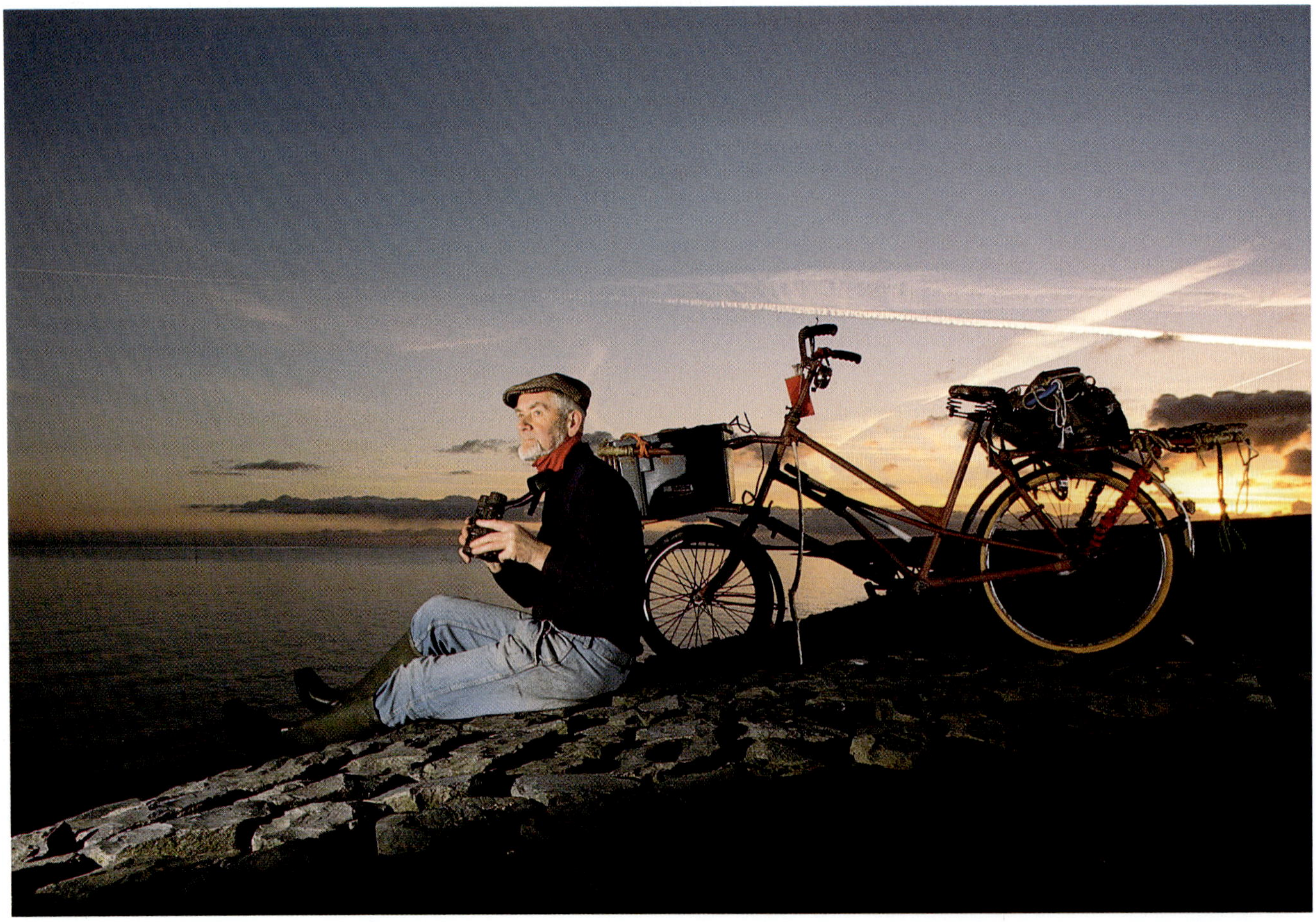

Flashmeters

If you are using studio flash lighting, a flashmeter all but guarantees perfect exposures, though that's not all it's useful for. You can also use a flashmeter to take accurate incident light readings from your hotshoe mounted flashgun.

The TTL exposure systems used in modern SLRs are so advanced that they can both measure and control the light from your hotshoe mounted flashgun. So you could be forgiven for thinking that a hand held lightmeter capable of measuring flash light is an unnecessary additional expense. Nothing could be further from the truth.

For a camera to measure flash exposures, you must use a dedicated flashgun. But what if you are using studio flash? These are connected to the camera by simple synch cords and do not link up with the camera's TTL metering system. A synch cord merely synchronizes the firing of the flash to the firing of the shutter.

It is possible to calculate flash exposures using the power of the flash unit, the distance of the light from the subject and the film speed. But this technique is time consuming, open to error and is complicated by the use of light modifiers, such as umbrellas.

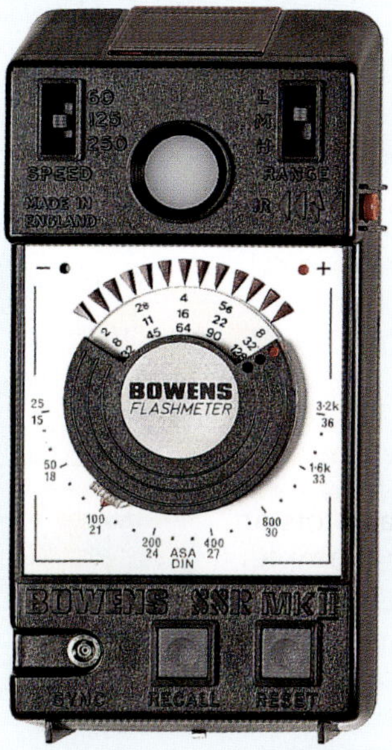

▶ Basic flashmeters are accurate to a half, or one third, of a stop. They are often slower to use than more advanced models, but they are also considerably cheaper – the cheapest types cost a tenth of the price of a top range meter.

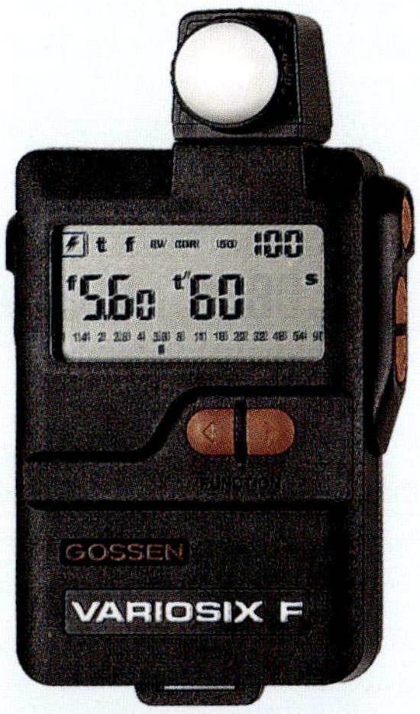

▲ You don't have to spend a fortune on a flashmeter to buy a well specified model. This type has a LED display, can measure ambient and flash light, and is accurate to one tenth of a stop.

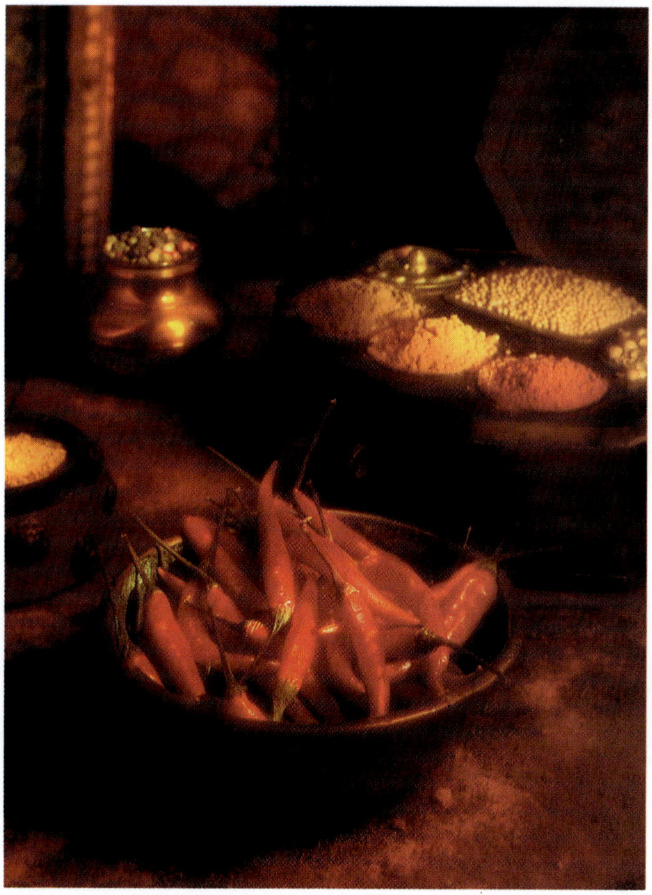

◀ For this shot, the photographer took flash readings from all areas of the composition. This enabled him to set an exposure that maintains the fine balance between the highlights and shadows. A flashmeter is essential for a complex lighting set up like this.

Use a flashmeter

A better idea is to use a flashmeter. These are used in the same way as a hand held ambient lightmeter – that is, those that measure constant light sources, such as daylight and tungsten lighting. The difference is that flashmeters can measure the brightness of the brief burst of light output by a flash unit. This lasts for a fraction of a second and is too fast for ambient lightmeters to cope with.

Flashmeters can also be used with hotshoe mounted flashguns. While TTL flash systems cope admirably with most subjects and lighting conditions, they are still prone to the same mistakes as any lightmeter that measures reflected light. For example, a scene that's made up of dark tones fools the meter into overexposing the picture. Filling the frame with a very light toned subject has the opposite effect.

The advantage of a flashmeter is that it comes with a diffuser dome and can be used to take incident flash light readings, whereby you measure the brightness of the flash light falling on to your subject, rather than the brightness of the light it reflects. Metering in this way avoids the problems of uneven lighting or non-average tones influencing the overall exposure.

Choosing a flashmeter

Probably the first question to be answered when it comes to buying a flashmeter, is how much you are prepared to spend. This will depend upon how much you expect to use the meter, and the type of pictures you are using it for.

There is a wide range of factors affecting the price of a flashmeter, and lots of points to watch out for when you are deciding which model to buy.

Measuring range The capability to measure a wide exposure range is especially important if you are likely to be using very powerful flash packs at close range. The output from these packs is too bright for many flashmeters to measure.

Some flashmeters are supplied with a second diffuser, which extends the meter's range by up to five stops. A meter which measures from EV -2 to EV +18 on ISO 100 film can cope with all but the most powerful flash packs. But for very powerful lighting your meter needs to measure up to EV +23 on ISO 100 film.

Accuracy Many basic flashmeters measure exposures to the nearest half a stop. This is fine for print film, which has a wide exposure latitude, but if you are shooting on slide film your meter needs to be accurate to the nearest third of a stop.

The most expensive flashmeters are accurate to the nearest tenth of a stop. But this degree of accuracy is unnecessary unless you use flash packs that can be adjusted in tenth stop increments.

Metering modes Some flashmeters have a fixed diffuser and are limited to taking incident flash light readings. Others let you take incident and reflected flash light readings.

More advanced flashmeters give readouts for both ambient light and flash. This saves you having to carry two meters around with you.

A few flashmeters accept accessories for specific metering applications. For example, you can attach a small diffuser on a bendy metal arm for taking incident light readings from small, difficult to reach areas of the frame.

Basic flashmeter

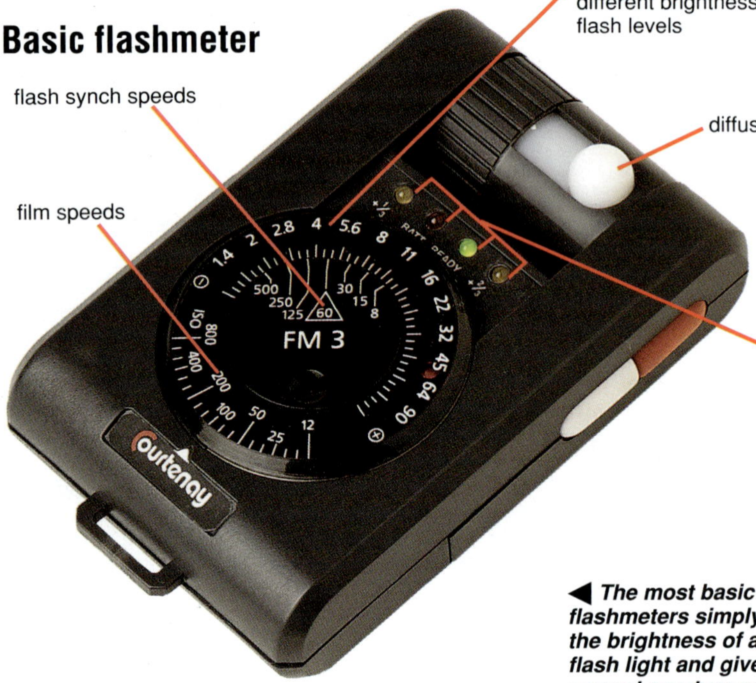

◀ The most basic flashmeters simply measure the brightness of a burst of flash light and give you the correct aperture setting for an accurate exposure. On this inexpensive model, you can read off the required aperture setting for a correct exposure at a variety of shutter speeds, ranging from 1/8th sec to 1/500th sec.

Advanced flashmeter

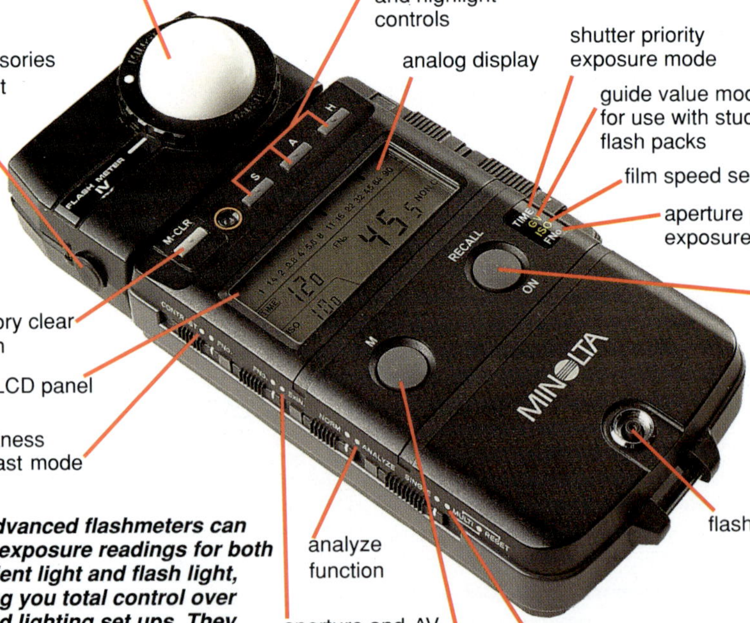

▶ Advanced flashmeters can give exposure readings for both ambient light and flash light, giving you total control over mixed lighting set ups. They also tend to be more accurate and reliable, and some feature a range of advanced metering modes, which add to the versatility of the meter.

Advanced metering modes

Top of the range flashmeters are expensive because they are designed and constructed to give accurate and reliable service for years, despite heavy use. These flashmeters also offer a variety of features and metering modes that increase their versatility.

Multi-flash mode In this mode, flashmeters can give a cumulative reading for multiple flashes. This is useful when you need to fire a low powered flash several times to build up the exposure, so that you can set a small aperture for maximum depth of field.

On some flashmeters you can even key in the aperture you require. Then you simply fire the flash once and the meter displays how many times you must fire it to give the chosen aperture.

Memory function This allows you to store separate exposure readings. You can use it to compare readings – for instance, when you are calculating the brightness range in a scene.

Analyze function The most sophisticated flashmeters can display the proportion of continuous and flash light making up the exposure. This enables you to control precisely the ratio of daylight or tungsten lighting to flash, to alter the overall feel of a shot.

Guide value mode This mode is most useful with studio flash packs that let you increase flash output over a considerable range. However, you can use it with any flash. You simply key in the required aperture and fire the flash unit. Then press the GV (guide value) control and the meter tells you by how much you must increase flash output for a correct exposure at your chosen aperture setting.

Highlight and shadow controls When you set your flashmeter to the highlight metering mode and meter from a brightly lit area, the exposure reading is automatically balanced towards a high key exposure. The meter displays an exposure that's approximately $1^{1}/_{2}$ stops brighter than average. The shadow metering mode does the opposite – it reduces the exposure to give a low key shot.

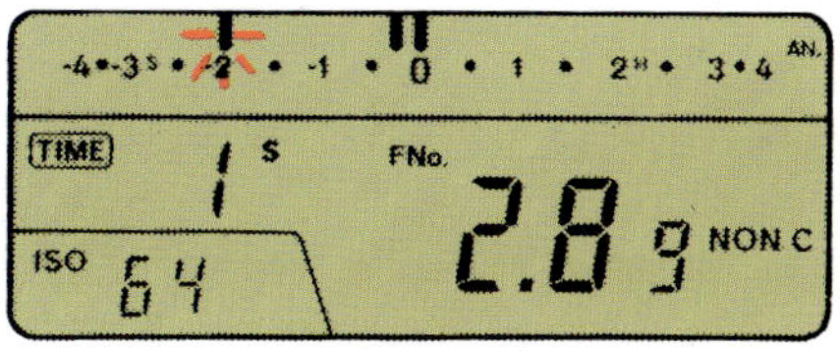

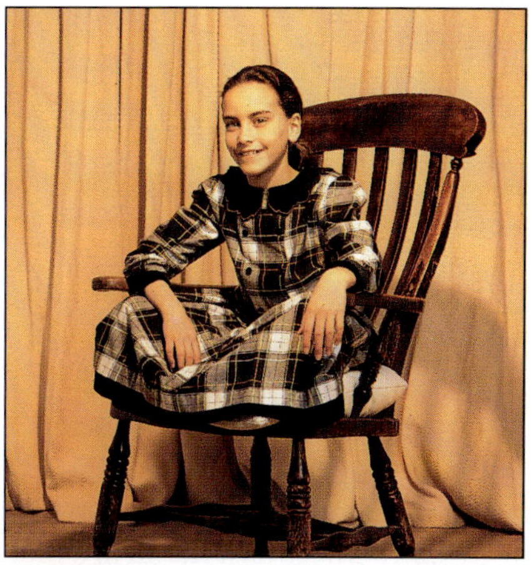

▲▶ *The analyze function found on some flashmeters shows the proportion of continuous and flash light making up the overall exposure. It is useful for mixed lighting set ups. The flashing marker shows the proportion of flash light, and the stationary marker shows the proportion of ambient light. Here, tungsten lighting is the dominant light source, giving the picture a strong orange cast.*

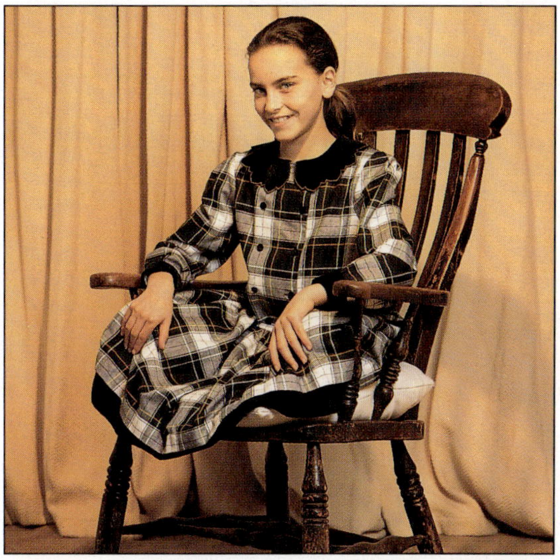

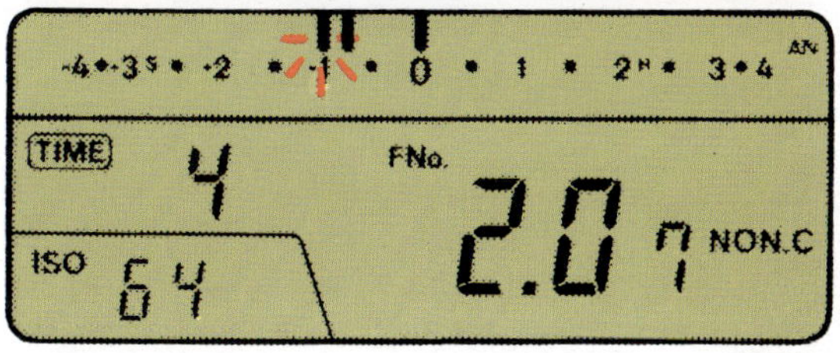

◀ *For this shot, the proportions of tungsten and flash light are almost balanced. This gives the portrait an attractive warm glow. To obtain balanced lighting, the proportion of tungsten light was reduced by increasing the shutter speed – from one second to one quarter of a second. The LED display clearly shows that the flashing marker has moved towards the stationary marker, so that they are next to each other. This indicates that the proportions of tungsten and flash light are almost equal.*

▼▶ *To gain a more neutral result, the proportion of flash light was increased further. To do this, the photographer increased the output of the flash. He adjusted the flashmeter's GV control upwards, which moved the flashing marker closer to the zero position. He then read off the GV number and increased the flash output by this amount – in this case two stops.*

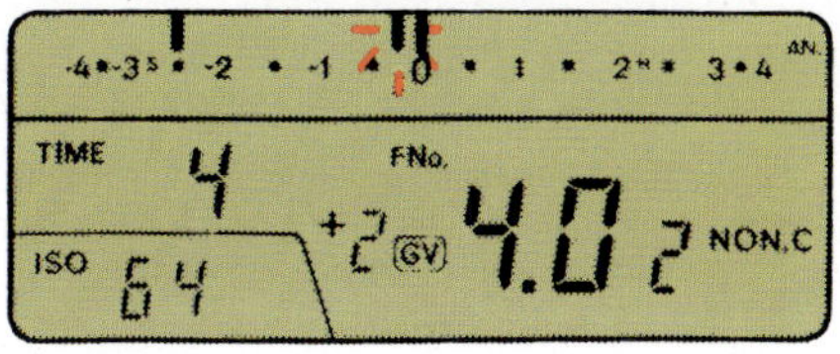

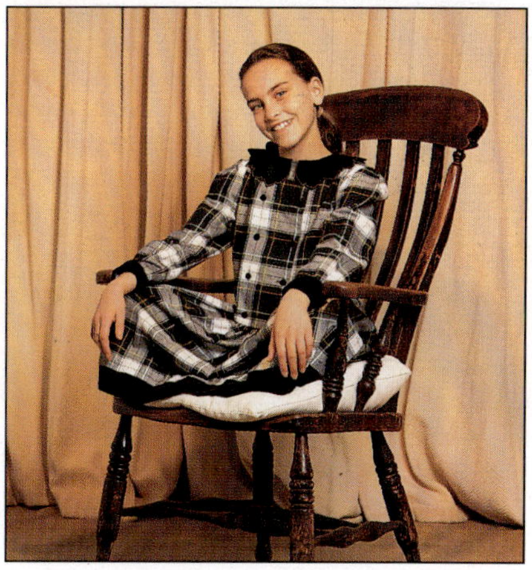

How to take a reading

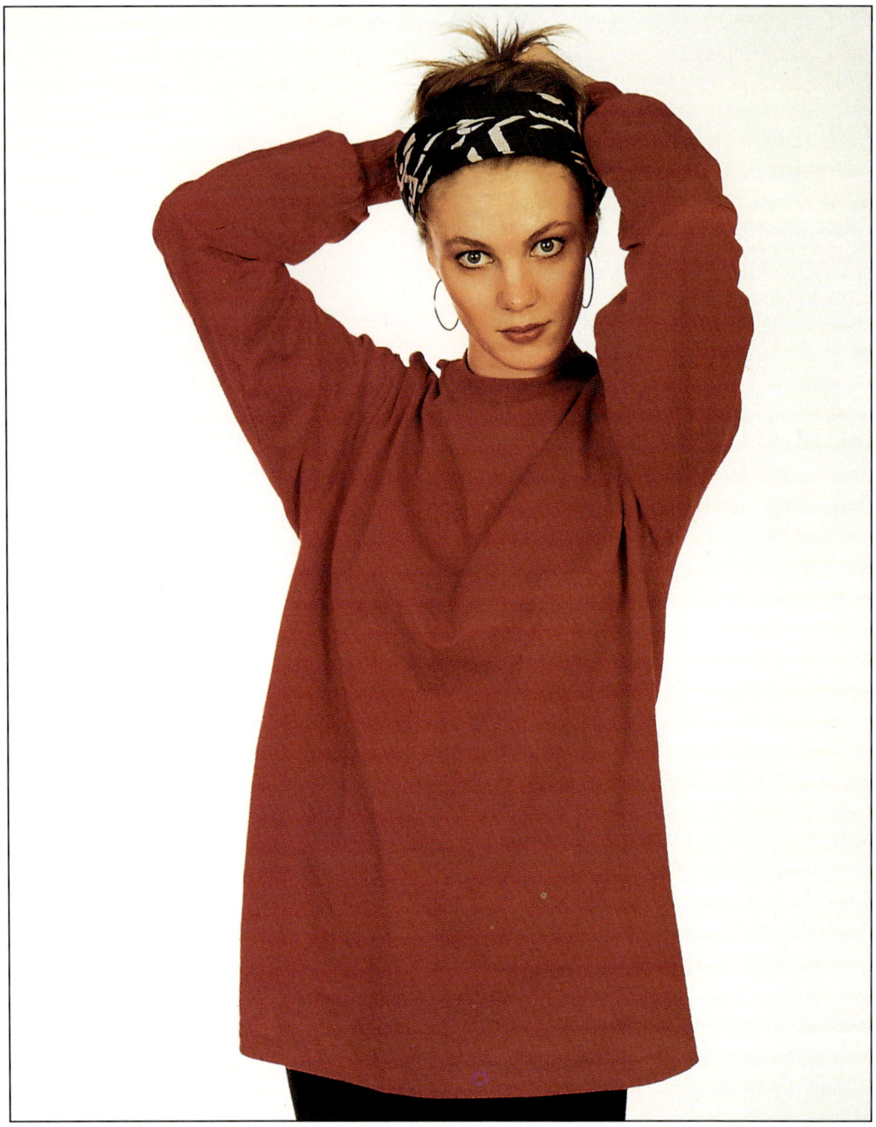

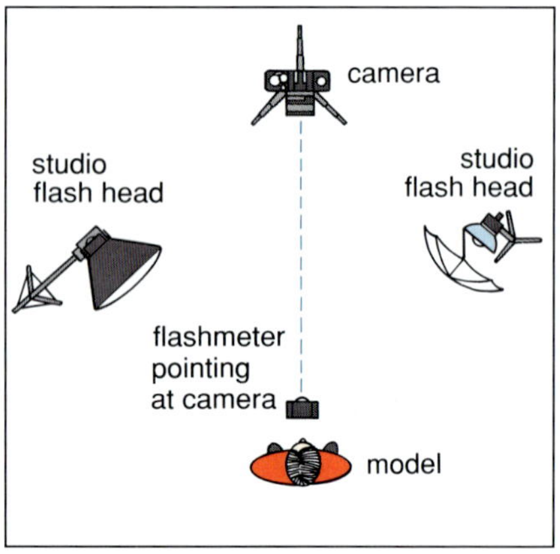

◀▲ ***To take an incident reading, hold the meter in front of your subject, with the diffuser pointed straight at the camera. If you're using more than one light, as in this shot, don't be tempted to point the meter at your main light – keep it pointed at the camera, so that the lighting from both flash heads is taken into account.***

Most flashmeters are easy to use, as long as you follow a few simple guidelines. You may take a little longer to master all the functions on a top of the range model, but these are unnecessary for the majority of picture taking situations anyway.

Before you take a reading you must key in the speed of the film you're using and the shutter speed you've set – bearing in mind that this must not be faster than your camera's highest flash synch speed.

If you are going to take an incident flash light reading, hold the meter in front of your subject, and point the diffuser at the camera. It is easy to make the mistake of pointing the diffuser at the main flash unit, but this leads to inaccurate readings.

For a reflected flash light reading you must remove the diffuser, and in some cases fit a special metering accessory. You then point the flashmeter at the part of your subject you want to take a reading from. Make sure this is a mid-tone unless you are deliberately trying to achieve an under or overlit picture.

When you are ready, press the metering button on the flashmeter, or press the test button on the back of the flash. The method you use depends on whether you are shooting in cord mode (when the flash is linked to the meter by a synch cord) or non-cord mode – see Linking up.

Once you've fired the flash the meter indicates the correct aperture setting. How it does this depends on the meter you are using.

The final step is to transfer the aperture setting suggested by the flashmeter to your camera's lens.

Linking up

BACK TO BASICS

You can take an exposure reading with a flashmeter in two different ways. In cord mode the meter is linked to the camera by a synch cord – in the same way that you link a flashgun to the camera. When you press the metering button on the flashmeter, it automatically fires the flash and measures the brightness of the light. You can then read off the exposure.

This is the easiest method to use as you don't need an assistant to fire the flash, while you hold the flashmeter in position. However, it may mean trailing long lengths of cable between the meter and the camera.

The other way to take a reading is to set your flashmeter to non-cord mode. This primes the flashmeter to measure the next burst of flash. As soon as a flash fires, the meter makes a reading.

Flat lighting for portraits

The soft, even illumination that is characteristic of flat lighting is an essential technique to master. It's one of the best ways that you can obtain a really flattering portrait.

Lighting is one of the key factors of a good portrait. It should be seen as a creative tool that can be used to show how you want to portray your model.

For instance, hard lighting is effective if you want to highlight the confident or assertive nature of your subject. If, however, you want to emphasize the gentle and romantic side of your model, flat lighting is more appropriate.

This makes flat lighting especially suitable for much conventional portraiture as well as most glamour work. It gives soft and flattering portraits which have a wide range of mid-tones and no deep shadows or bright highlights.

Harsh shadows, especially, tend to distort facial features. A diffuse, apparently directionless light is usually much more appealing. In particular, skin textures can look very striking if they are evenly and softly lit. So facial close-ups and nude studies also look good when flat lit.

Variety of locations

Flat lit portraits can be done at a variety of locations. On an overcast or hazy day, you can obtain good flat lit portraits outside.

If it is important to have the convenience of working indoors, a particularly good location is a conservatory or greenhouse. Sometimes these have frosted glass roofs which help to flatten light. If not, you can attach tracing paper over the glass.

Window light

It's also possible to take portraits with reasonably flat illumination using window lighting indoors. To do this, you must use reflector boards to bounce light on to the side of the subject in shadow. Again, you can hang diffusing materials over the windows – such as tracing paper or even net curtains – to help flatten the light.

However, to have absolute control over the lighting in your photograph, working in a studio with artificial lighting is best.

▶ Flat lighting is a key ingredient in a glamorous beauty portrait. Note how the shadows on the model's face and neck are relatively soft. This effect, together with natural looking make up and soft focus filtering, produces an image that flatters your subject.

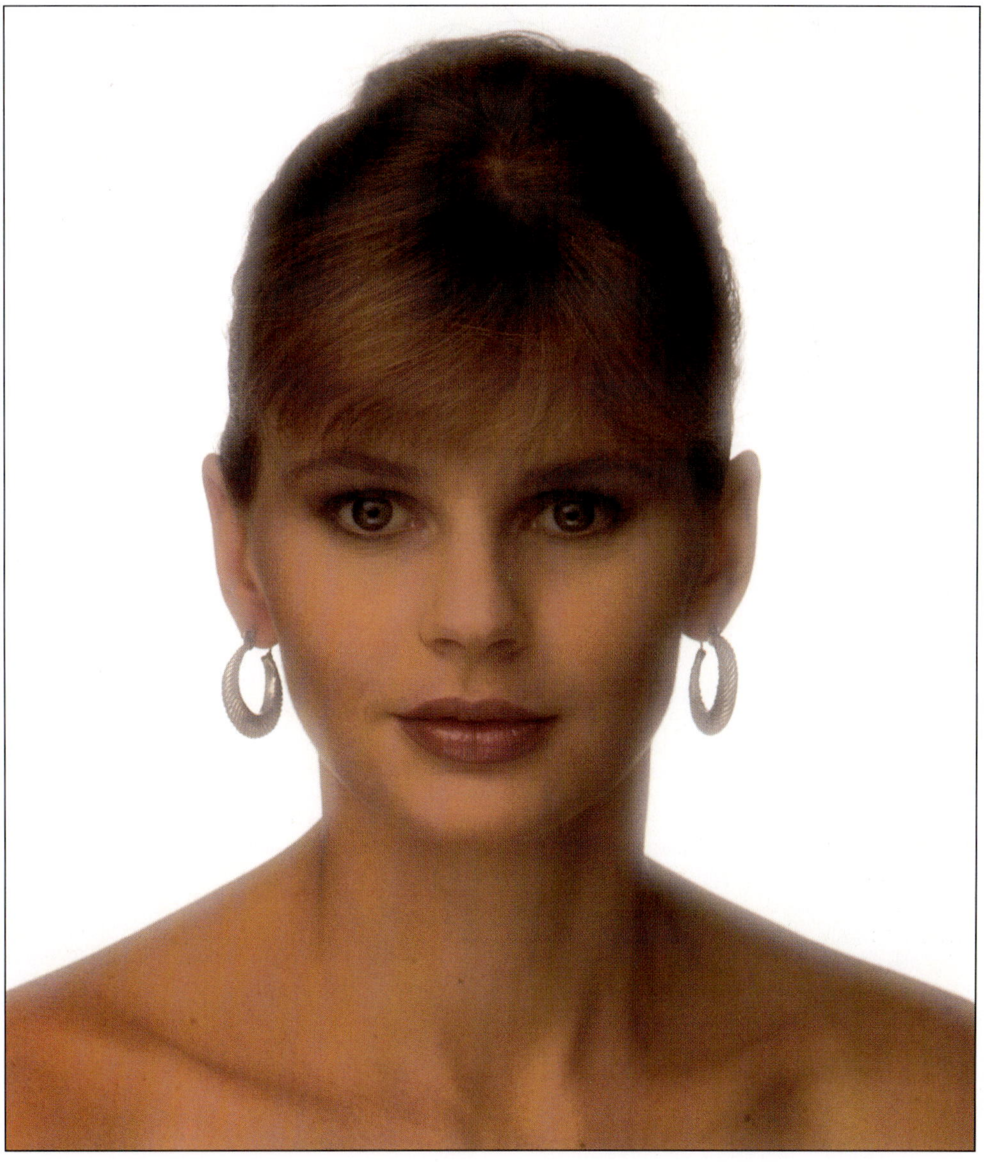

Angle of light

Flat lighting basically depends on two factors: the angle of light and the quality of light. The angle of light will depend on where you place the lights you are using.

If you are using just one light, the ideal position is just straight on and slightly above the model. If you have your main light at an angle, you are obviously going to have the shadow of the nose raking across the subject's face and one side in shadow.

Try to install your light about a metre above the camera on a boom stand. Don't have the light too high as this will cause pronounced shadows under the nose and chin. And certainly don't position the light beneath the camera unless you want the type of lighting associated with horror movies.

Using two lights

If you have two lights, they should be placed on either side of the subject at an angle of about 45°. For absolutely flat lighting, the two lights should have equal intensity. That is, if they are equally powerful sources of light, they should be equal distances from the model.

This is a departure from standard portrait lighting where one lamp usually works as key light and one as a fill light. In this standard set up, the fill lightens the shadows. However, the goal of flat lighting is to eliminate the shadows altogether.

You may find that giving both lights equal importance creates a portrait that is too flat and that you need some of the modelling effects given by shadows. Under these circumstances, position one lamp slightly nearer to the model than the other.

Diffused flash at an angle

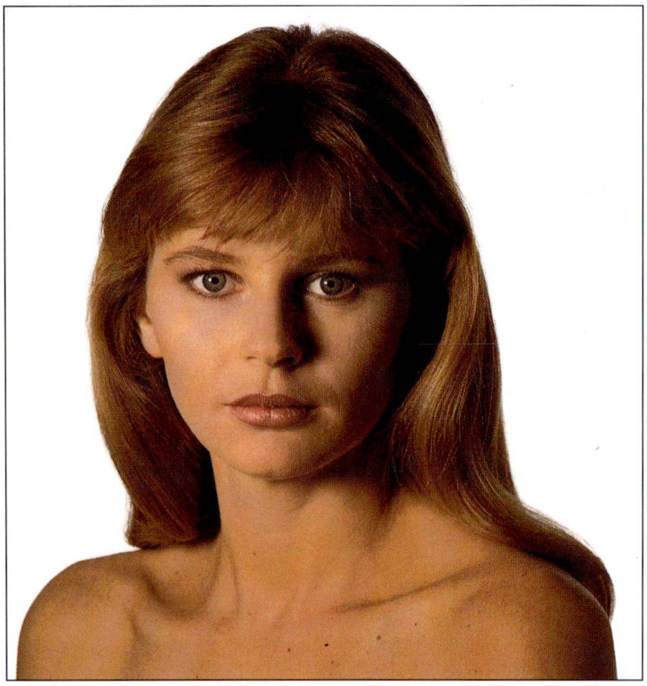

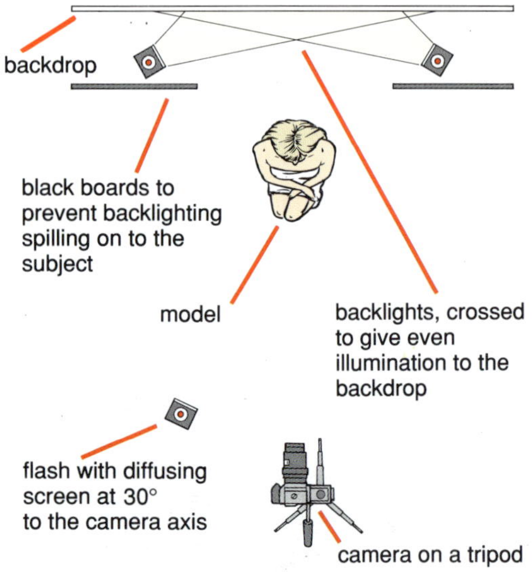

This photograph was taken with a flashgun at about 30° from the camera axis. The flash had a diffusing screen attached to the front of it. However, because of the oblique angle of light, the nose has created a hard shadow and the left hand side of the model's face is in shadow.

Diffused flash straight on

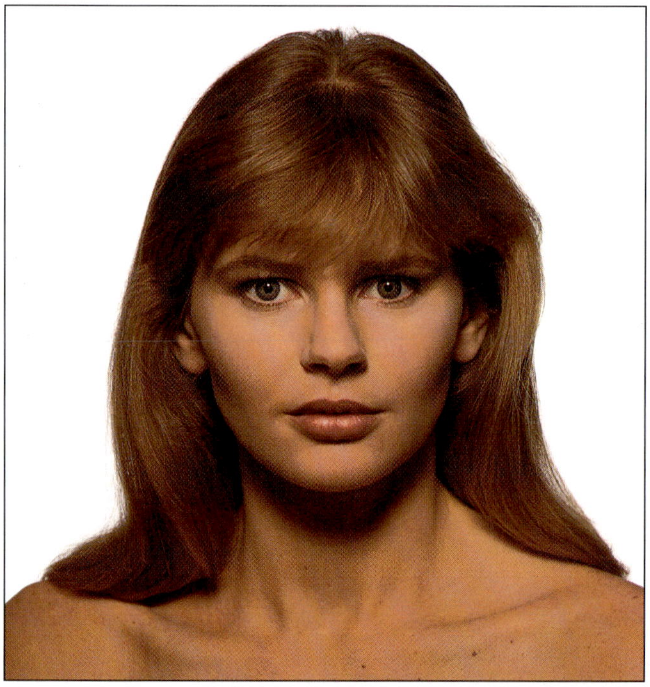

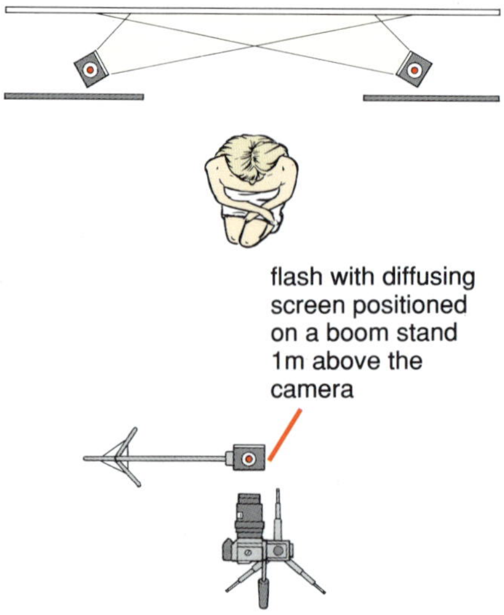

The same flashgun has produced a slightly flatter light when square on to the subject, above the camera. However, there is still a lot of contrast between the highlights on the bridge of the nose and the cheekbones and the heavy shadows under the chin and along the jaw.

Quality of light

To obtain flat lighting, you need as diffuse a light as possible. There are many ways in which you can diffuse conventional sources.

If you're lighting with tungsten photofloods, try using a soft reflector which has a metal disc in front of the lamp to reflect and spread the light.

If you only have a single flash head, you can bounce the flash off a white surface which will spread and flatten the light. If you have a synch cord, you can remove the flash from the hotshoe and use your own made up diffusing screens (see page 45, Portable flash in the studio).

Studio flashes can be fitted with umbrellas to soften the light. You can set up the flash so that the light is thrown into the brolly and then back on to the model. There are three linings to choose from – white, silver and gold. White gives the softest light, while gold gives the warmest.

Alternatively you can fire the flash through a translucent umbrella. This set up generally gives softer light than silver or gold lined reflective versions but a slightly harder light than white lined reflective umbrellas. You can also fit studio flashes with casings in which diffusing screens can be attached.

For the flattest lighting, it's best to use a softbox. Sometimes, these are self-contained units which give a large, even spread of light. On others the flash is housed in a box which is generally lined with silver material. At the front, they have at least one diffusing screen.

Large softboxes are expensive – they can come in sizes of up to two metres by one metre. Therefore, these are best to hire only for specific shoots when you need really flat lighting.

Small softbox straight on

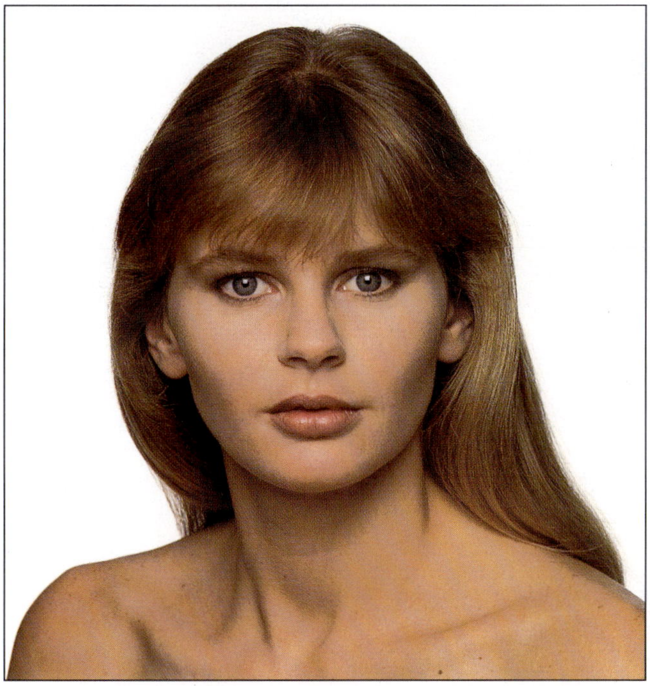

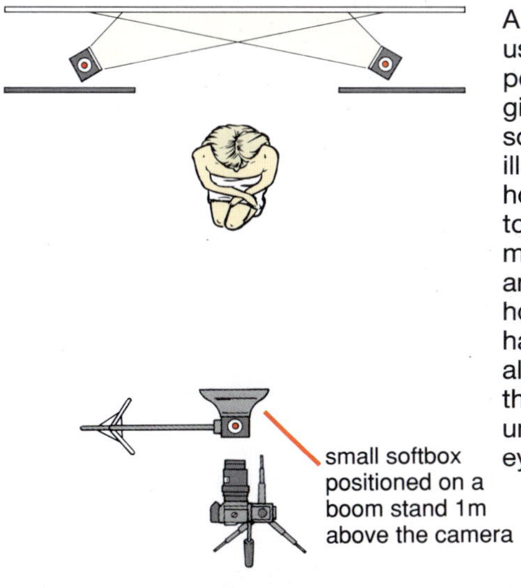

A small softbox, used in the same position, has given much softer illumination. Note how the skin tones appear much more even and delicate, and how the shadows have lightened along the line of the jaw and under the eyebrows.

Large softbox straight on

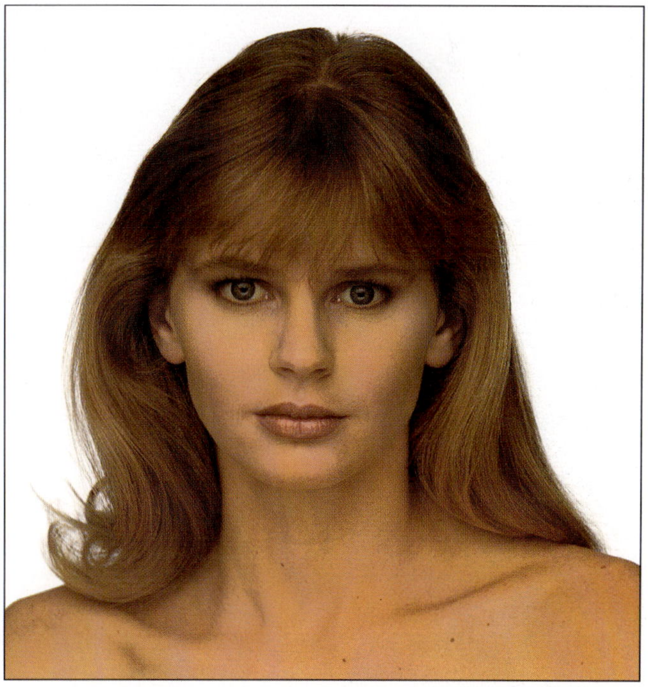

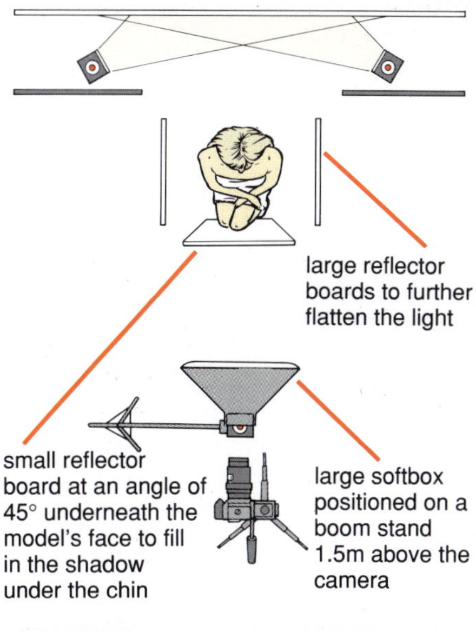

A large, professional softbox above the camera eliminates virtually all contrast in the skin tones. The photographer has used a small white reflector underneath the model's face to remove the shadow beneath her chin. Larger reflectors were used to the sides to further flatten the lighting.

Glamorous touches

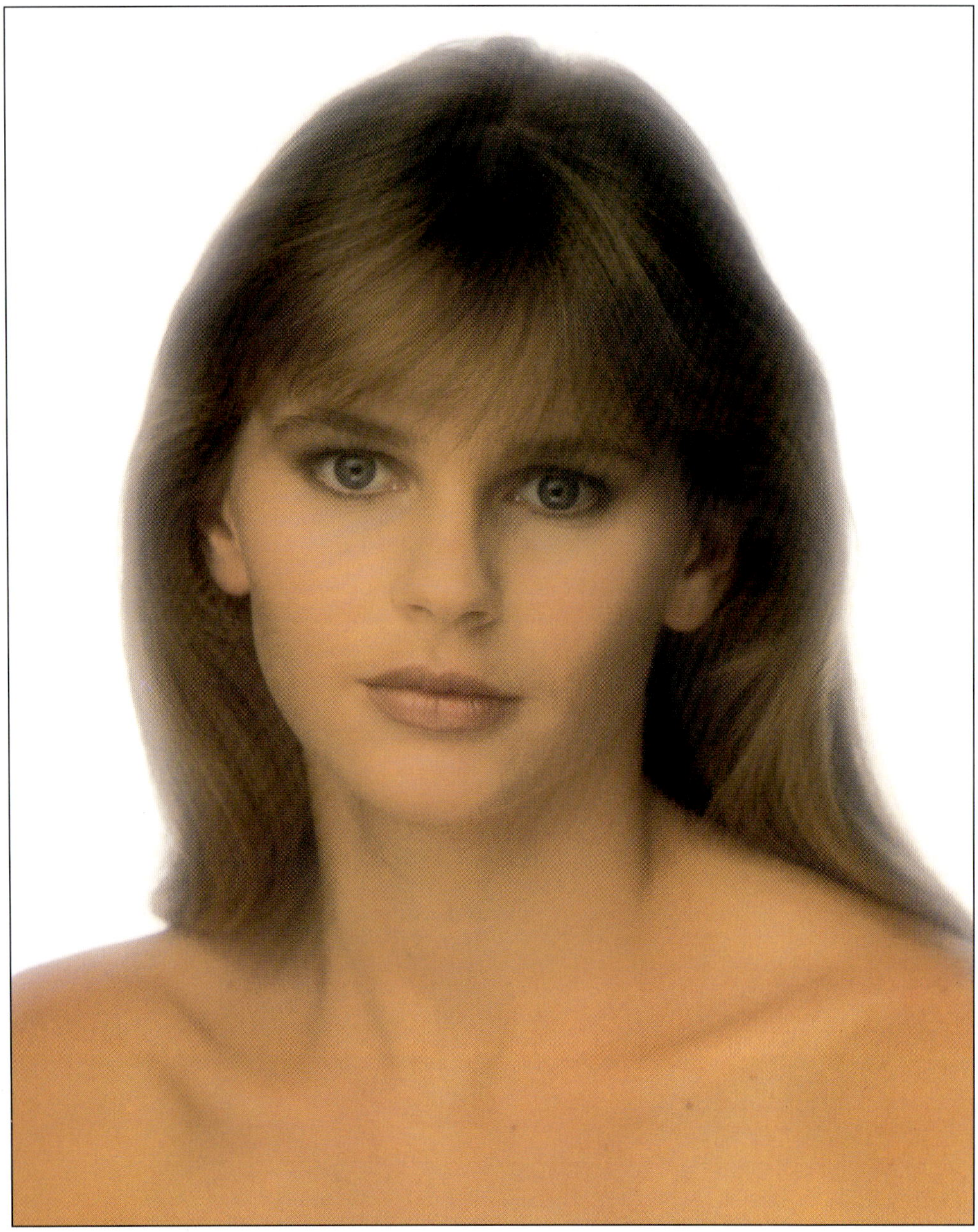

◀ ***Soft focus works very well in combination with flat lighting. Here the photographer used a filter to obtain the dreamy soft focus and also slightly overexposed for the high key effect.***

> **Tip**
>
> ### Make up
>
> The whole point of flat lighting is to give the model's skin tones a soft and delicate appearance. Therefore, try to have the model's make up as natural as possible. Flat lighting with garish make up can look very incongruous. Also, if your model is bare shouldered, apply make up to the neck and upper chest to avoid a harsh line between bare and made up skin.

Flat lighting is particularly suited to glamour shots. Take a look at photographs of models in lingerie or period costume to see just how often flat lighting conditions are used in glamour work.

To complement the flat lighting, therefore, you might want to use a few specific glamour techniques. The most obvious is soft focus – this works in perfect harmony with flat, diffuse lighting.

The easiest way to achieve soft focus is by using filters. However, watch out for some of the cheaper soft focus filters which tend simply to throw the image out of focus. Other, more expensive, soft focus filters brighten the highlights without noticeably lessening the sharpness of the shot.

Remember, you can experiment with a variety of materials to obtain different soft focus effects. Some of the old Hollywood glamour shots were softened with a black stocking over the lens; others were made using special soft-focus lenses.

Overexpose

Another glamour technique is to overexpose in order to 'clean up' the skin tones. Try overexposing a few flat lit portraits by half a stop.

Remember, if you take a reflected light reading from Caucasian skin tones, it should always be about half a stop brighter than the overall exposure anyway. This is because you want white skin to be lighter than a mid tone.

High key

For a really high key portrait, therefore, you might want to overexpose by a stop. This will make any blotches or blemishes on the skin much less obvious. However, always take a series of bracketed exposures to be sure of getting the right tone.

Hard lighting

A hard lighting set up produces bold, sharp edged shadows. Although it is less than ideal for most female portraiture, it can be extremely effective for male subjects.

For a conventional portrait, you generally need soft and flat lighting. However, to make your portraiture different, why not try hard lighting?

Hard lighting is characterized by deep, sharp edged shadows. Often with hard lighting you lose detail in the highlights and, more commonly, in the shadows. This can add to the weight and formality of a portrait.

The hardness of a light depends on its size and its distance from your subject. On a clear day, the sun produces very hard lighting because it's so far away from the earth. You *can* take portraits in direct sunlight. But sunlight is unpredictable and you can't control it to the extent thay you can control studio lighting.

So it's best to do a hard lighting portrait in the studio where you have control of the lighting. If you don't have professional lighting equipment, try using your slide projector. A projector light casts very hard shadows, and an 80a filter over the lens matches light almost to daylight.

Choice of subject

Unless you are doing a series of portraits in which you want the light to be consistently hard, it's probably not a technique you want to use for all your portraiture.

Use it when you want to enhance a particular quality of your subject's character. Hard lighting can suggest a sitter's bold, confident nature; contrasting shadows and highlights give the image a confrontational feel which is perfect for an assertive character.

You can also underline the sitter's moody aspect – hard lighting can involve a lot of gloomy shadows, which give a sombre feel. A hard light can even evoke a sinister mood, as in horror films and old black and white gangster movies.

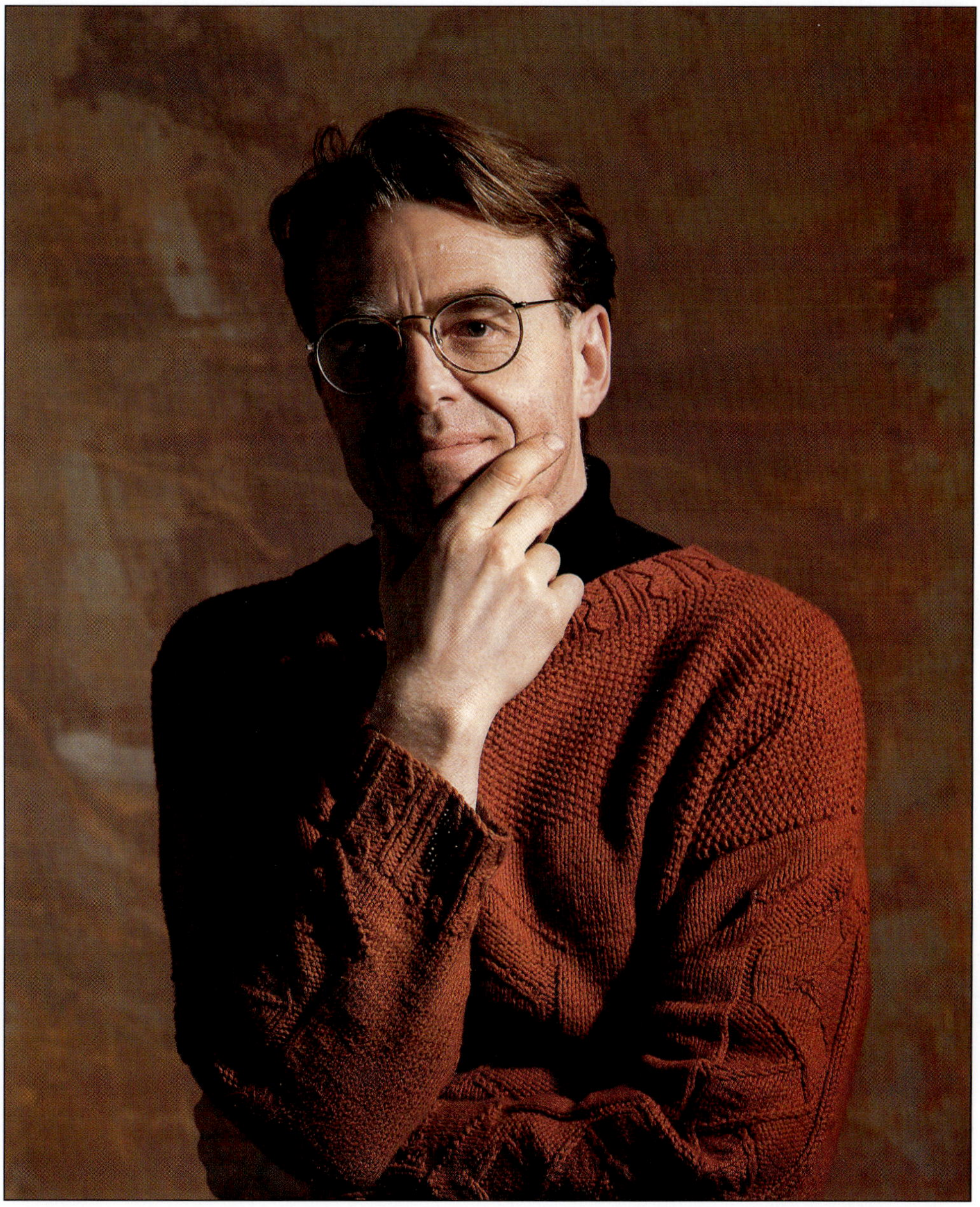

◀ ***A hard lighting set up gives bold, punchy photographs in which bright highlights contrast with deep shadows. It can give strong, hard hitting male portraits.***

Tip

Backgrounds

Choose a background carefully. An airy, bright white background is often at odds with the low key nature of a hard lighting set up. On the other hand, a dark toned background usually looks more imposing and effective. However, having the background absolutely black by using, say, a black velvet backdrop is usually not a good idea. That's because the shadow areas of the subject are likely to be indistinguishable from the background.

Hardening the light

You can obtain a hard light for your shot whether you are using flash or tungsten illumination. Flash lighting, which comes from small, gas filled tubes, and tungsten lighting, which comes from tiny halogen lamps, are both naturally hard light sources if they are not diffused in any way.

With flash lighting, the more tightly coiled the gas filled tube, the harder the light is. Narrow, polished dish reflectors can be added to a flash head to direct and harden the light further.

A honeycomb grid (used in three of the photos below and on the next page) can also be fitted on to a flash head to straighten the light. These grids come in various widths, the wider versions providing a more pointed light source.

If you're using tungsten lighting, tungsten-halogen lamps with a coiled filament give you a harder light source than the cheaper photopearl or photoflood lamps (see page 22).

Attaching a polished reflector directs and hardens a tungsten

Flash with softbox

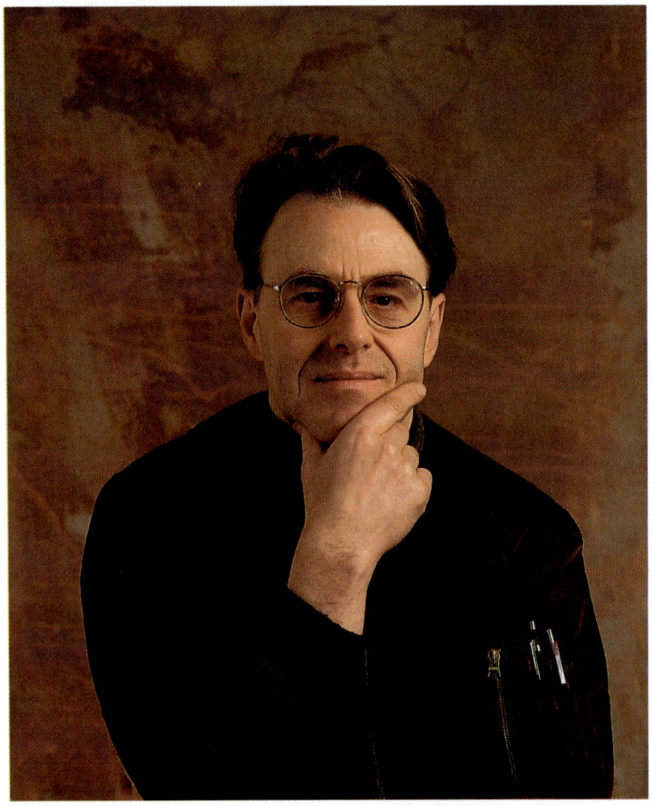

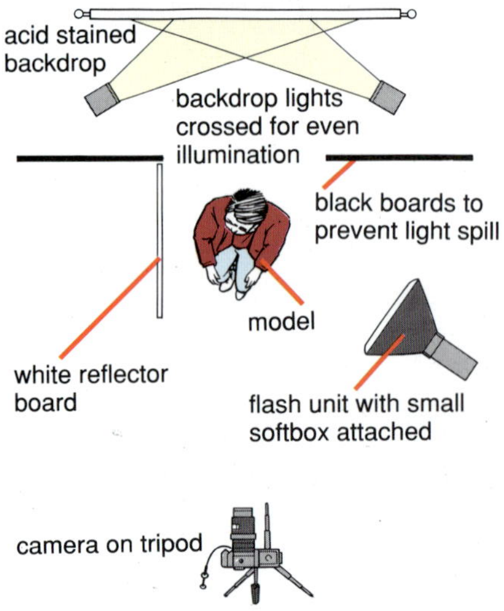

The first shot was taken conventionally with a flash unit in a small softbox at 45° to the subject and a white board throwing light back on the other side. The result is soft shadow areas on the left hand side of the face and hand.

Flash with honeycomb grid

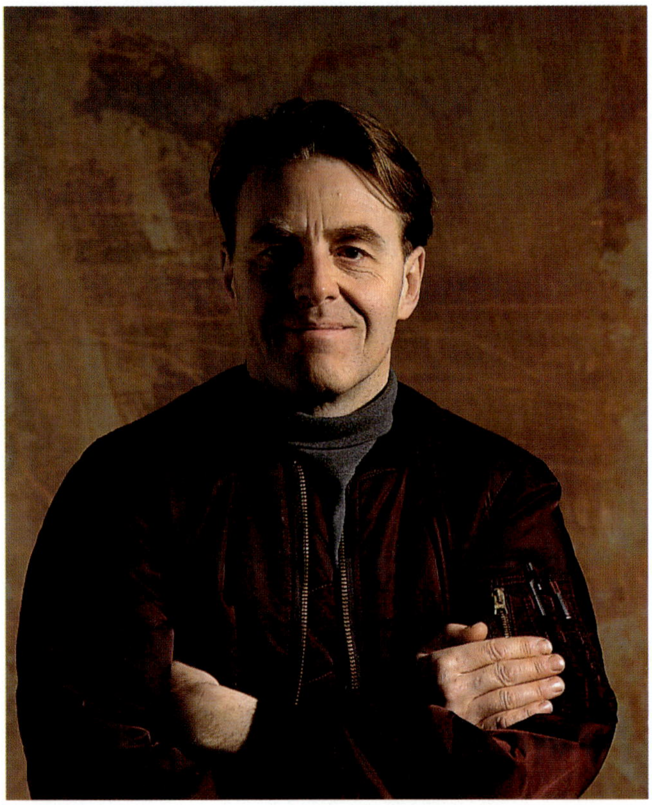

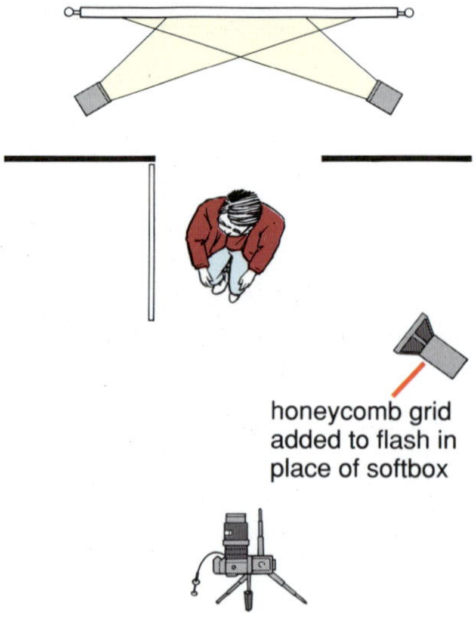

Using a honeycomb grid on the flash has limited the spread of light. The result is considerably harder and deeper shadows. The reflector board, however, has still filled in a narrow band of light on the extreme left hand side of the subject's face.

light. Even better is a spotlight housing. This has a curved reflector at the back and a lens which focuses the light.

With a spotlight, remember that you'll obtain the hardest light when the beam is at its broadest setting. Focusing a narrow beam of light will produce softer shadow edges. If you want to light a small area evenly and with sharp edged shadows, first focus a broad beam and then restrict it with barndoors or a conical, snoot attachment.

Some of the most dramatic effects with hard lighting are when the lamp is as far away from the model as possible. This can give an almost moonlit appearance.

Also try experimenting with the angle of your hard light. A low hard light throws shadows into the eye sockets and above the chin, giving an eerie, horror movie appearance to your model. If you're taking a profile shot, try having the hard light front on to your sitter. This gives a bright rimlight around the outline of their face.

Reflector moved back

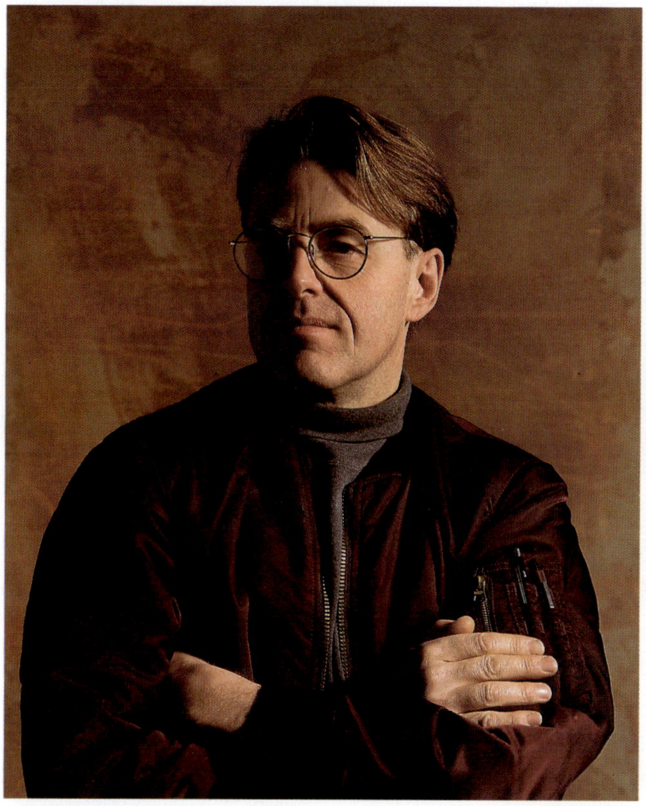

Moving the reflector board away from the model has removed most of the fill-in light on the left of the model. There is still some detail in the shadows on the left hand side of the face, especially beneath the glasses, because of light spill from the surroundings.

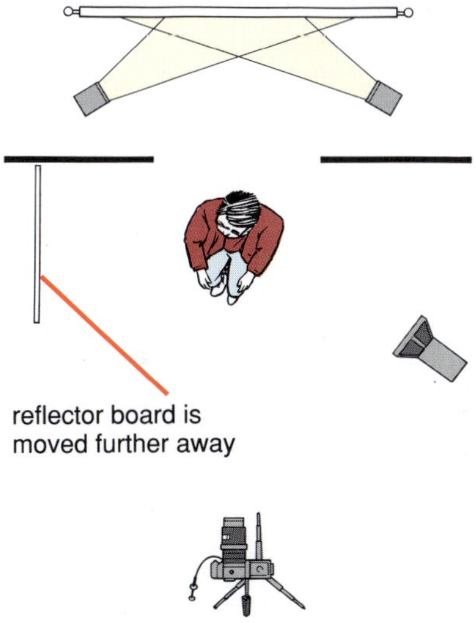

Black board replaces reflector

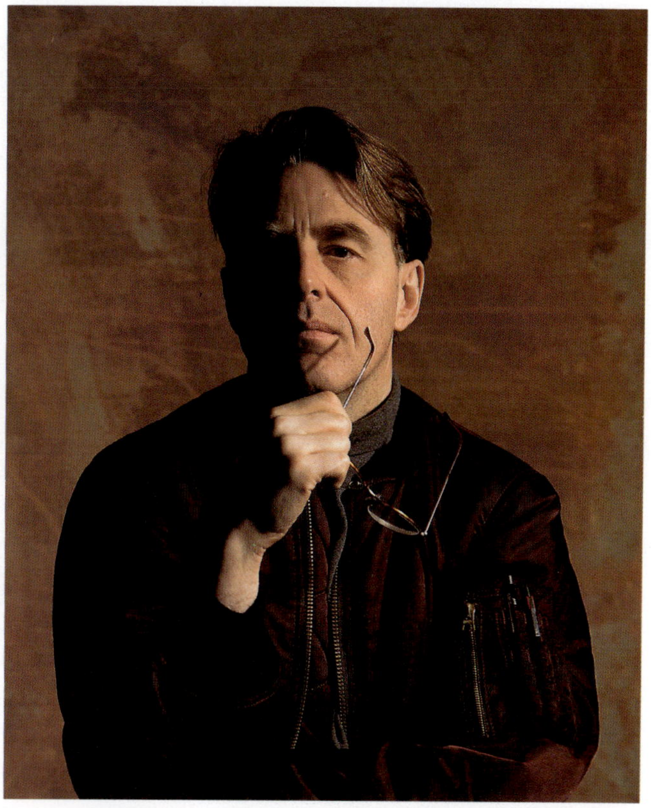

Using a black board instead of a white one has prevented any light reaching the left hand side of the face. The blocked in shadows have given the image a sombre and ominous feel. Note the hardness of the shadow of the glasses on the chin.

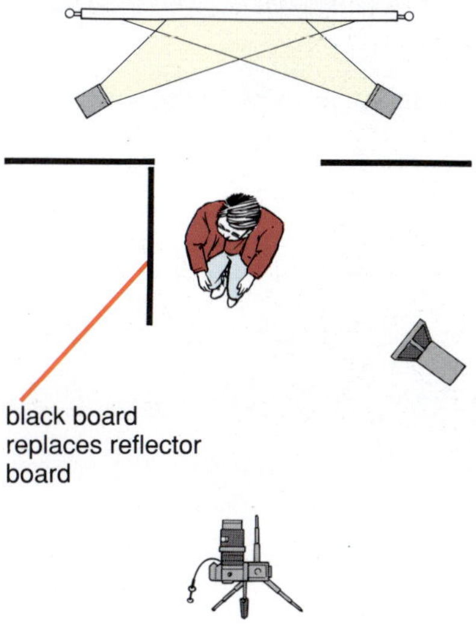

Black and white

Although good results are possible with colour film, hard lighting gives its most dramatic effects when you load up with black and white. There are no distracting colours to take the viewer's attention away from the lighting effects you've achieved. And in any case, hard lighting, with relatively few mid tones, often looks much more hard hitting in black and white.

Choose the type of film carefully. If you're using conventional print film, pick a slow one – preferably ISO 25. Slow film is characteristically sharper and more contrasty. The increased grain of fast film softens the image and will tend to work against the sharp edged shadows of hard lighting.

For the best results, develop the film yourself. A fine grain developer increases sharpness but tends to lower contrast. The best choice is probably a high definition (also called acutance) developer. It boosts development at the edge of shadow areas, giving the image a bold, sharp appearance.

An unusual alternative is to use black and white slide film. The advantage of slide film is that it's considerably more contrasty than prints made from print film and it also tends to give richer tones.

You can buy black and white slide film that is specially processed by the manufacturers, or you can develop print film by reversal process to obtain slides. However, it's a great deal easier to use instant picture film. With Polaroid's PolaPan, you process the film in a portable developing unit so you don't require any darkroom facilities.

PolaPan film is very delicate so it's best to have your slides copied straightaway. To obtain warmer tones, try developing PolaPan in PolaChrome colour chemistry.

▶ PolaPan slide film gives very contrasty results which are ideal for hard lighting set ups. Note how detail has been lost on the hand and the right side of the model's face. In colour, lost highlight detail often looks disconcerting but in monochrome it can add punch and impact.

▼ When developed in PolaChrome colour chemicals PolaPan takes on a warm tone. The tone helps give the photograph a more intimate and less intimidating feel.

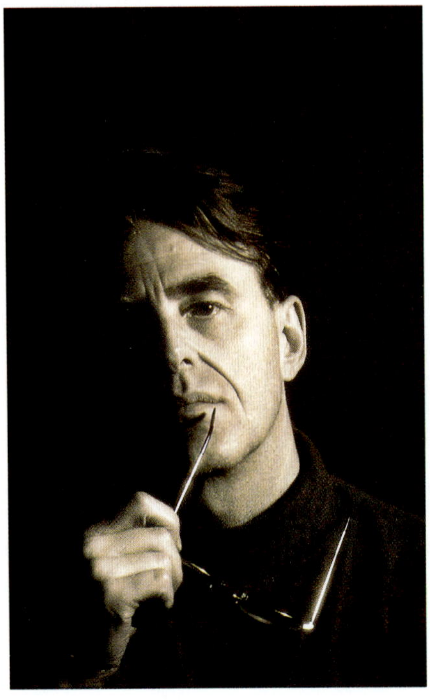

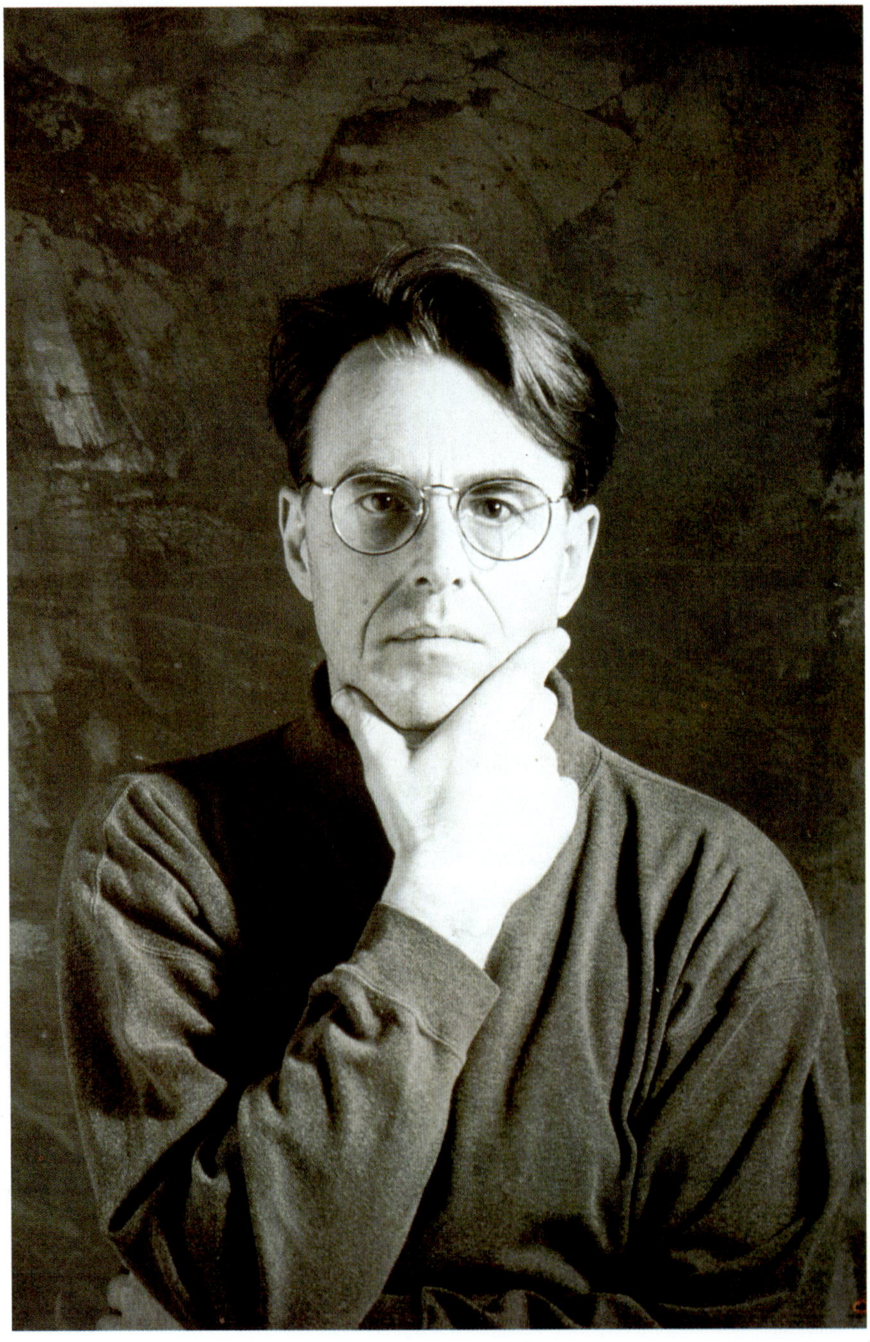

Jane Bown – Professional portraiture

Paradoxically, you can learn a great deal about lighting – about what looks natural and what does not – by studying the work of an expert in available light photography.

"I was delighted when Samuel Beckett gave me permission to photograph him. When I got to the Royal Court, however, he'd changed his mind. I needed the picture, so I went to the stage door and confronted him. Luckily he relented, and leant against a wall glowering at me while I quickly took three frames in very poor light."
Taken on an Olympus OM1 with a 50mm lens on Kodak Tri-X ISO 400 black and white print film at 1/60th sec and f2.8.

Jane Bown has been providing the *Observer* Sunday newspaper with distinctive and highly effective portraits of politicians, celebrities and people in the news for well over 40 years. She joined the paper after finishing a two year photography course in Guildford and was initially used as a general staff photographer. The specialization in portraiture, which now dominates her work, came only later.

'The first portrait I took for the paper was a study of the English philosopher Bertrand Russell in December, 1949', she recalls, 'but photographing people was only part of my job at that time. I was sent on all sorts of assignments, and I wasn't that good at taking portraits to begin with. I suppose I improved a bit when I began to specialize in them.'

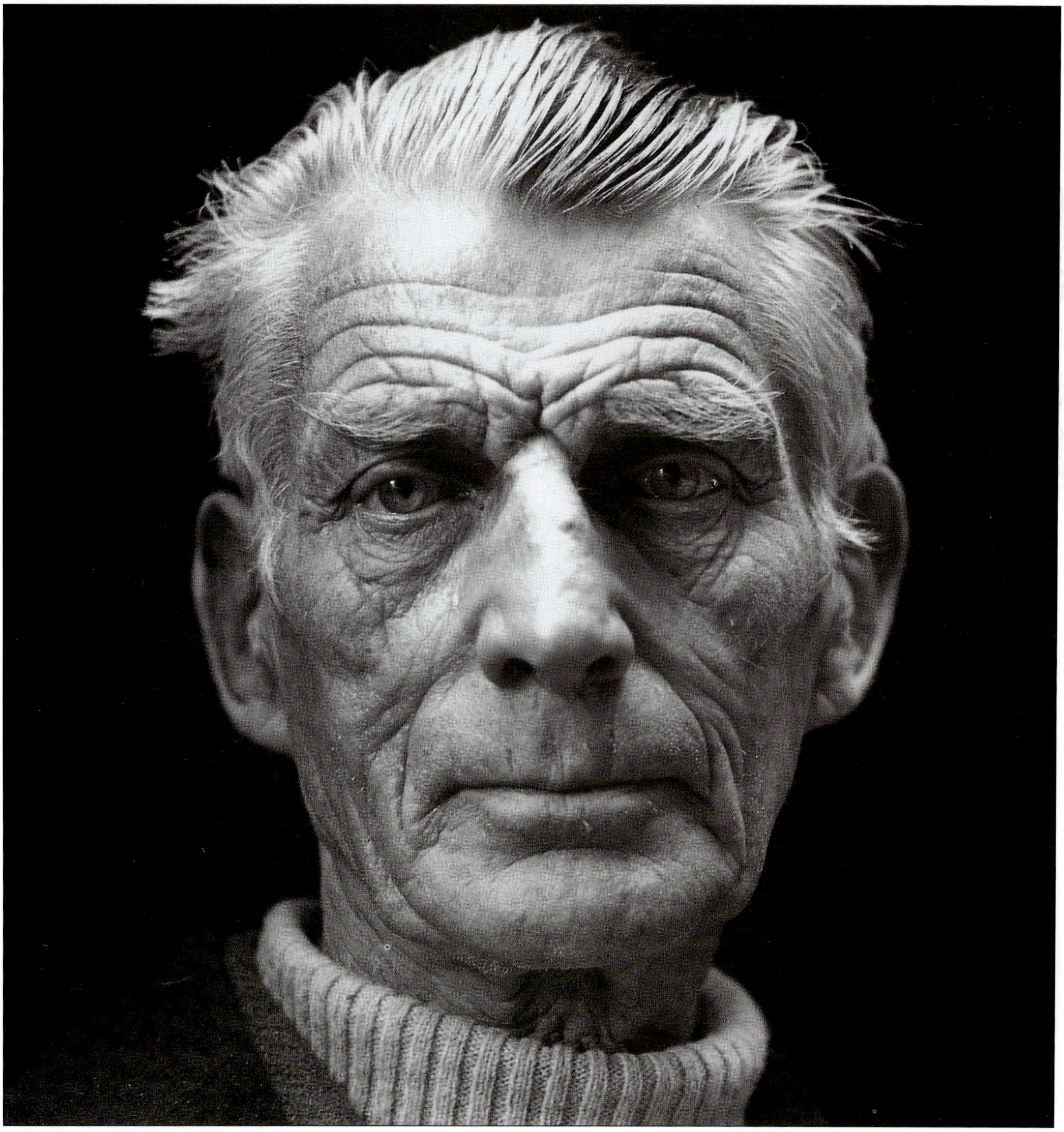

Soft light

She has always preferred natural to artificial light, and uses window light whenever possible. The benefit of this approach is clearly apparent in her pictures: the soft window light brings out every detail in her subjects' faces, and is descriptive without being too searching. 'Daylight is so much kinder to faces than flash', she explains, 'which I find very harsh and unforgiving. Besides, if you turn up at a shoot with a van load of lights and equipment, you're immediately going to build up a barrier between you and the subject.

'If I'm working with a journalist, I try to arrive ten minutes early so I can suss the location out and dictate where the subject sits in relation to the light. Then ten minutes after the writer arrives I'll leave. I rarely need more than 20 minutes on a picture. I tend to avoid shooting during an interview, though, because some of the journalists don't like you snapping away while they're talking.

Reliable technique

'I know a lot of photographers like to shoot nine or ten rolls of film on a subject', says Jane, 'but I rarely shoot more than a roll and a half. My first instincts are always the best, and if I'm going to get a shot right I usually get it right early on. Because I always shoot on Tri-X and usually photograph people beside windows, my exposure is nearly always the same – 1/60th of a second and f2.8. If I ever write a book I'll call it 1/60th and f2.8!

'I know the Olympus OM1 is practically extinct, but they're great cameras and I stick with them because they're so reliable. I've always preferred black and white for portraits, but recently the *Observer* has insisted that we all shoot in colour and black and white on all shoots. I've been looking for a colour film that performs as reliably as Tri-X does, but exposing accurately hasn't been easy. I may have to invest in a hand held meter!'

"I took this portrait of Marty Feldman in an old Irish pub in Kilburn where he'd arranged to meet a journalist who was going to interview him. There was no time problem there – he was relaxed, very helpful and in no hurry at all. The light in the pub wasn't the best, but I was able to cope with it. We had quite a few drinks that day!"
Taken on an Olympus OM1 with a 50mm lens on Kodak Tri-X ISO 400 film at 1/60th sec and f4.

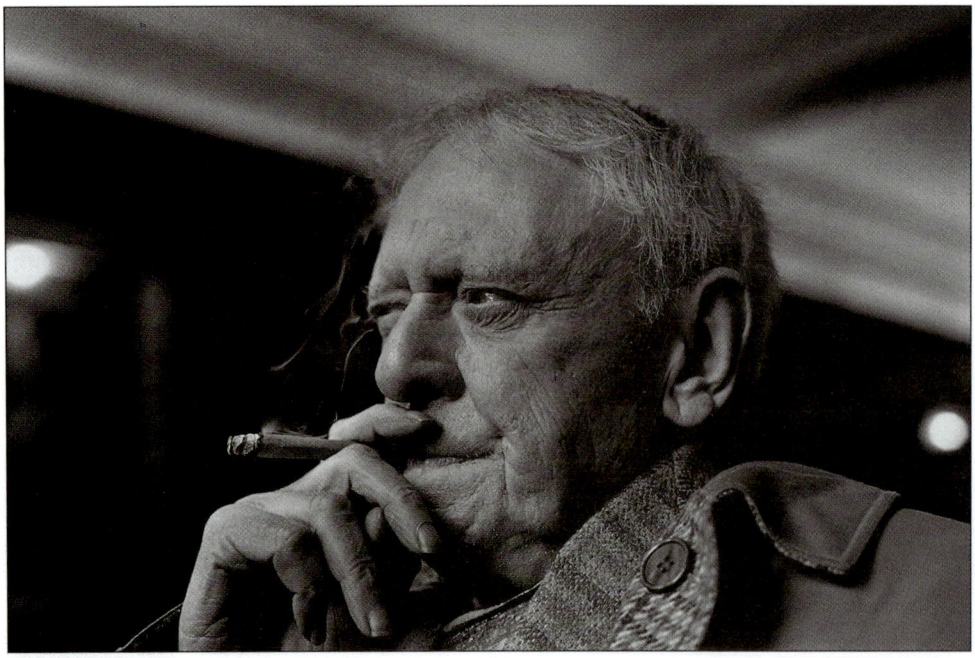

"This shot of Anthony Burgess proved to be extremely difficult to take. He was very aloof for a start, and was involved in a deep conversation with a journalist that I didn't have the nerve to interrupt. The sun was glaring in through the window and causing a lot of problems, and I didn't think I was going to get anything out of the shoot. I just had to fire ahead and hope for the best. In the end I was very surprised and pleased with the results."
Taken on an Olympus OM1 with an 85mm lens on Kodak Tri-X ISO 400 film at 1/60th sec and f2.8.

Technical details

Jane uses natural light for indoor portraits whenever possible. 'If there's a window in the room I'll try to make sure the subject ends up sitting beside it so I don't need any artificial light. You get more interesting detail with window light, which is more diffused and even than flash. Sometimes you struggle for light, but I'd rather do that than lug lots of lights around that intimidate the subject and take ages to set up.'

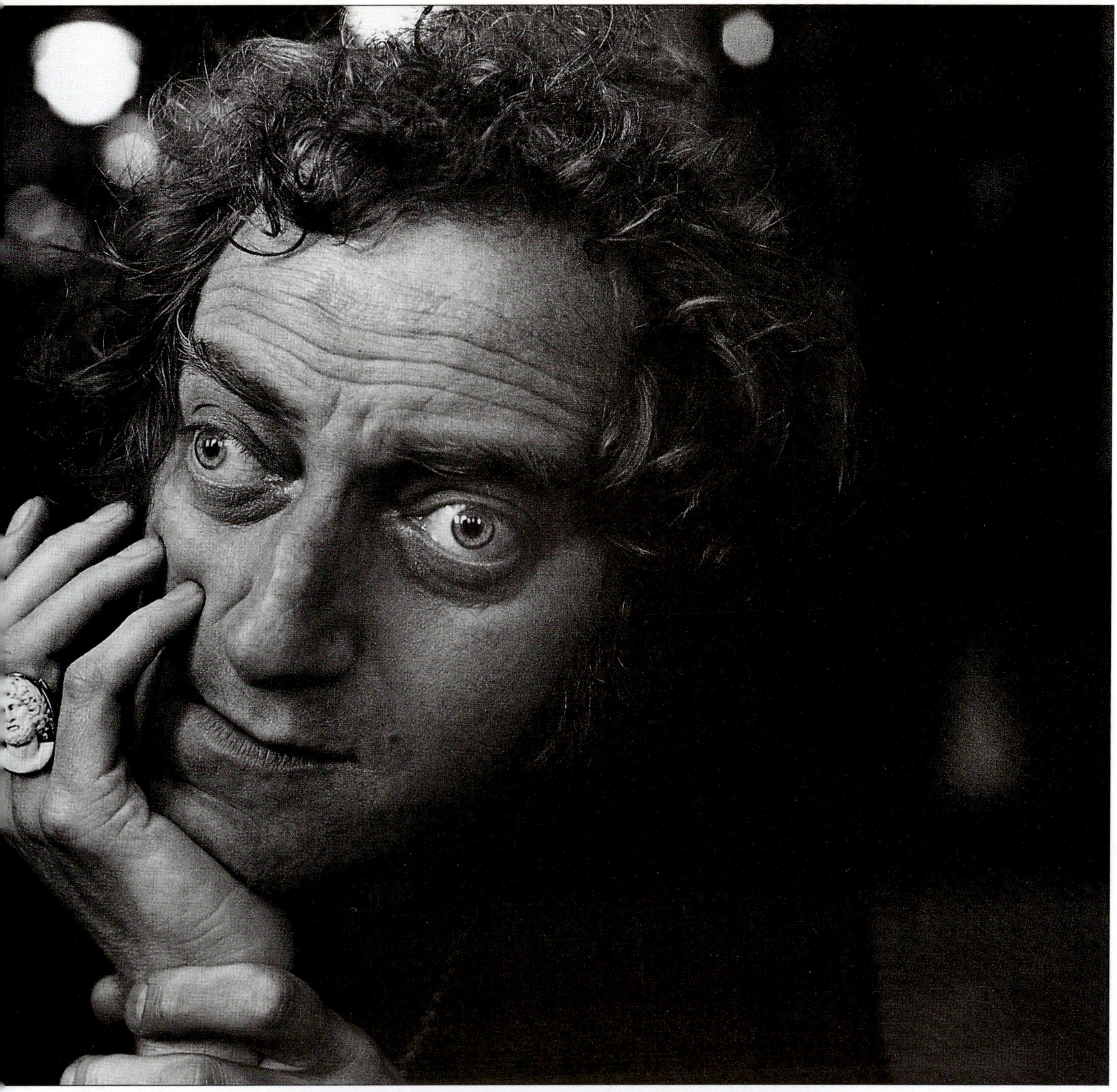

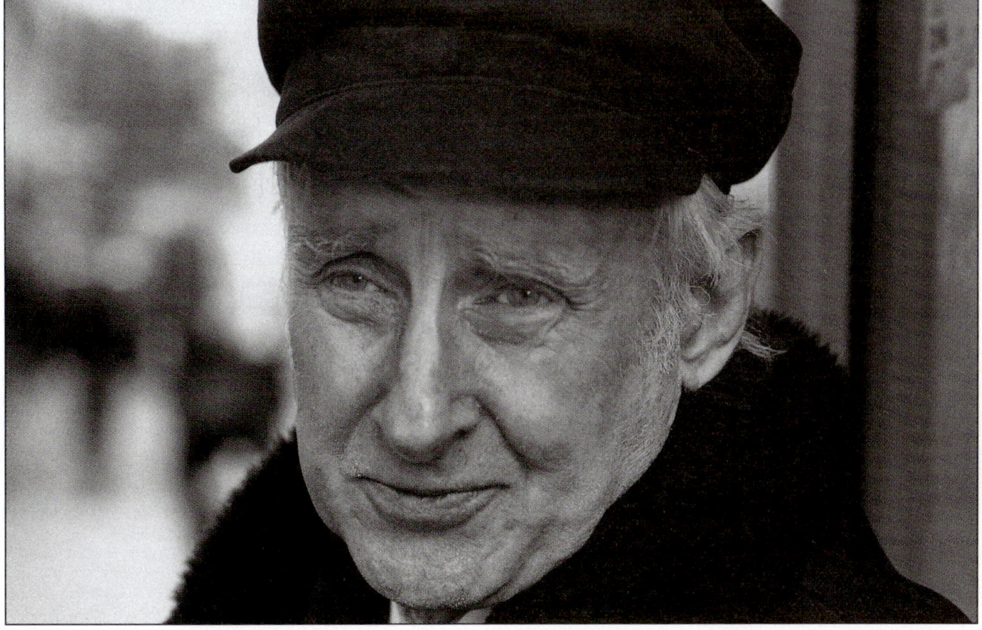

"I took this shot of Spike Milligan at one of his book launches. There were lots of people around and he wasn't in a very co-operative mood, so I knew I'd only have a minute or two at the most to get a picture. The light in the book shop was terrible, so I took him outside and asked him to sit on a bus stop seat. He did it under great sufferance, but I like the result because he looks rather sad."
Taken on an Olympus OM1 with an 85mm lens on Kodak Tri-X ISO 400 film at 1/250th sec and f5.6.

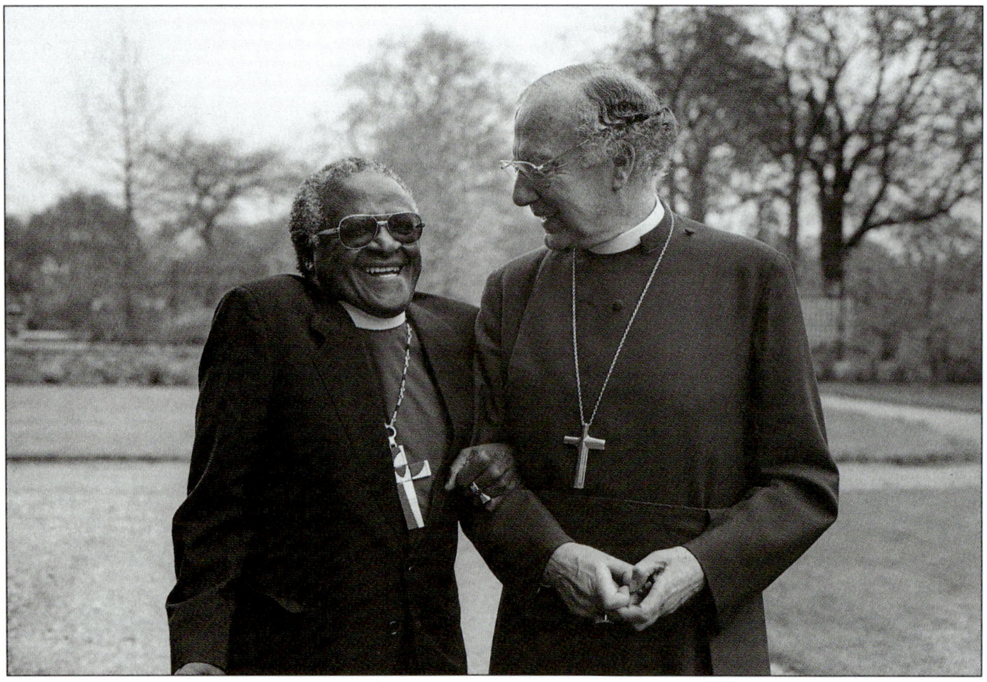

You can do it

Jane Bown has a gentle way of approaching subjects, because she finds that the less threatened they are the more relaxed they become. 'I like to work almost unnoticed', she explains, 'and I'm very instinctive about when the person is getting bored, so I try not to let them get restless.' If you're taking portraits at home, remember that subjects get bored very quickly. By keeping the set up simple, your sitter will feel more relaxed and you'll get your picture quicker.

"This picture of Archbishops Runcie and Tutu was taken at a press photocall with about a hundred photographers." Despite this unpromising start, Jane got a really spontaneous image. "It's not a situation I usually enjoy, but I had a good relationship with Dr Runcie. I'd photographed him many times before so he made sure I got the chance to take this picture. Archbishop Tutu is great value from the photographic point of view as he's always so animated." Taken on an Olympus OM1 with an 85mm lens on Kodak Tri-X ISO 400 at 1/250th sec and f4.

"To begin with, Arthur Scargill was quite a difficult subject", Jane commented about the famous miners' leader. "He turned up in this very smart car and was very bossy and intimidating, ordering everyone about and telling me exactly where he wanted to be photographed. But once we got into a room on our own he turned out to be very helpful and awfully nice. Photographing him in front of that painting was actually his idea." Taken on an Olympus OM1 with a 50mm lens on Kodak Tri-X ISO 400 at 1/60th sec and f2.8.

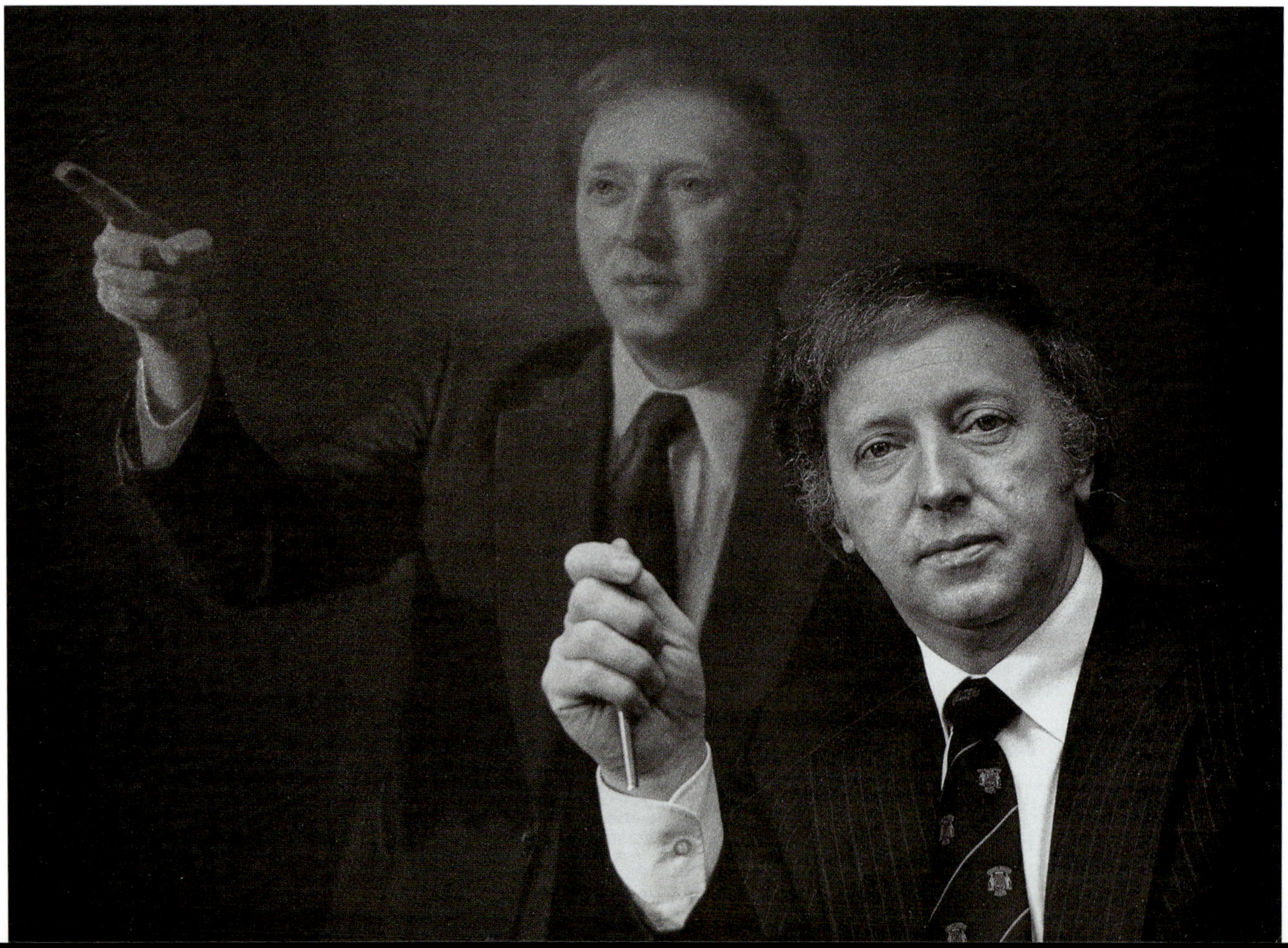

Choosing your background

Whether you're photographing a studio portrait or a still life, your choice of backdrop can make or break the shot.

Ringing the changes with backgrounds needn't cost a fortune. If you want to buy specially designed backgrounds, there's a huge range of colours and materials to choose from – but you can make your own just as easily. Have a look at published photographs for inspiration. Try to guess what the photographer used for the background, then see what you can use around your own home.

The subject you want to photograph determines what kind of background is appropriate. The backdrop material also has a great bearing on the shot's atmosphere. For example, a highly reflective, metallic surface can give a clinical feel to a shot, while a textured rug in a neutral shade can contribute an 'olde worlde' sense.

Multi-purpose backgrounds are a good idea: by lighting or arranging them in different ways you can completely transform the background appearance. This lets you use the same material with various subjects or to create different moods. Lighting your background is dealt with on page 73.

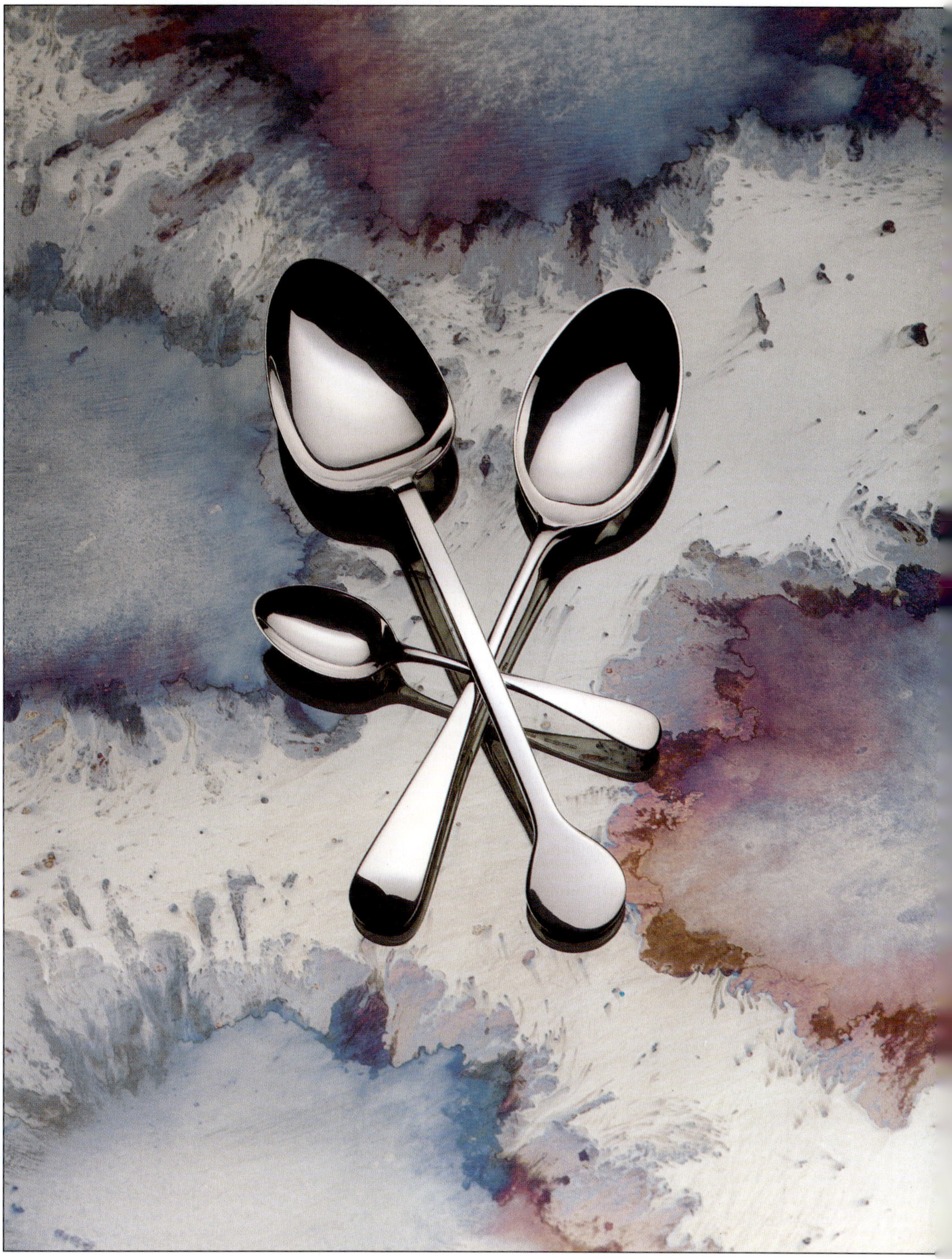

▶ ***Ordinary kitchen cutlery is transformed into a stunning picture with the aid of this improvized background. The photographer made use of an oiled mirror which displayed an attractive sheen. The spoons were polished to remove every trace of dirt and fingermarks, then carefully positioned by a gloved hand to avoid further marks. A large softbox provided the lighting.***

Suitable backdrops

There are a few points you should bear in mind before selecting background material. Remember that the background shouldn't compete with the subject, so you'll find it's easier to work with neutral shades like grey or beige to start off with. Equally, don't buy a very expensive backdrop if it's in an unusual or very noticeable design – if you use it all the time, all your shots will look the same.

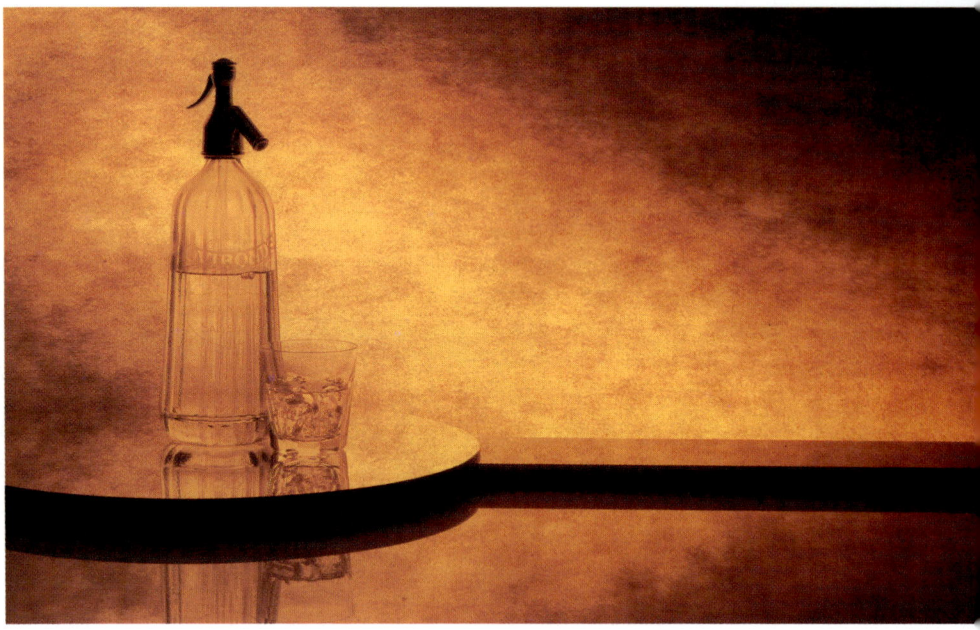

▶ ***All the colour in this minimalist shot comes from the backdrop, which was achieved by shining a single strip light through spray painted background paper. This picks out the fibres in the paper, making it appear textured. The soda siphon and glass are positioned on a circular mirror which in turn lies on a slab of marble.***

Shades of grey

Keen photographers use purpose designed backdrop rolls (available from large photographic shops) because they provide a large, seamless backdrop – there's no join between the wall and the floor. They are available in a huge range of shades and can be one colour or graduated.

Rolls are available in sizes ranging from 1.3m to 3.6m wide by 11m or more in length. Smaller sizes are available for tabletop set ups. They are quite expensive, so store your roll where it won't be torn or damaged – any creases show up as shadows in the final picture. If part of the roll gets grubby, simply tear off that bit.

If you buy only one of these backgrounds, choose a mid-grey colour. Depending on the lighting, it gives the impression that it is black, pale grey or almost white.

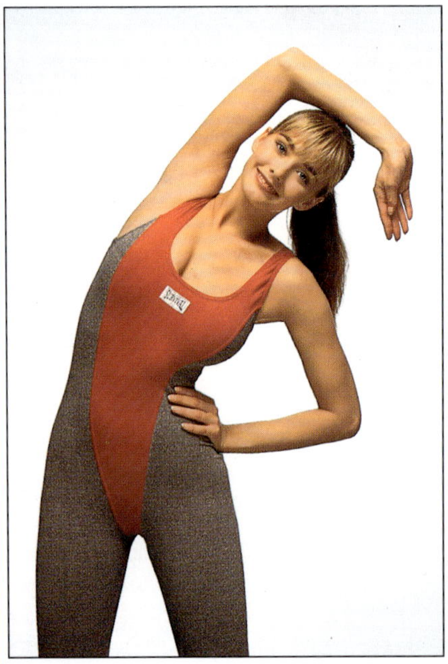

▲ ***In these three shots, the same grey backdrop paper was used. The model was about 3.5m from the background and illuminated by a softbox. Here, two lights trained on the roll create an off-white backdrop.***

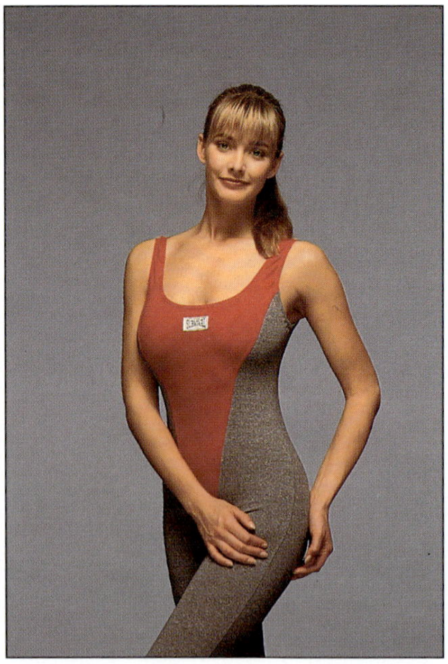

▲ ***Same girl, different background. The model appears unchanged because she receives exactly the same exposure. However, reducing the power of the lights on the background by three quarters turns it mid-grey.***

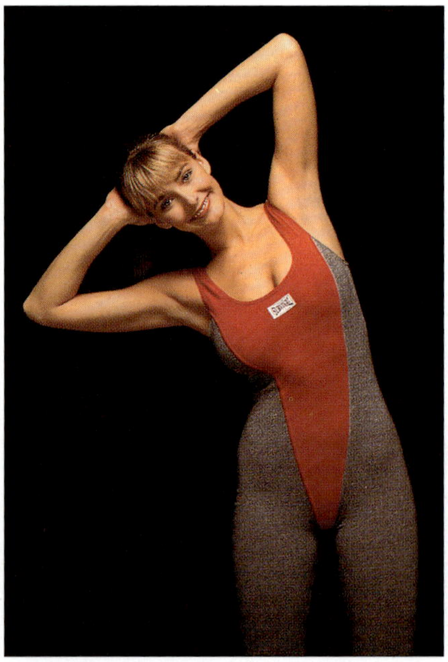

▲ ***The lights trained on the background were switched off. The model was again lit by the softbox – black boards either side of her reduced the chance of light spill. The background now appears to be a solid black.***

Pure black

For a simple but very effective background, black is an ideal colour. Use velvet, if possible, as its surface absorbs light, unlike black paper, which can have a shine that spoils the final shot.

Smooth the material out or arrange it in drapes. Make sure that it's spotless – use a clothes brush to remove any specks of fluff. A pure black background makes double exposures easy, or for a dramatic portrait, dress your model in black so that only the face is visible.

Painted canvas

To give your pictures an attractive painterly feel, buy a canvas background. They are available ready-coloured in lots of shades or you can paint your own.

Spray on a number of different shades of aerosol paint or dab paint on with a small brush for a more interesting, semi-textured feel. You don't have to go right to the edges of the material – only cover the part that appears in the final shot.

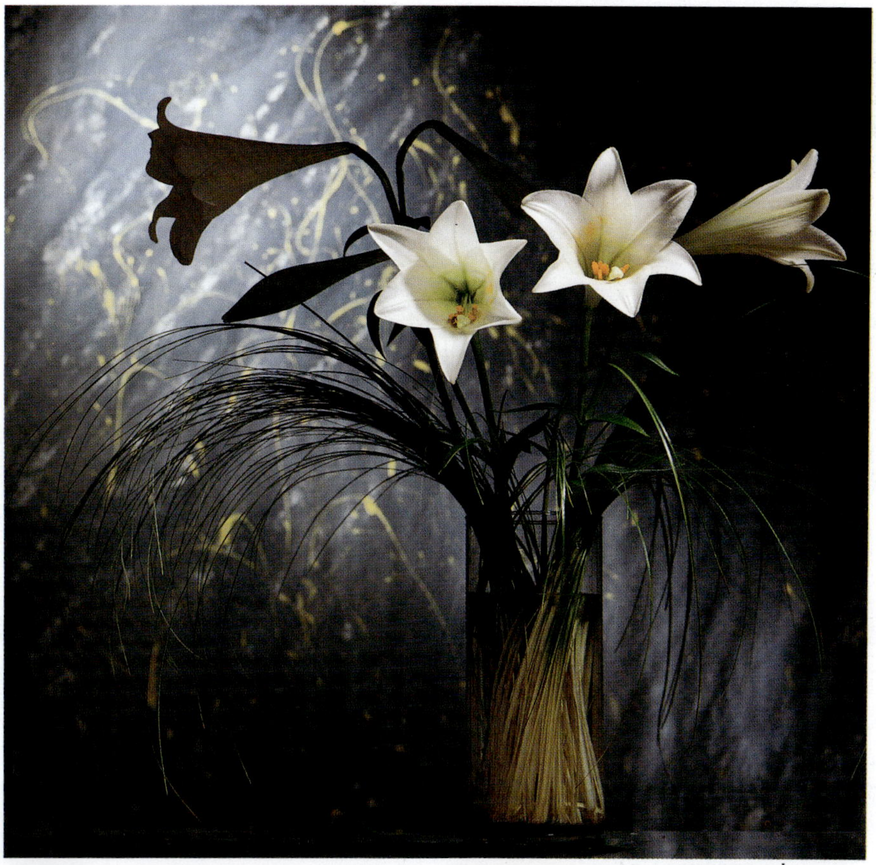

▲ ***Some backgrounds look unconvincing if they are perfectly sharp. Opening up the aperture to make the backdrop out of focus, as here, can work wonders. Paint, in a colour which toned with the inside of the flowers, was splattered on to a piece of material to give a flecked appearance.***

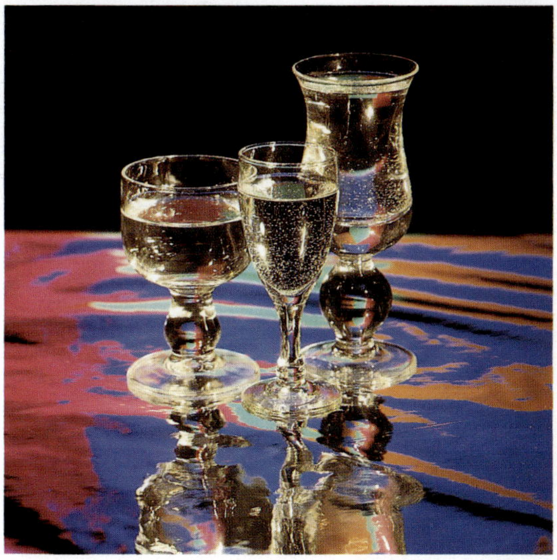

◀ ***These wine glasses are standing on a sheet of plastic film which has a reflective surface. A special ultra-violet (black light) bulb made the reflective material glow with distinctive colours, and the sheet was left wrinkled to distort the reflections.***

Tip: Cheap plastic

If you don't want to buy a special sheet of plastic, a piece of glass painted black or any colour you choose is a good substitute. With the painted side away from your subject, you can create stunning reflections that add the finishing touch to the shot. Remove the paint from the glass, repaint it a different colour and you have a brand new background. Bear in mind, though, that flexible plastic allows you to curve the background, unlike glass.

Plastic

Add an extra dimension to still lifes by showing a reflection of the subject – it's easy if you use a sheet of dark acrylic underneath the arrangement.

Hi-tech subjects are especially suitable for this treatment. Or you could use transparent plastic and light the set up from underneath for a bright background without shadows.

You can buy plastic sheets from builders' supply and specialist shops. They are quite expensive, so don't buy one above tabletop size unless you really need it.

Rest the translucent sheet over two chairs with a gap in the middle – that way you can position a light underneath the sheet if necessary. Opaque sheets can be rested on a tabletop.

One big advantage of plastic is that it's easy to wipe clean after the shoot. This is especially useful if you're shooting messy still lifes of food, for example.

Handle the sheets carefully as they are very easy to scratch. You may also find the surface attracts dust because of static electricity – use an anti-static polish to attack the problem.

Improvize

You can save money by making backgrounds from materials found around the home or bought cheaply. All it takes is a little creative thinking. Keep an eye open for likely backgrounds when you're out. Here are some ideas:

❑ **Coloured paper** Suitable for close-ups and small subjects. For larger subjects, use plain wallpaper. Scrunch up tissue paper then smooth it out for a contoured surface – you could even shine a light through it from behind, to create a background that glows.

❑ **Fabrics** Dye an old bed sheet, iron it and hang it up in folds behind your subject. This has the advantage of allowing you to create the exact colour which you want. Textured materials like hessian are another good source, or you could use curtain material if you need to cover a large area.

❑ **Metal** A rusty sheet of metal creates an interesting backdrop! Or try making lots of scratches on a sheet of steel with wire wool for something even more unusual.

❑ **Building and decorating materials** Bought from the local builder's yard, DIY store or garden centre, these include wood offcuts, cork matting, paving stones and marble slabs. The size you buy depends on the size of subject you want to work with.

A range of backgrounds

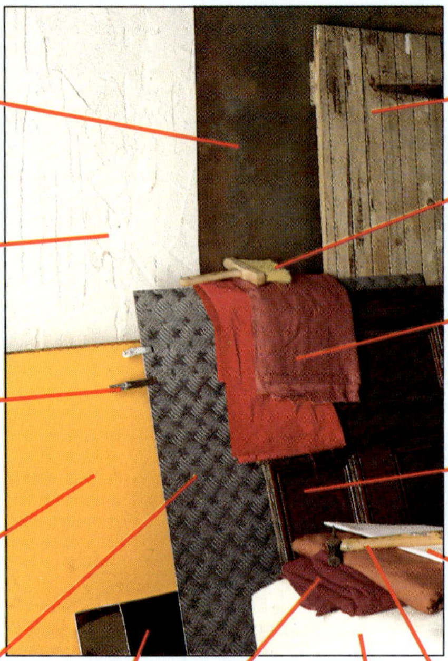

▲ ***A professional studio photographer needs to keep a good selection of backgrounds of different sizes, types and colours in the workplace at all times. That way he or she can be ready to photograph a wide range of subjects in different ways as required.***

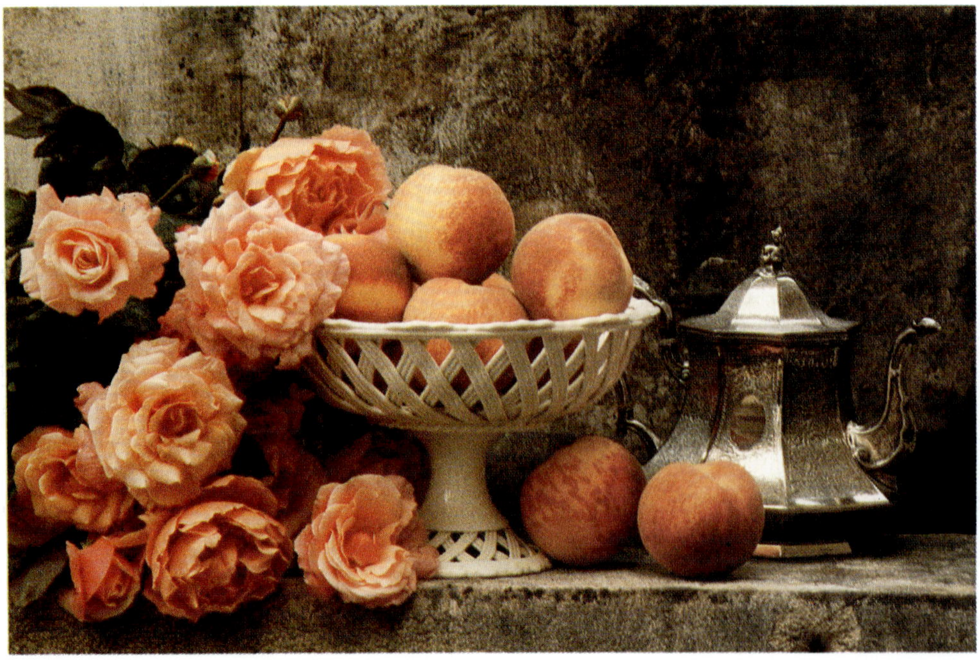

◀ ***Inside or out, keep your eyes open for ready-made backdrops wherever you go. Here the photographer spotted a good setting for a still life shot, and later returned to it with her subject.***

Tip **Rubbish**

Junk shops are full of likely objects that could make cheap, improvized backgrounds. Anything fairly flat has possibilities – for example, an old desk top, or slate or ceramic tiles.

Even background lighting

Achieving an even and balanced background light is one of the basic skills of studio photography – but getting it right is not as easy as you might think.

Even background lighting normally has one of two uses. Used on its own or with a small amount of frontlighting, it provides the setting for a silhouette. Used with a stronger front or sidelight, it gives a clean, bright and distraction-free background, so that your attention is focused on the main subject.

Knowing how to control the evenness and shape of the lit area is an important skill to master. The larger the background, the more difficult it becomes to obtain a constant illumination from one side to the other.

Relative size is important

The first thing you must decide is the area of background that you want in the frame and the intensity of the light on it. This all depends on the size and type of your subject.

For example, photographing a fashion model against a white wall will provide you with more lighting problems than photographing a tiny model soldier against a sheet of white A4 paper. This is because of the extra volume of light needed to provide such a large, shadow-free backdrop.

It helps to keep the background area to a minimum, particularly if your lighting resources are limited. Don't be too ambitious to begin with – this is a difficult technique and you cannot expect to get it right first time.

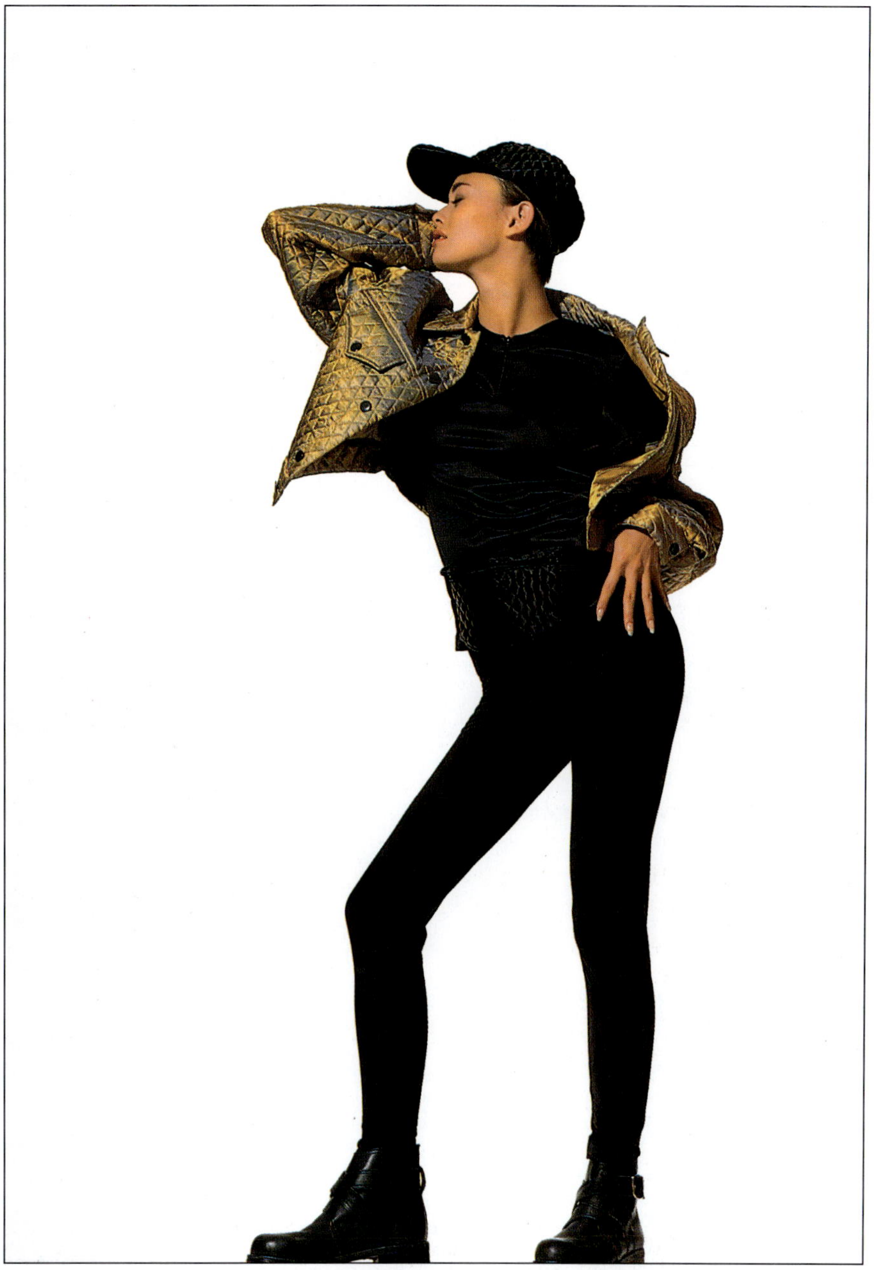

▲ ***Many advertising shots feature unobtrusive white backgrounds, so that text can easily be inserted around the picture when it's published. Here, with no distracting background to catch the eye, your attention is directed straight to the model and her clothes.***

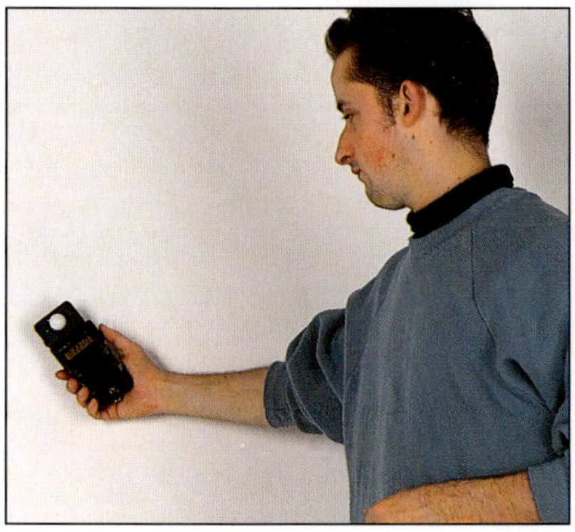

◀ ***If you do a lot of studio photography, buy a hand held incident lightmeter. Use this meter to check that the lighting is even. With the diffusing dome directed at the camera, readings at all four corners and at the centre should be within half a stop of each other.***

Crossing the beams

For an even background, aim the beams of light at opposite sides of the backdrop. They will cross, which gives you more even edge-to-edge illumination.

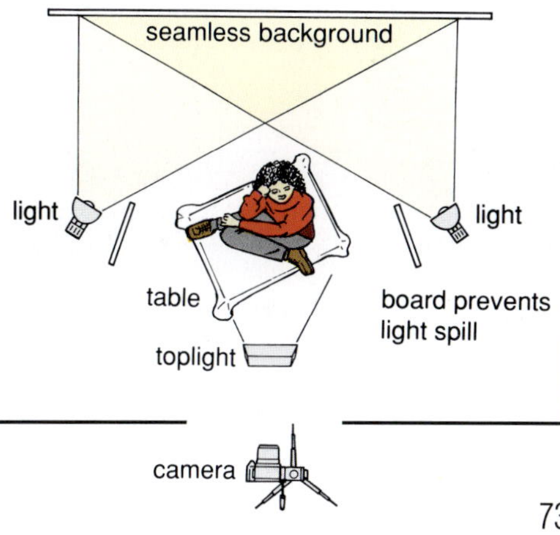

The perfect background

A large area of white backdrop looks most effective if it is lit so that it appears as clear film on a slide, or solid black on a negative. However, this is definitely the most difficult background lighting technique to master.

The ideal solution is to use a professional studio. Here, you can light the background with two powerful strip lights – one on either side. Or you can use four flash heads aimed into umbrellas – a pair on either side of the background, with one at about head height and the other below it.

A white background needs an extra stop or two of light, compared with the average exposure for the subject, to ensure that it is recorded as white, and not grey.

A large mid-toned background is easier to light. You can make do with only a pair of lights, as any unevenness is less noticeable than on a white backdrop. Also, the lights don't need to be as powerful – as the exposure for the subject and the background is the same.

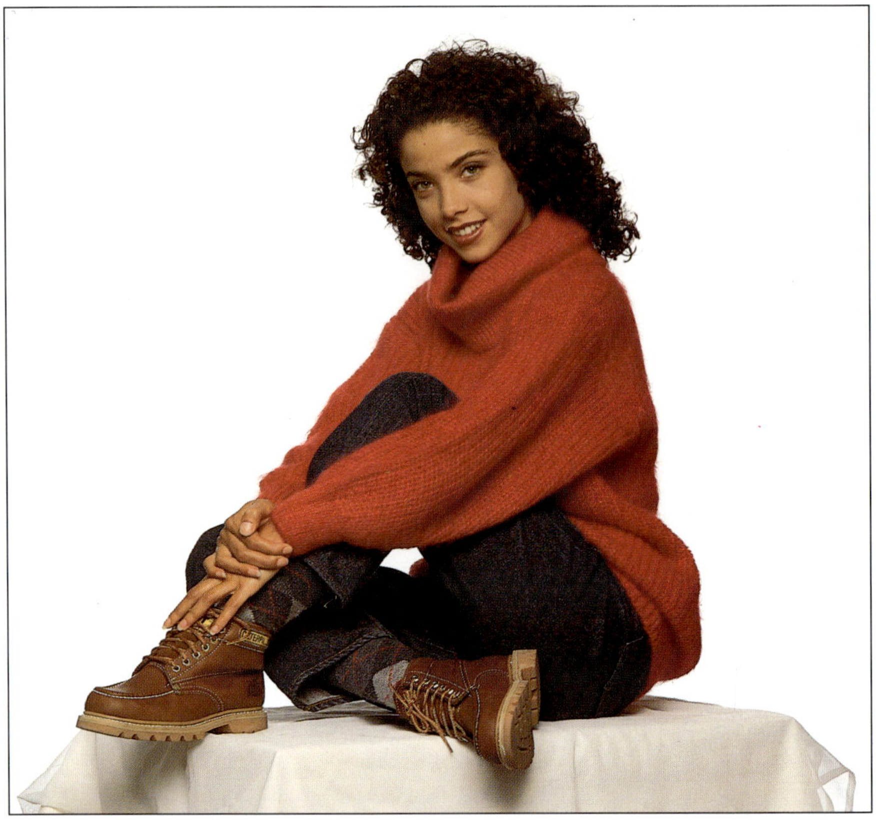

▲ ***On this slide the background appears transparent.***

Problem 1: dark corners

What if you don't have access to sophisticated studio equipment? You may have only two tungsten lamps or flash units, and want a portrait where the background is evenly lit and without shadows.

The common fault of dark corners is caused by placing the lights too close to the background. You obtain a nice even light in the centre, but only a dirty grey in the corners.

If you move the lights away from the background for a more even spread, there is a fall off in the brightness of the background lighting. This may mean that you can't maintain the balance between the exposures for the subject and the background.

The solution is to reduce the area of background that you have to light. Make the shot smaller, utilizing the area of the background that you have managed to light evenly. This means you'll probably have to close in for a head and shoulders shot, rather than a full length portrait.

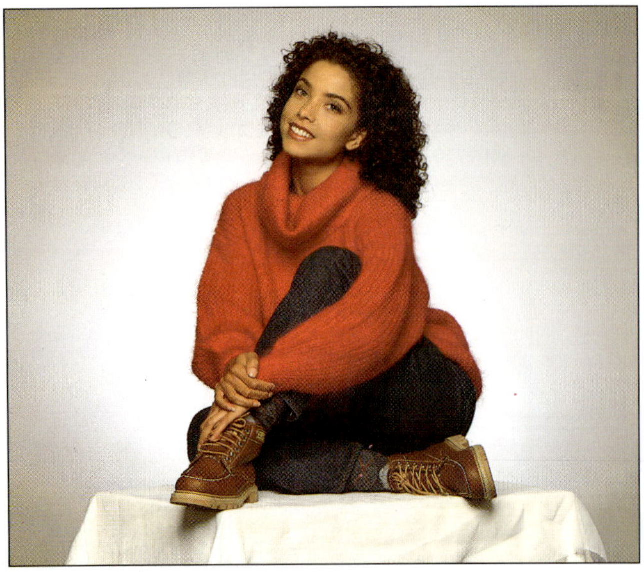

◀ ***Sometimes this kind of background lighting can look attractive, but here the photographer wanted an even background with no dark shadows.***

▶ ***To improve the background, the photographer moved the camera nearer to the model so that he could take a tight head and shoulders portrait. That way only the evenly lit central part of the background is visible.***

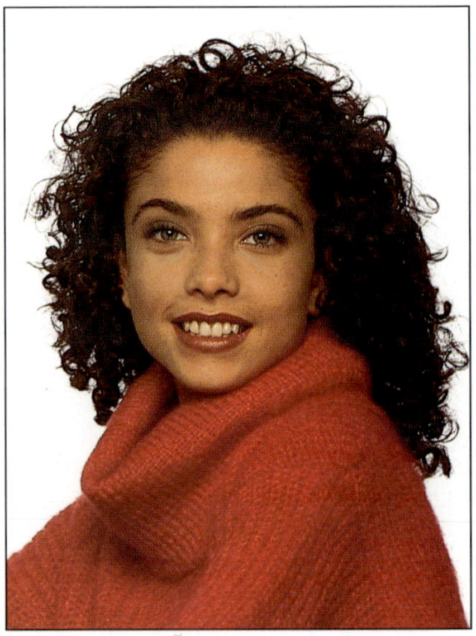

Problem 2: background too bright

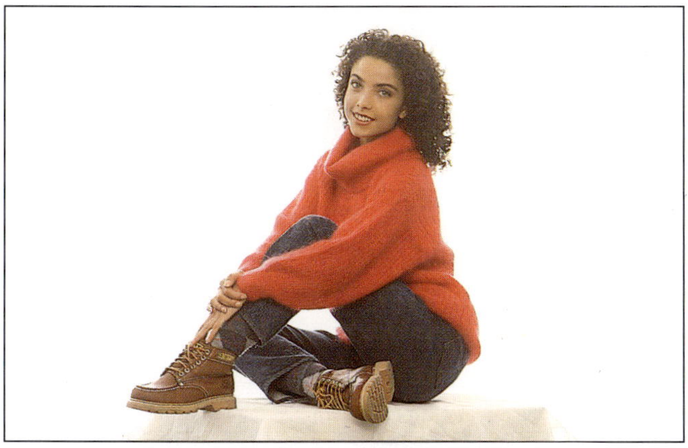

In this picture, the background looks bright, white and even, but it's too bright. The light reflected from the background causes flare around the subject. This gives a washed out image, which lacks contrast between the subject and the background.

The solution is simple – reduce the power of the background lights. However, not all studio lights can be adjusted for intensity. If this is the case with yours, the same effect can be achieved by just moving the lamps further away from the background.

Problem 3: background too dark

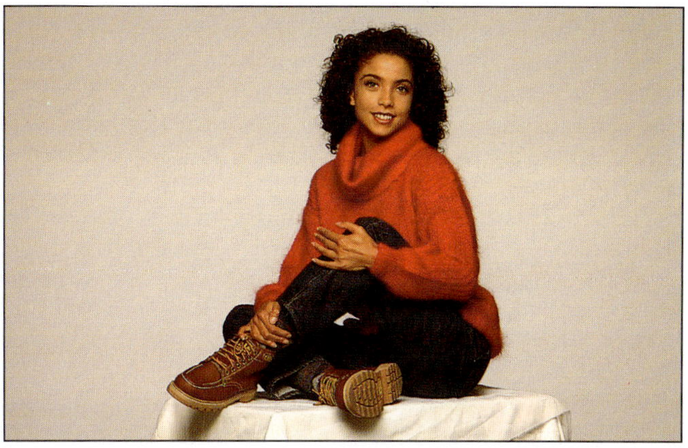

In this case, moving the lights away from the backdrop, to give flat and even lighting, has underexposed the background.

The solution is one of three things. You can move the lights closer to the background to light a smaller area evenly – and close in for a head and shoulders shot.

Otherwise, reduce the brightness of the light on your subject. This way you can maintain the subject to background lighting ratio.

The final option is to buy, or hire, extra lights.

Problem 4: dark centre

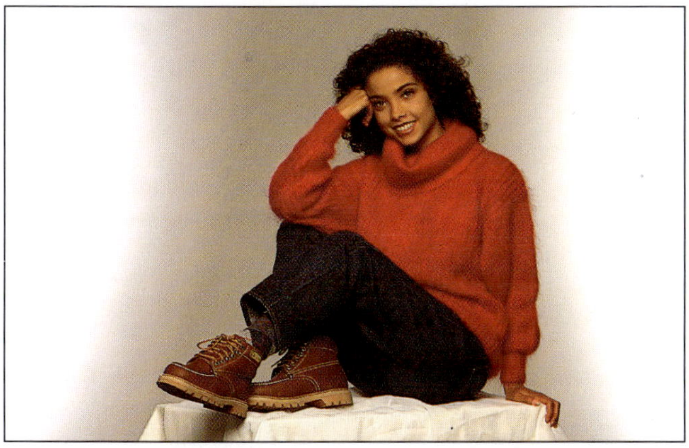

Here the sides of the backdrop are bright enough, but the centre is in shadow.

There are two reasons for this. Firstly, the subject is too close to the background.

This means it is difficult to obtain the correct angle from the background lamps without the light spilling on to the model and causing her to be overexposed in the final shot.

Secondly, the lamps are far too square-on to the background. As a result they are giving spots of intense brightness rather than pools of more even and balanced light.

The solution is to move the subject away from the background. This allows you to position the background lights so they are at a more oblique angle to the background. It also reduces the risk of flare.

Remember also to cross the beams so that they give a more even spread of light.

Problem 5: flare

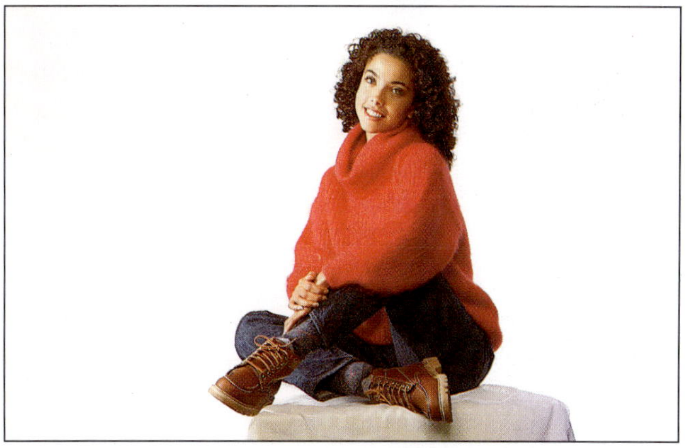

This problem is not at first apparent. The background appears evenly lit, but owing to lack of space in the studio, the subject is positioned too close to the background lighting units. The result is that light spills on to the subject and overexposes her face.

The solution is to use flags. These are matt black boards, cards or sheets placed between the lights and the subject, to ensure that light intended for the background doesn't illuminate anything else.

There are two methods of flagging lights. The first is to put large pieces of black card, black polystyrene board, black sheeting or similar materials between the lights and the subject.

If this proves to be impractical – perhaps because of the cramped conditions in which you are working – try fitting hinged barn doors on to the lights themselves.

Extra exposure

When the brightness of the background lighting is insufficient for a correct exposure, one solution is to give the background extra exposure. This may be difficult with a moving subject, but it is simple on a still life, because the subject is stationary.

With tungsten lamps you need to expose the background for longer. First, black out the studio. Then switch on the background lights and take an exposure reading. Next, make a long exposure using the camera's B setting.

After the correct exposure time, replace the lens cap and turn the lights off. Then switch on the subject lights and make an exposure for the subject.

You can use a similar procedure with flash, except that extending the exposure time has no effect. To give extra exposure you need to lock the shutter open and fire the flash several times.

To increase the exposure by one stop, you need to fire the flash twice. To increase the exposure by two stops, fire the flash four times and to increase the exposure by three stops use eight flashes.

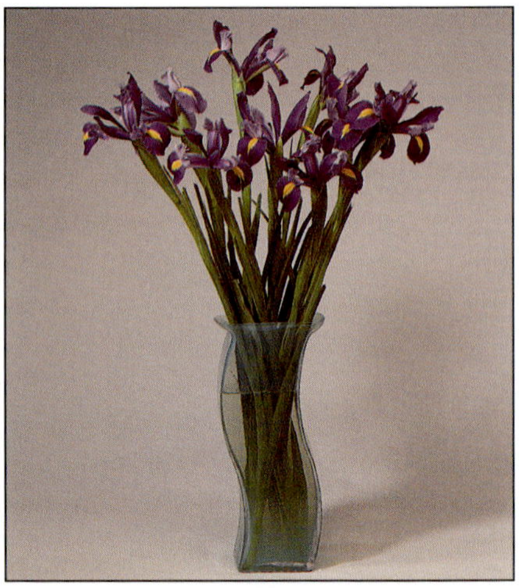

▲ ***A simple study of flowers is spoilt by two things – the background appears off-white and there's a distracting shadow.***

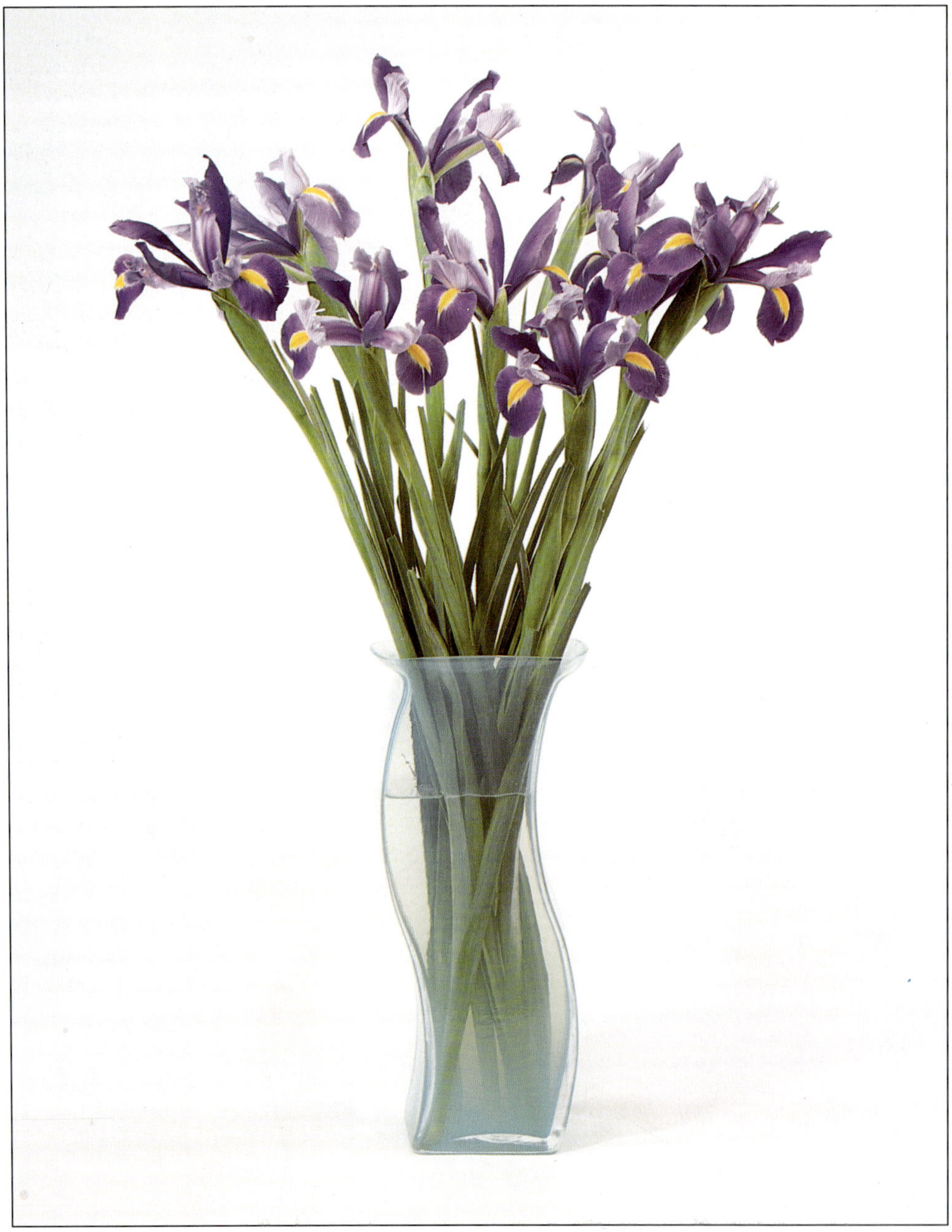

◀ ***For an even, white backdrop, the tungsten lamps on the background were left on for five times as long as those on the flowers.***

Tip **Using acrylics**

A good alternative to sidelighting seamless backdrop paper is to backlight an acrylic sheet. Owing to its superb diffusion properties it is easy to obtain an even spread of light across quite large surface areas.

Unfortunately, acrylic sheet is expensive, and it scratches easily. However, an ordinary lightbox (roughly 50cm x 1m), used for viewing slides, makes an ideal background for small still life pictures because of its bright, white and even light.

It is even possible, when shooting small still life arrangements, to use two lightboxes to effectively sidelight a large sheet of white seamless paper.

Creative background lighting

Once you have mastered the techniques involved in creating even background lighting, you are much better equipped to experiment with creative background lighting.

In the studio, you can experiment not only with different ways of lighting your subject, but also of lighting the background. For a standard portrait you may want a simple, evenly lit background. But for greater impact with portraits and with other subjects, you may wish to try some more ambitious lighting techniques.

Background lighting can be done in two ways. You can create *direct background lighting* by shining lights through a translucent backdrop from behind. However, this needs a large studio to accommodate the lights behind your backdrop, and you can't use an opaque background. The easier and more conventional way to light the backdrop is to use *reflected background lighting* – that is, to shine your lights from the front.

Creative background lighting can be done relatively easily with reflected backlight. In portraiture, if your key light is highlighting the right hand side of your model's face, try lighting the backdrop from the left hand side. This will give a strong, well balanced image.

Graduated background

Another idea is to light the background from below, so that the bottom of the backdrop is well lit and the light tapers off towards the top – an effect known as 'raking up'. To do this, you will probably need at least two backlights if you want to ensure that the light does not fall off to the sides as well as to the top.

With two backlights, point them at the bottom of the backdrop using a crosslighting technique – that is, point the left hand light at the right hand side of the backdrop and vice versa. Otherwise, you may want to invest in a studio strip light that provides an even amount of illumination over a wide area, so that fall off to the sides is not a problem.

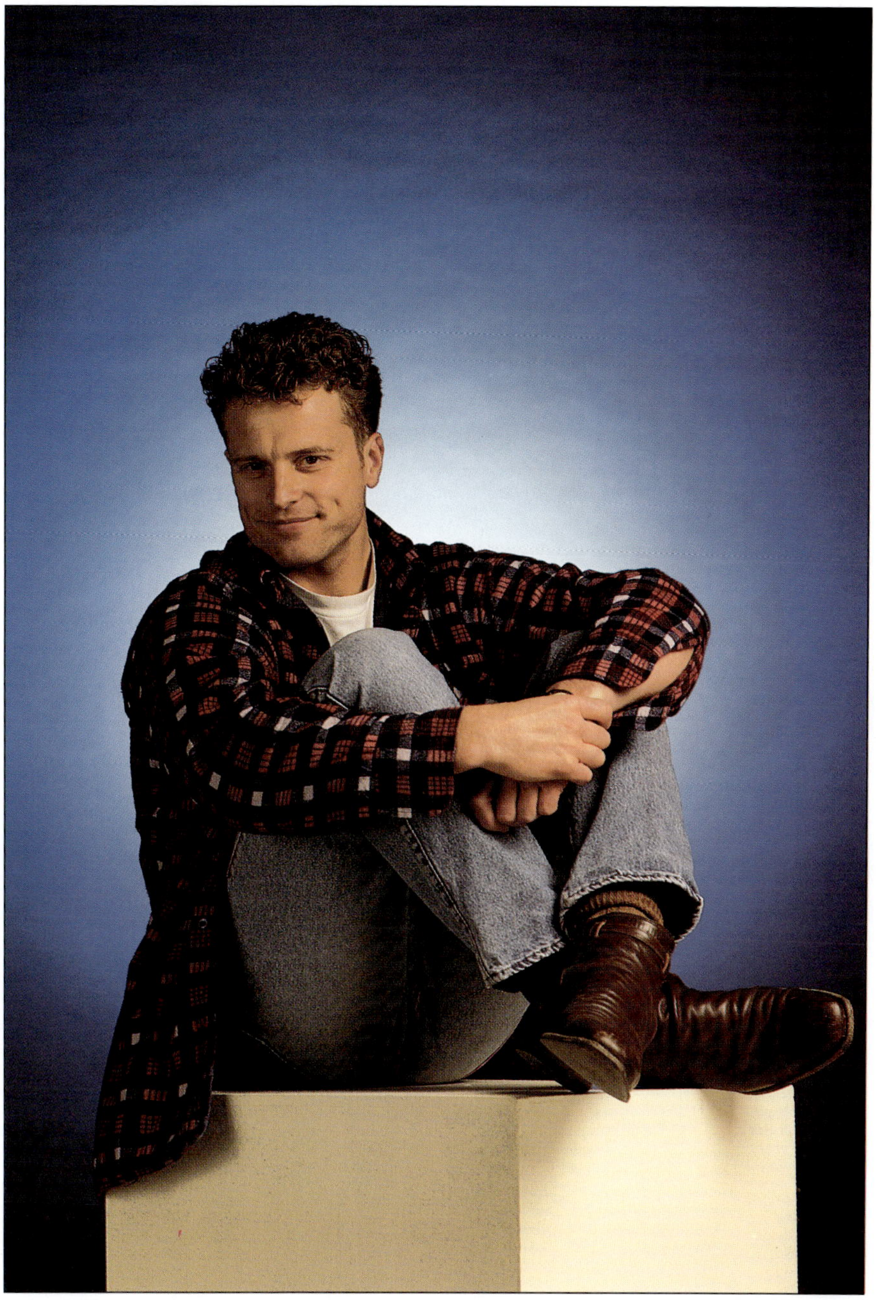

▲ ***A hot spot, together with a coloured backdrop, gives a sense of impact to a studio portrait.***

Hot spot with colour

In this shot, a spotlight was placed behind the model and pointed at the backdrop to create a hot spot. Reflector boards, placed parallel to the backdrop, helped prevent any light spilling from the backdrop on to the subject. These boards, together with the silver reflector, also helped illuminate the model evenly. A smaller reflector, beneath the main light – a soft modelling lamp – highlighted the right hand face of the plinth.

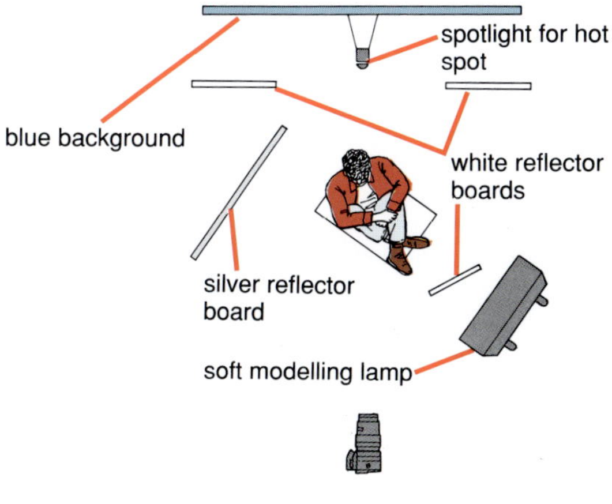

Hot spot

A hot spot was used on a plain white backdrop in this photograph. Even without a coloured background, the hot spot gives a pleasing halo effect and also helps draw your eye towards the model at the centre of the image.

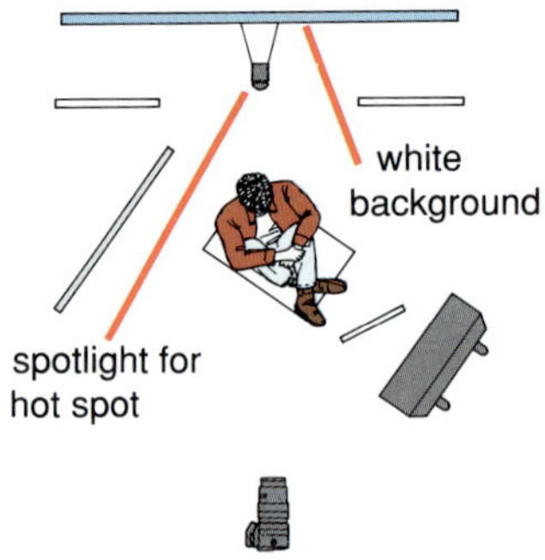

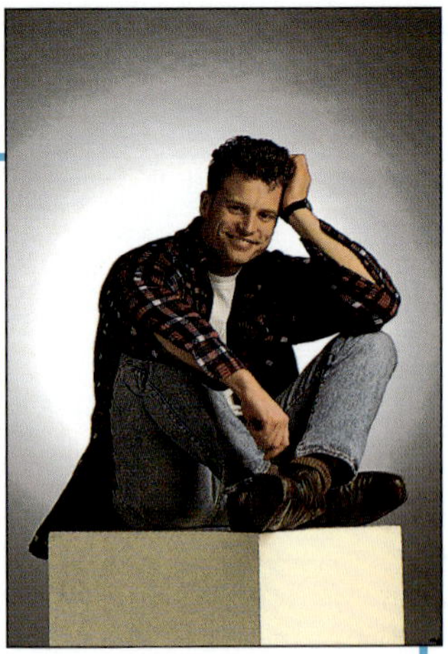

Beware of flare

As background lighting may 'spill' from the backdrop, protect your lens from flare. Use a lens hood and, if necessary, stick opaque tape around it to mask down to the photo's edge. Make sure that you can't see the tape through the viewfinder.

If you are taking a photo of a still life on a table using this technique, you can hide the lights from view underneath the table. The well lit bottom half of the backdrop will draw your eye down towards the subject.

Hot spot

A concentrated spot of light projected on to your backdrop – often called a 'hot spot' – can look very effective in both still life and portrait studies.

When you are combining many objects in one still life, you may want to highlight the central object. Use the concentrated light on the backdrop behind the main object and it will almost appear to cast a 'shadow of light'. For a portrait, a hot spot on the background gives a pleasant halo effect.

You can achieve a hot spot using a photoflood lamp fitted with a reflector dish. For a really pronounced concentration of light, use a spotlight – that is, a lamp with a lens to focus the beam of light.

Raking up

This raking up effect was achieved by positioning a studio strip light behind and beneath the subject. The strip light was directed at the bottom of the backdrop so that illumination fell off gradually towards the top. The long length of the strip light ensured that illumination did not fall off to the sides as well as to the top.

Raking down

To achieve the raking down effect, the strip light needed to be positioned above the subject. The photographer used heavy duty stands to hold the strip light in place. The reflector boards parallel to the backdrop are black-backed to prevent the backlight from the strip light spilling from the boards on to the lower half of the backdrop.

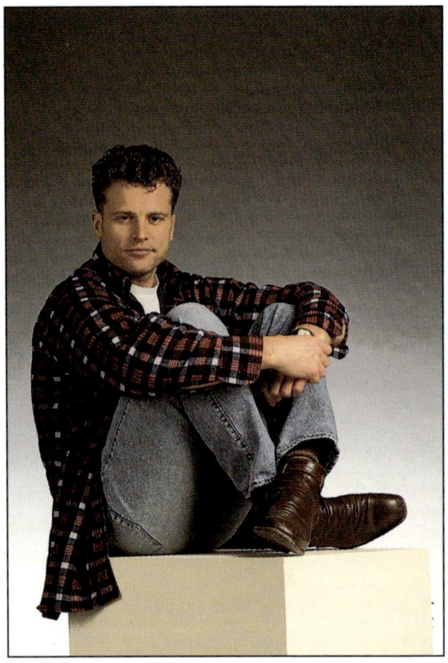

▲ ***Raking up without colour.***

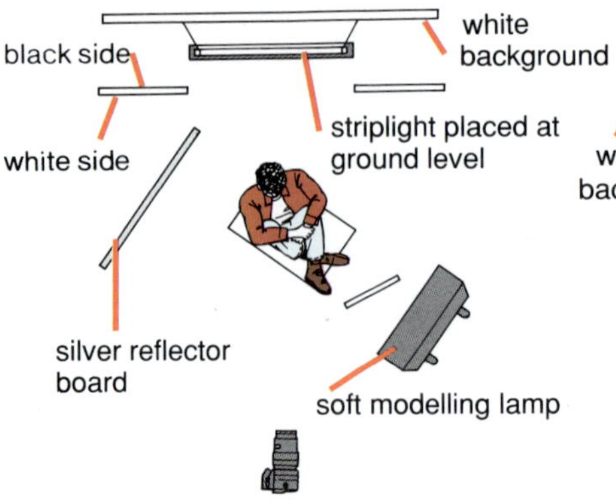

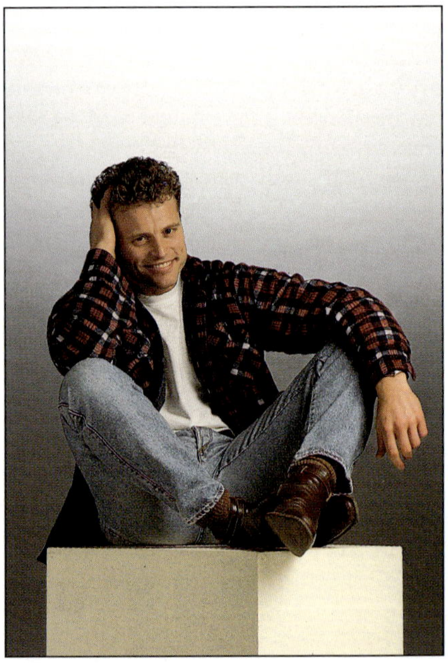

▲ ***Raking down without colour.***

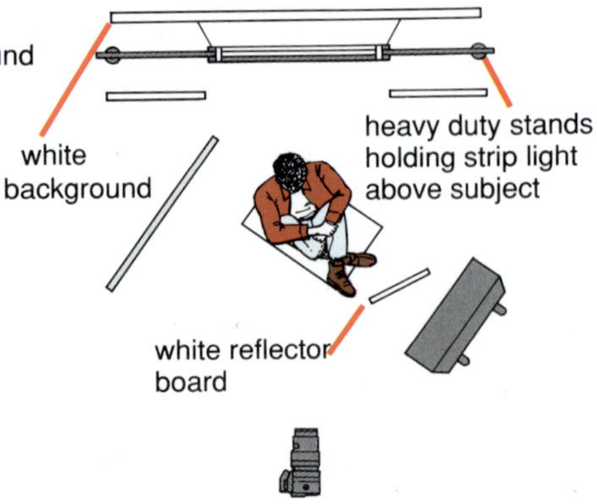

Tip

Subtle backlighting

If you don't want the backlighting to become too intrusive in your shots, make sure that:

❑ the background is out of focus. Use an aperture large enough so that the background falls out of the depth of field.

❑ the backdrop is made of a soft, unreflective material rather than a hard, shiny one. This will help diffuse the light. Try professional acrylic sheet, seamless backdrop paper or even a cotton bed sheet.

Adding colour

The easiest way of adding colour to the background is by using a coloured backdrop. However, for more versatility, try using gels over your backlights. Gels are flexible, coloured acetate filters. They can be attached over lights with special gel mounts.

There are endless colour possibilities with gels. If you want to romanticize a portrait, for instance, try a pink gel. To obtain stronger hues, fit two gels on one lamp. If a yellow gel doesn't give the golden glow you want, use two yellow gels. You can also combine different colours – for instance, a light with a blue gel together with a light with a green gel to create an 'underwater' feel.

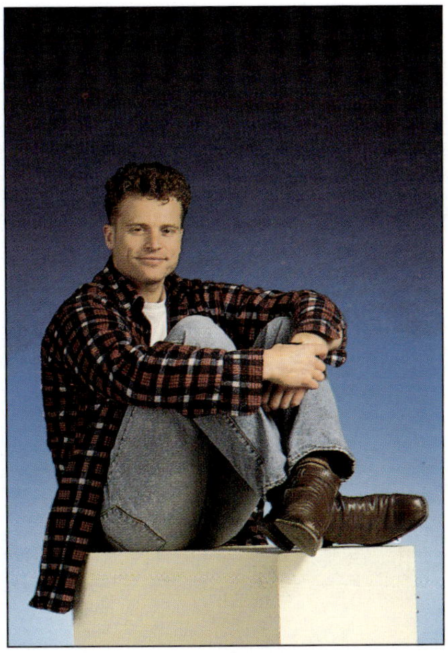

▲ ***Raking up with a blue backdrop.***

Coloured backdrop

The most conventional and convenient way to add background colour is to use a coloured backdrop – although this does not offer the imaginative possibilities of gels. For this image, the photographer used the raking up technique with a blue paper backdrop.

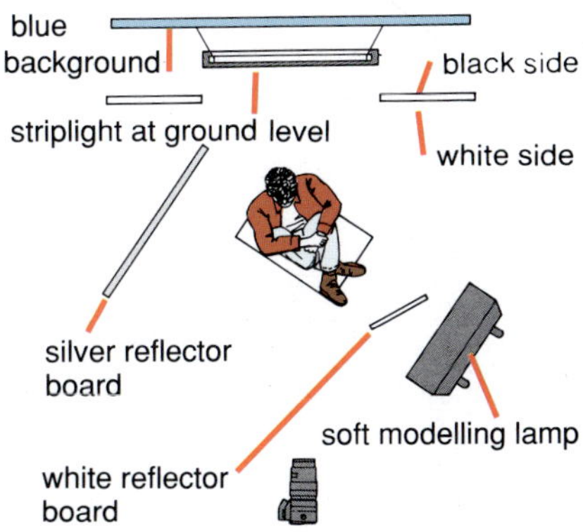

Multicoloured backdrop

In this shot, two backlights were used – the left hand one with a blue gel and the right hand one with a red gel. They were projected on to a crumpled, white paper backdrop. The photographer made sure that the lights overlapped in the middle of the backdrop in order to create a third colour – mauve. This prevented a distracting strip of white backdrop from appearing behind the subject's head and also added further to the colourful impact of the photograph.

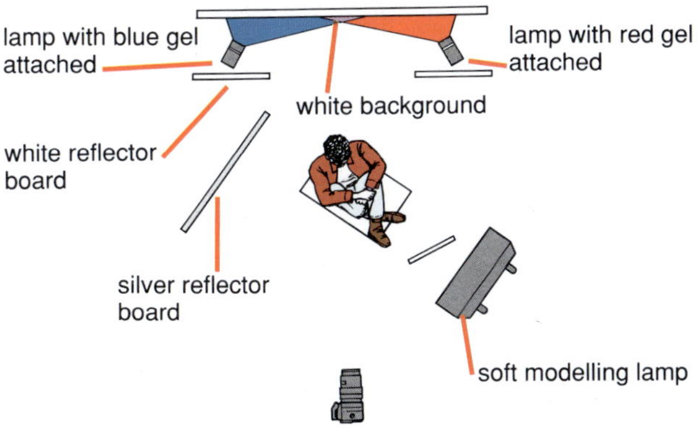

▶ ***Backlighting with coloured gels.***

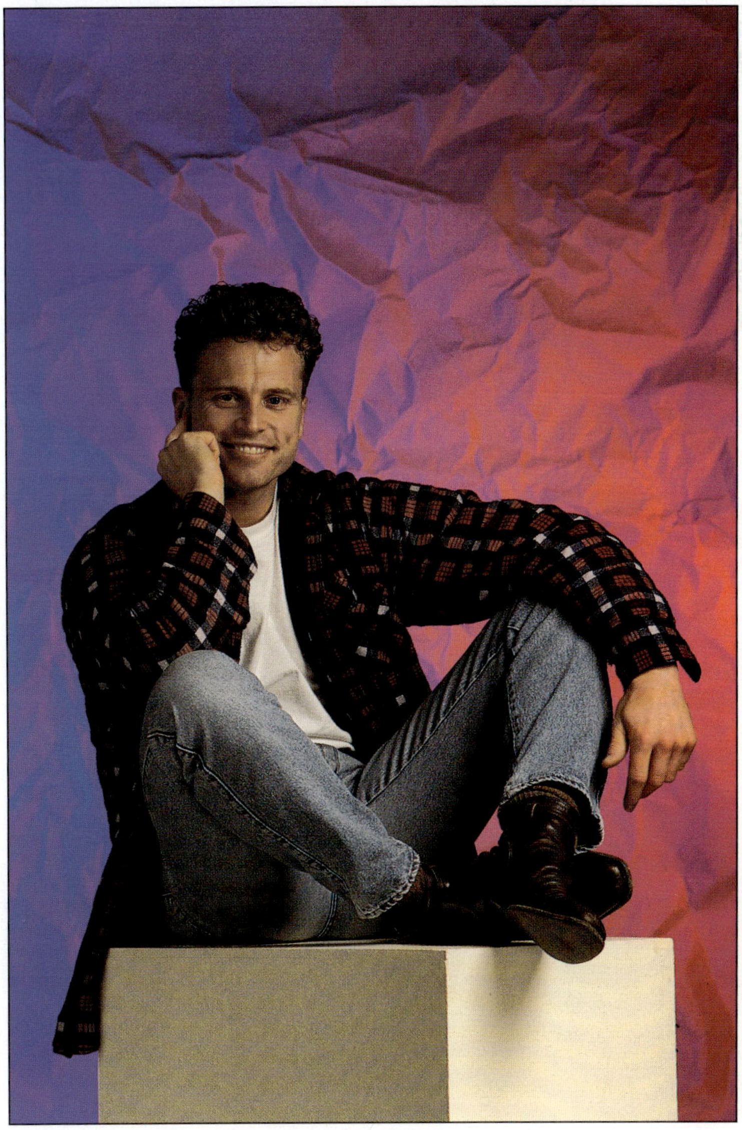

Tip: Exposure

Whatever background lighting arrangement you decide to use, don't let it fool you when it comes to exposure. Always take an exposure reading from close to your subject or take an incident light reading. Bracket exposures if you are not completely sure – you don't want to have to set up the whole shoot again if the subject is spoilt by the wrong exposure.

Projection

Throwing shadows on to a backdrop is an exciting way to enliven your studio shots. One way of doing this is to use metal masks known as gobos. Gobos come in many different forms – for instance, you can project an image of a castle or a cityscape, or create the effect of light coming through a window frame or palm fronds.

Gobos can be slotted into most professional spotlights. To put gobos on to most other lights, you must have attachments made up.

Remember, if you project gobos on to the backdrop from the front, you'll produce a distorted image. This is because your backlight cannot be square-on to the backdrop; if it is, it will shine directly on to the subject.

However, you can hide your backlight behind your subject and point it up to the backdrop. The bottom of the projected image will be a bit narrower than the top. This distortion, though, will be less than if you place the light to the side.

If you want to eliminate distortion completely, you should project gobos on to a translucent backdrop from behind.

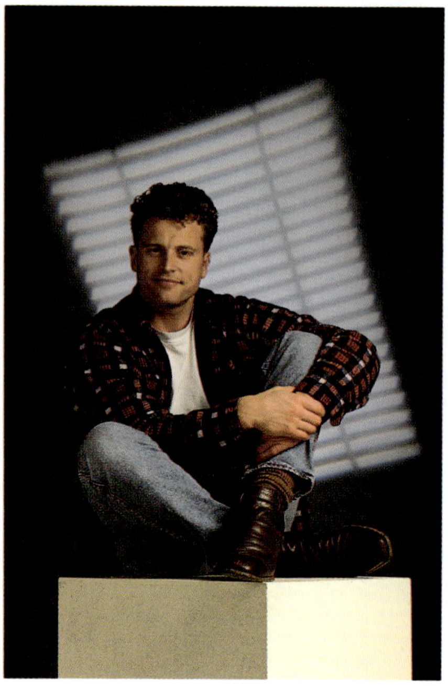

Using a gobo

To simulate light coming through a Venetian blind, a single backlight was fitted with a gobo. The backlight was positioned beneath and behind the model and pointed up towards the backdrop. For greater effect, the photographer has projected the image of the gobo at a slightly crooked angle. The low angle of the backlight has also caused the bottom of the image to be slightly narrower than the top.

◀ ***A Venetian blind gobo.***

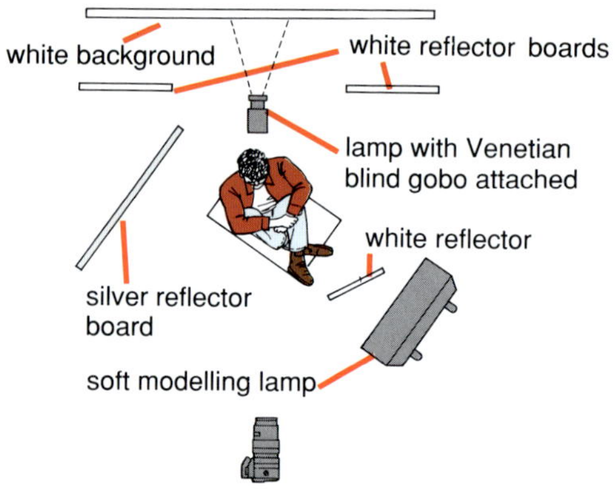

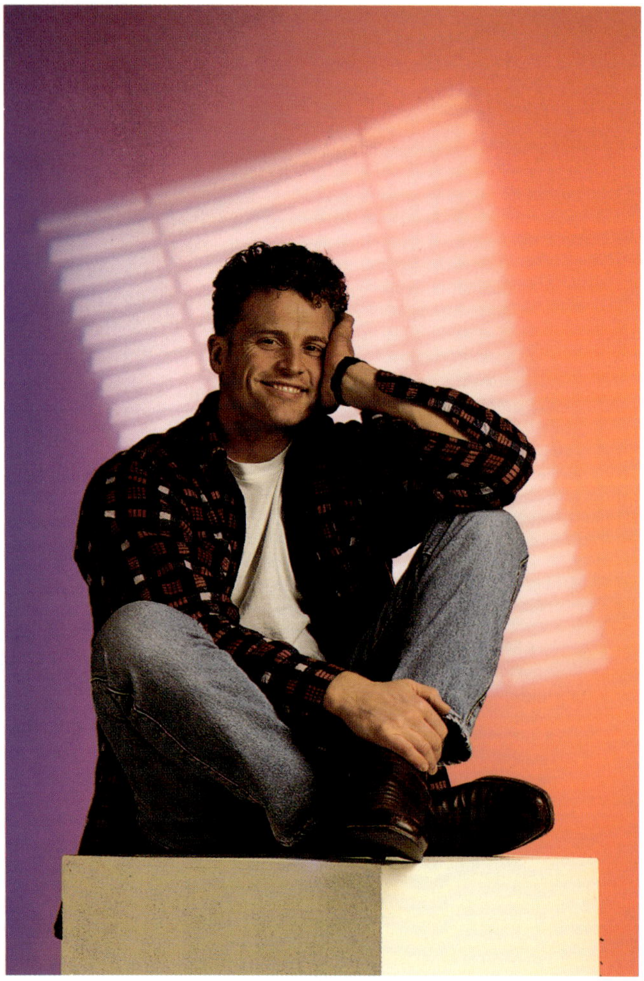

Tip: Use a photocopier

If you have access to a photocopier, you can create your own textured lighting effects. First, buy some clear acetate film in A4 size from a large stationers. Then load this into the photocopier's paper tray. Now you can photocopy whatever objects you want on to the acetate film. For instance, you may want to photocopy tree bark, your hand or a newspaper. Once you have an image on the acetate film that will create an interesting lighting effect, cut the film to fit a gel mount. Use a metal ruler and a craft knife to cut the acetate. Now you can project light through the acetate film as you would through a gel.

Gobos and gels

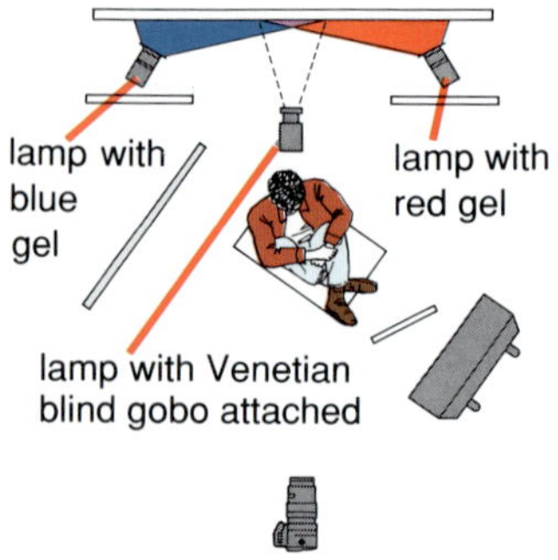

In this photograph, a backlight with a gobo was used in combination with backlights which had red and blue gels fitted. The lights with gels were positioned to the sides. By pointing these lights towards the bottom of the backdrop, the photographer has also achieved a very subtle raking up effect.

◀ ***Backlighting with a gobo and coloured gels.***

Glamour photography

Glamour photography requires soft, flattering lighting on the subject and unobtrusive but appropriate background lighting. Graham Finch leans how it is done.

I arrived at Harry Ormesher's studio feeling more than a little nervous. I'd never photographed a glamorous model before, and was quite daunted by the prospect. How would I light my shots, for example, and what would I ask the girl to do?

I relaxed a little when I met our subject for the day, Vida. She seemed very professional indeed, and quite comfortable in the studio atmosphere. All the equipment I could possibly want was at my disposal, so I asked Vida to get changed into one of her outfits and began setting up my shot.

An unflattering shot

I chose a bright blue background, which I lit with two small lights, one on either side. I decided to sidelight my model with one big studio light which I bounced off a silver umbrella. When Vida emerged wearing some purple lingerie, I started shooting.

I used a Nikon F801 with a 35-105mm lens together with Fuji ISO 50 daylight colour slide film, and synched the camera up with the lights. I said a few words to Vida before we started, but once I got going I concentrated on the composition and forgot all about her. In the resulting shots she looked uncomfortable and bored, the light was far too harsh and the background clashed badly with Vida's outfit.

Softening the light

When Harry took over he spent a long time getting the lighting set up exactly right. For his main light he bounced two big studio lights off two white polystyrene boards in front and to either side of the model. To fill in he used two small lights with umbrellas, one above and one below his line of vision. He then swapped the bright blue

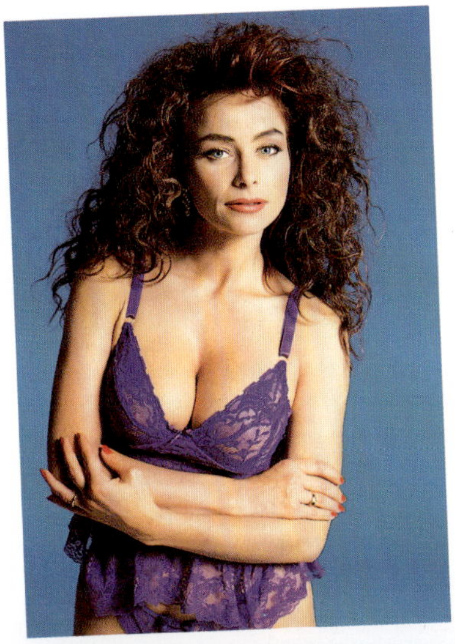

◀ *In Graham's shot the model's arms are folded in an uncomfortable pose that hides her shape. She looks bored, the blue background is totally unsuitable and the naked sidelight is unflattering to her face.*

1 A WARMER SHOT
Harry's first shot is a huge improvement. The background's much more appropriate, Vida looks relaxed and attractive and the light is perfect. By bouncing and diffusing he's created a warm, even light that's also soft and flattering.

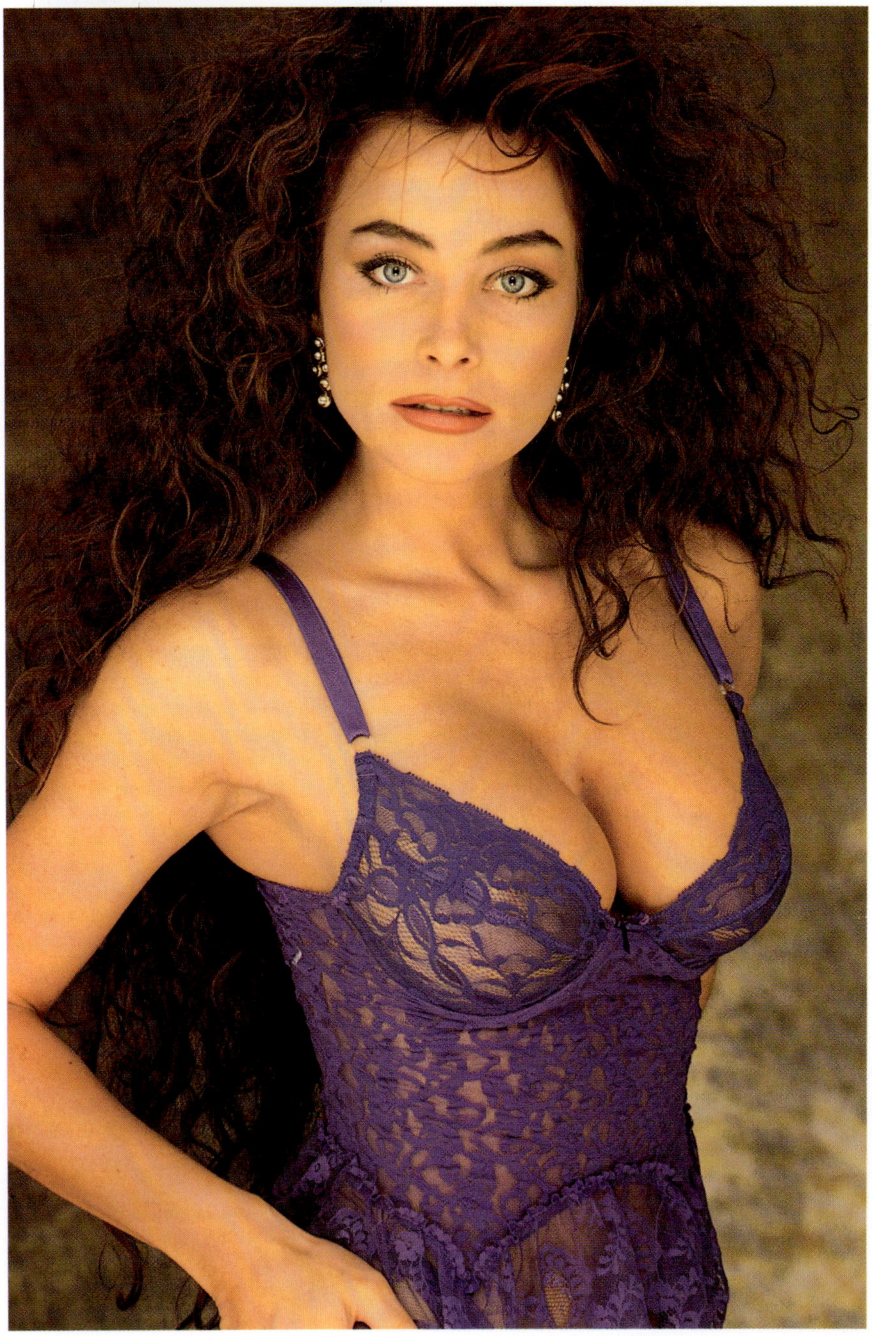

background for a tasteful canvas, which he lit from the left with a large light.

The effect of all this was to create a much softer and more flattering light that highlighted the body's contours without exposing the face too harshly. Harry used the same camera and film as I had, but switched to a 70-200mm zoom lens. When he was shooting he spoke to Vida all the time, encouraging her and telling her exactly what he wanted.

When he'd shot off a roll, Harry asked Vida to change into something different. Then he took a series of pictures of her sitting in a chair wearing white lace underwear. He used the same lighting set up and asked the model to try a variety of different positions until he found the pose he wanted.

A tasteful nude

When he decided to try shooting a subtle nude study, Harry changed the lighting set up completely. He toplit the shot by hanging a big softbox directly above Vida's head and bounced a light off a gold reflector on the floor in front of her to fill in the shadows.

He sat her on a wooden bench and asked her to lean forward and hide her face. 'Strong top light is excellent if you want to emphasise the shape of the body', explains Harry, 'but its hard shadows do the face no favours at all.'

To finish off, he took some flattering head and shoulder shots of Vida. He used four softboxes for this, and diffused them all heavily to make the effect even softer. He ended up with a strong light that was also soft and even enough to be complimentary.

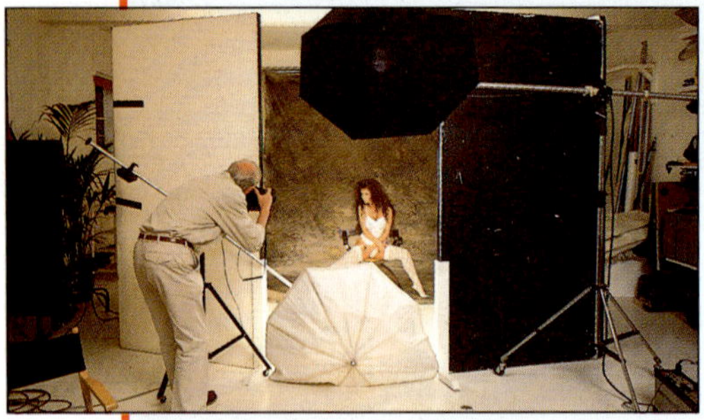

The set up

Graham and Harry were shooting in a small professional studio. Graham's shot was harshly and heavily side lit, but Harry created a far kinder light when he took over.

His basic set up for the first two shots was: two large bare studio lights on either side of the model facing away and bounced off two polystyrene boards, two smaller lights bounced off umbrellas above and below Harry's line of vision and a single light on the background.

He toplit the nude shot with a large softbox as described above. The portrait lighting set up is described on the following page.

Both photographers used Nikon F801s. Graham chose a 35-105mm zoom lens and Harry switched to a 70-200mm lens.

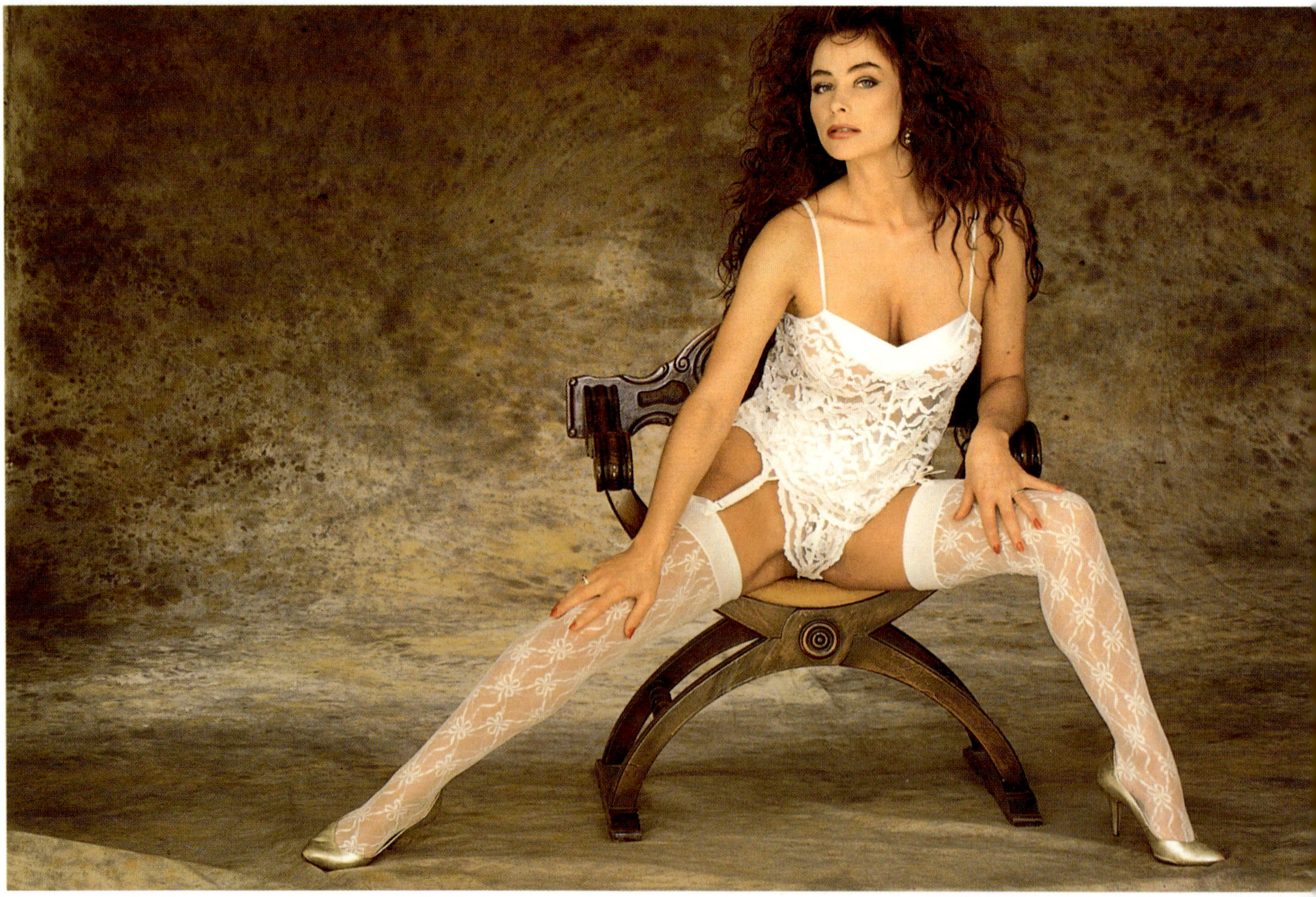

Tip: Creating a very soft light

When taking his close-up portrait, Harry was looking for the softest light he could find. 'I used four small softboxes to light the shot', he explains. 'They produce a nice soft light on their own, but to make it even softer I shone them through a double trace screen. This gave me a really kind light that's absolutely perfect for close-up glamour portraits. I made a hole in the middle of the screen between the lights and shot straight through it.'

Obviously you won't be able to achieve as perfect a light as this at home, but a modified version with domestic lamps and a smaller screen should be quite effective for a portrait.

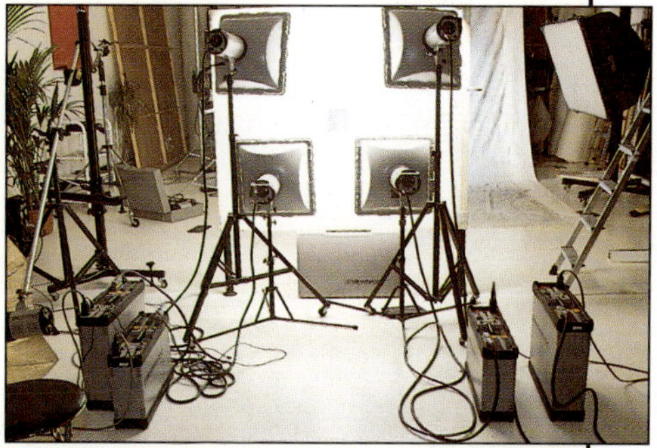

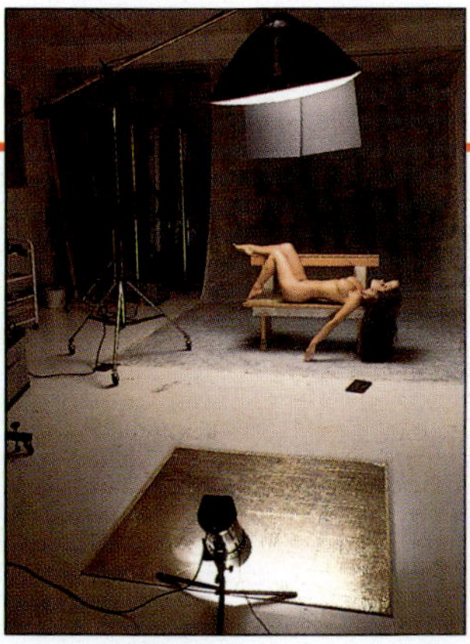

2 ◄ CHANGING THE POSE
Having asked Vida to change into a white outfit, Harry used the same lighting set up and background as before to create a totally different picture. He asked her to sit on a chair and then moved her around until he found the exciting pose he wanted.

3 ► TOPLIT NUDE
Harry then took an unusual and striking nude study which he lit from above. A big softbox directly over the model really picked out the body's shape, and a light bounced off a gold reflector in front of the set up filled in the shadows.

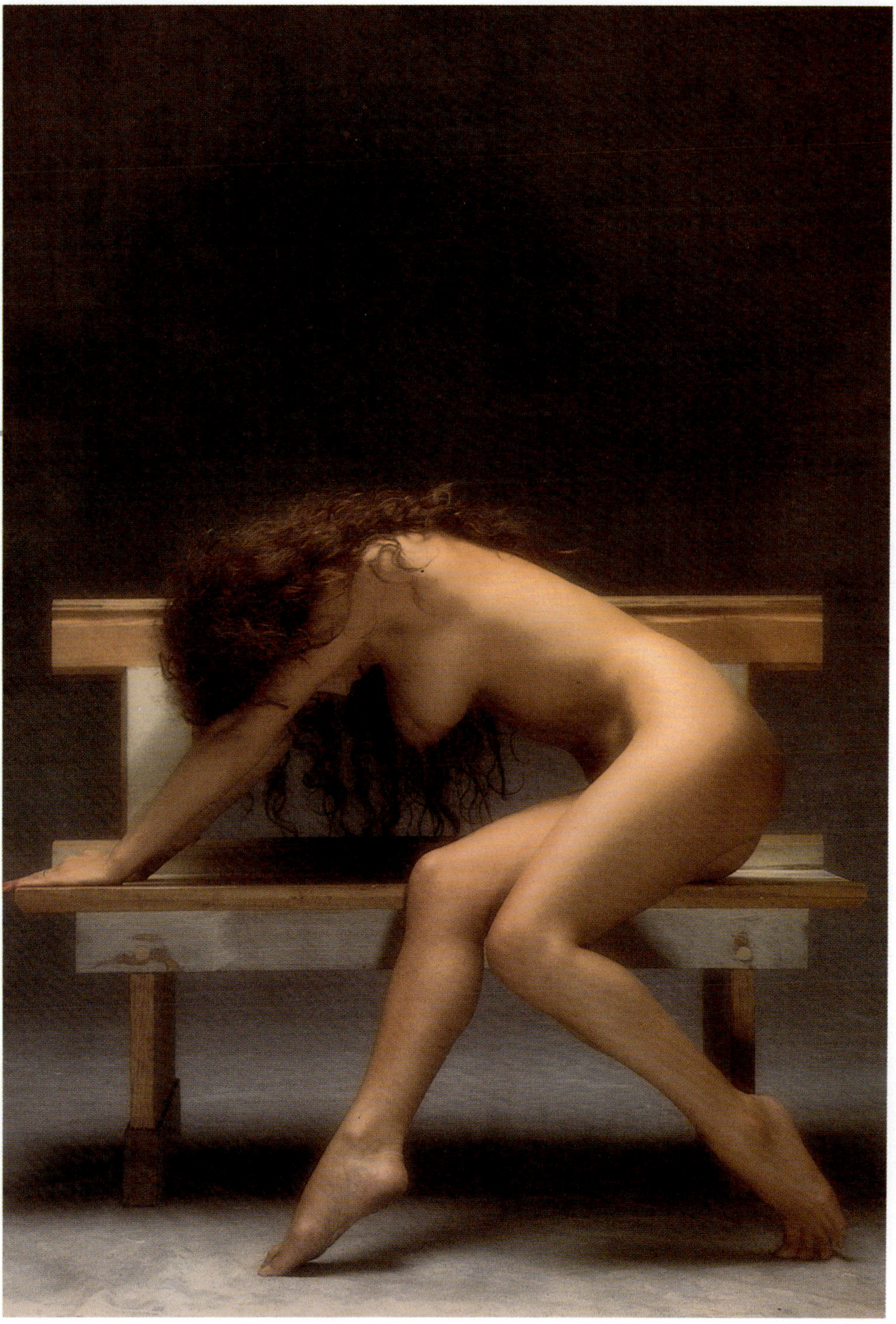

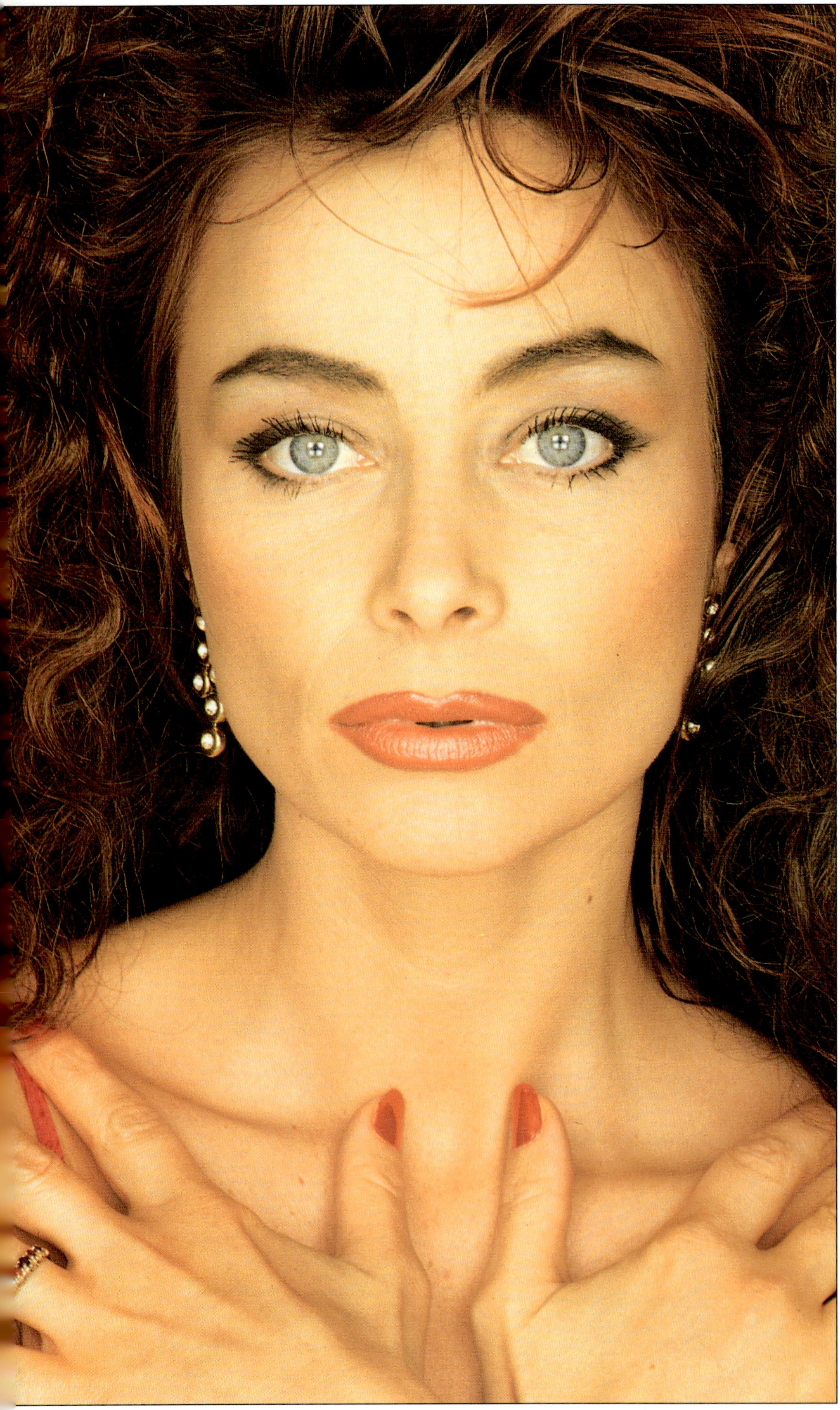

4 FLATTERING LIGHT Harry wanted to take a very close head shot to finish off, so he needed a light that was strong but not too harsh. He did this by diffusing four big softboxes through a double trace screen directly in front of the model and shooting in between them.

Compact tip

As you can see, elaborate studio beauty and glamour pictures like these are very much easier with professional equipment. With simple gear such as a compact camera, you'd be better off choosing an outdoor setting in a remote location.

SLR tip

It's hard to emulate beauty lighting at home – you'll avoid a lot of frustration and disappointment by renting a well-equipped studio. Make sure you've got all the facilities you need, as well as someone on hand to help you use unfamiliar equipment, before choosing a studio.

Photographing food

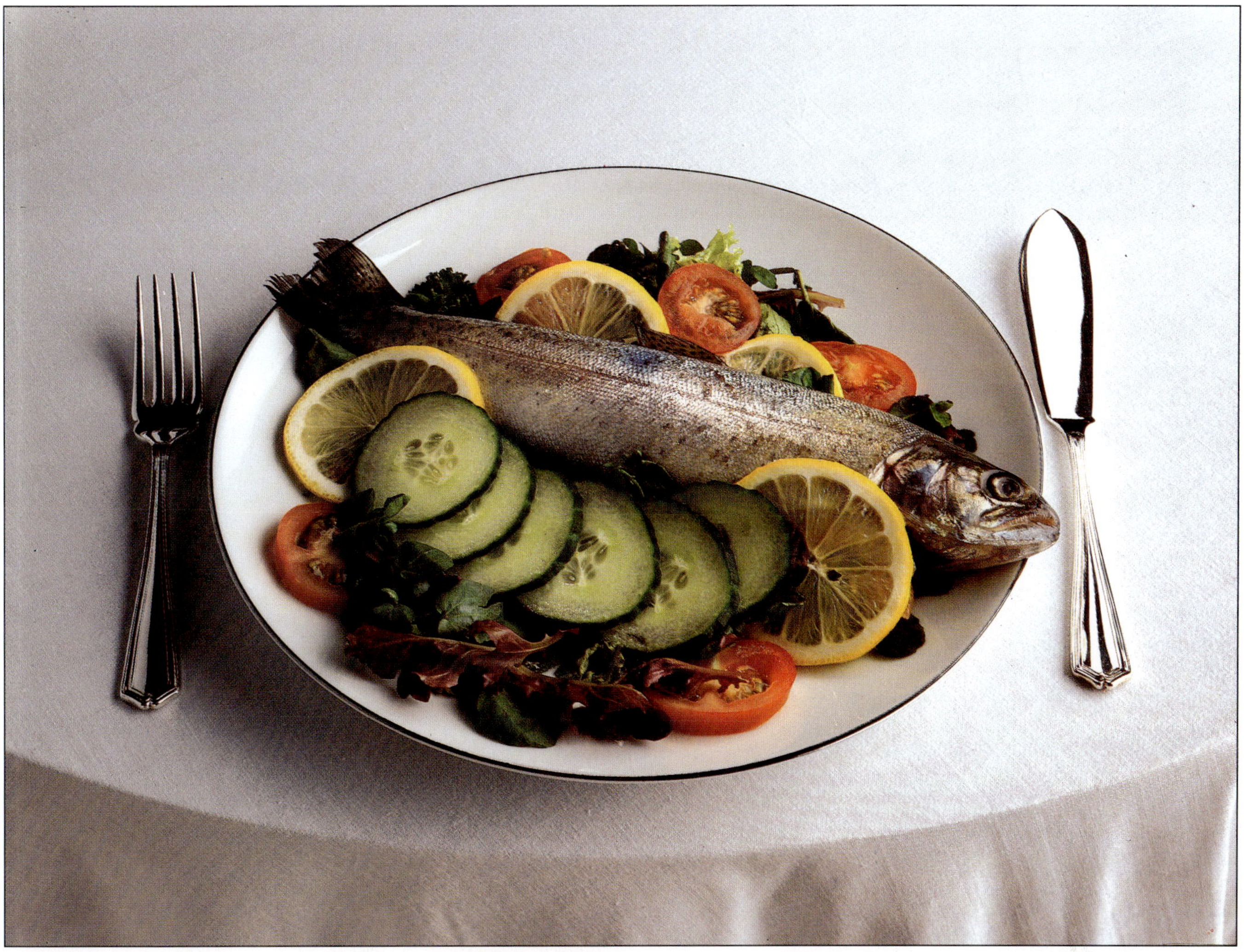

Lighting food is completely different from lighting for glamour, but it is (if anything) even more demanding. Seamus Ryan shows David Jones how it is done.

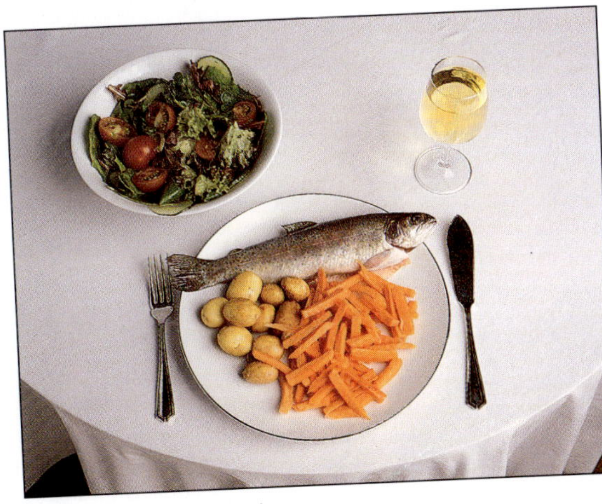

▲ ***Seamus found that when the trout was cooked it lost all the colour in the scales, so he decided to use a raw one coated in glycerine to make it look cooked. The garnish was carefully arranged by a specialist food stylist.***

◀ ***David was right to try an overhead shot. But the composition is full of empty spaces, the fish is being pushed off an overcrowded plate, the salad bowl looks messy and the wine glass is far too full. The front lighting does the food no favours either.***

Whenever I've tried photographing a spread of food at home, the results have been disappointing. However mouthwatering the food appears to the naked eye, it always ends up looking washed-out and inedible on film. So I asked still life and food photographer Seamus Ryan to show me how to light and shoot a simple meal effectively.

I soon discovered that food photography is a very specialized craft involving the subtlest of lighting techniques and some surprising ways of making the fare look more appealing. Indeed, on most occasions a home economist (a specialist food stylist) is present at shoots to ensure the food remains in absolutely perfect condition. Our home economist for the day found us some lovely fresh-water trout to photograph.

Perking up the food

The home economist tried cooking one of the fishes, but they actually looked more colourful and attractive raw. So she used a small paint brush to coat one in glycerine, so it looked cooked. She coated the vegetables, which were cooked but cold, in the same way to make them look as though they were covered in melted butter. She also made sure there were plenty of tomatoes at the top of the salad to give it colour.

A flat picture

With studio lights and equipment at my disposal, and food prepared by a professional, I thought I had a good chance of producing a decent photograph, so I started to arrange the set. The table was already covered with a white linen cloth, so I arranged a knife, fork and plate on it. Then I laid the fish out on the plate and surrounded it with carrots and potatoes.

Finally, I put an attractive looking bowl of salad above it on the left hand side and a glass of wine on the right to balance the shot. I then turned my attention to the lighting. I frontlit the scene with a big softbox, and used a reflector on the other side of the set up to throw light back on the food.

Then, using a step ladder to get an overhead viewpoint, I used a Sinar P 5 x 4 large format camera fitted with a 150mm lens and

The set up

The food that Seamus and David used was prepared by a home economist. They covered a round table with a carefully ironed tablecloth and shot down on it from above. They both used a Sinar P 5 x 4 large format camera and a 150mm lens, but Seamus used Polaroids to get his lighting right. David frontlit his shot with a softbox, but Seamus sidelit his from the right with a big reflector on the left, and used a spotlight to pick out the main plate. He also used several tiny reflectors on the table itself to give more light to the bowls of vegetables.

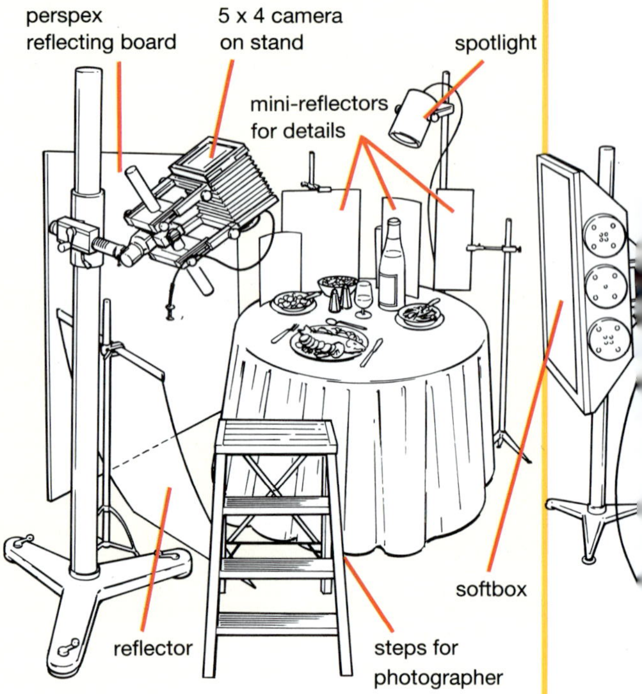

BUILDING UP THE SHOT

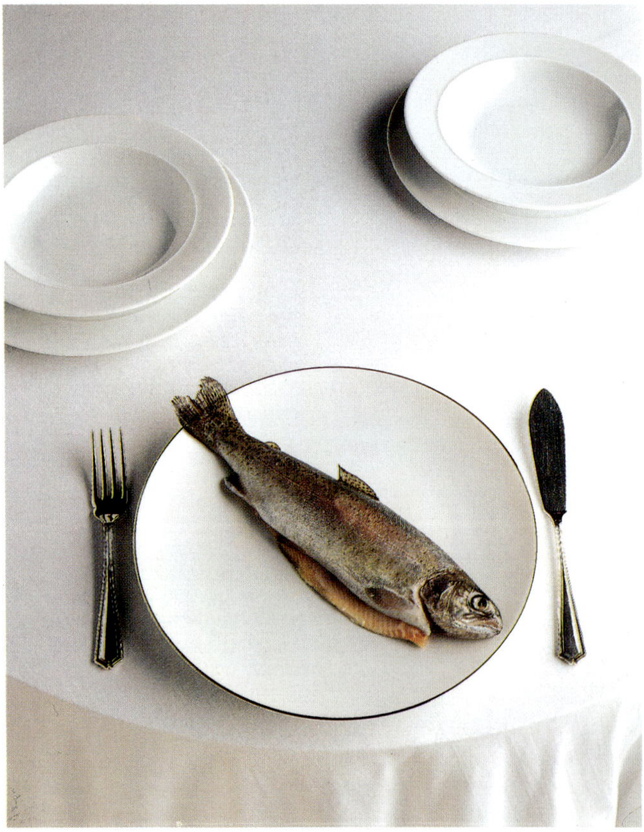

1 THE BASIC COMPOSITION
Before he laid out all the food, Seamus used empty plates to work out the basic shot he wanted. He put the main plate in the foreground, and placed a plate for vegetables on either side at the top of the frame to balance the composition. He sidelit the set up from the right.

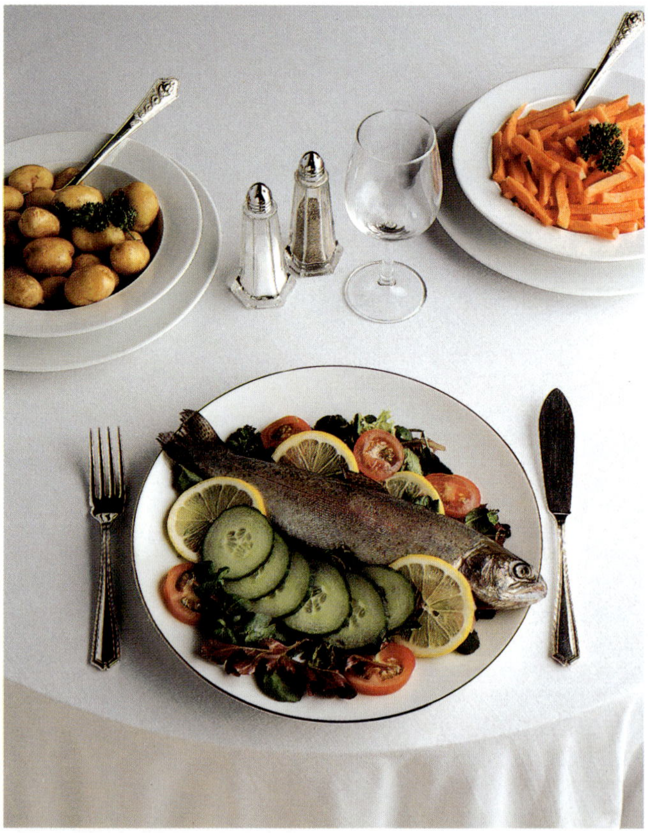

2 ADDING THE FOOD
The carefully arranged garnish made the fish look far more appetizing, and the carrots and potatoes added colour to the background. Seamus used salt and pepper cellars and a wine glass to fill the gap in the middle, but there's still a lot of empty space at the back.

Ektachrome ISO 100 slide film to shoot the scene. If I'd taken a Polaroid first I would have realized that the light was flat, the composition full of empty spaces and the plate itself far too overcrowded. But I'd never used a large format camera before and the upside-down viewfinder image confused me.

Balancing the composition

When Seamus took over he cleared my set up and started from scratch. To begin with he used empty plates to get his set up right before he thought about food. He used the same camera, lens and film as I had, but took Polaroids to make sure each stage was correctly lit.

He chose a slightly lower angle, and sidelit his set up with the softbox on the right and a perspex reflector on the left. He placed the fish in the middle of a plate in the foreground and arranged a garnish around it. He then added a plate of potatoes and a plate of carrots above it, and filled the gap in the middle of the table with a wine glass and salt cellars.

The finishing touches

When Seamus had brought in the wine bottle and salad bowl to fill the gaps at the top of his shot, he concentrated on adding the finishing touches to his lighting set up. To make the main plate really

Tip: Keeping food fresh

'If you leave food sitting around under the lights for too long', says Seamus, 'it will look very tired by the time you get around to shooting it. This is a serious problem when you're working under big studio lights. The best thing to do is to keep the food fresh in the kitchen and work out your lighting and composition without it. When you're ready, bring in the food and shoot it as quickly as you can. This is worth doing even if you're using domestic lamps to light your shot.'

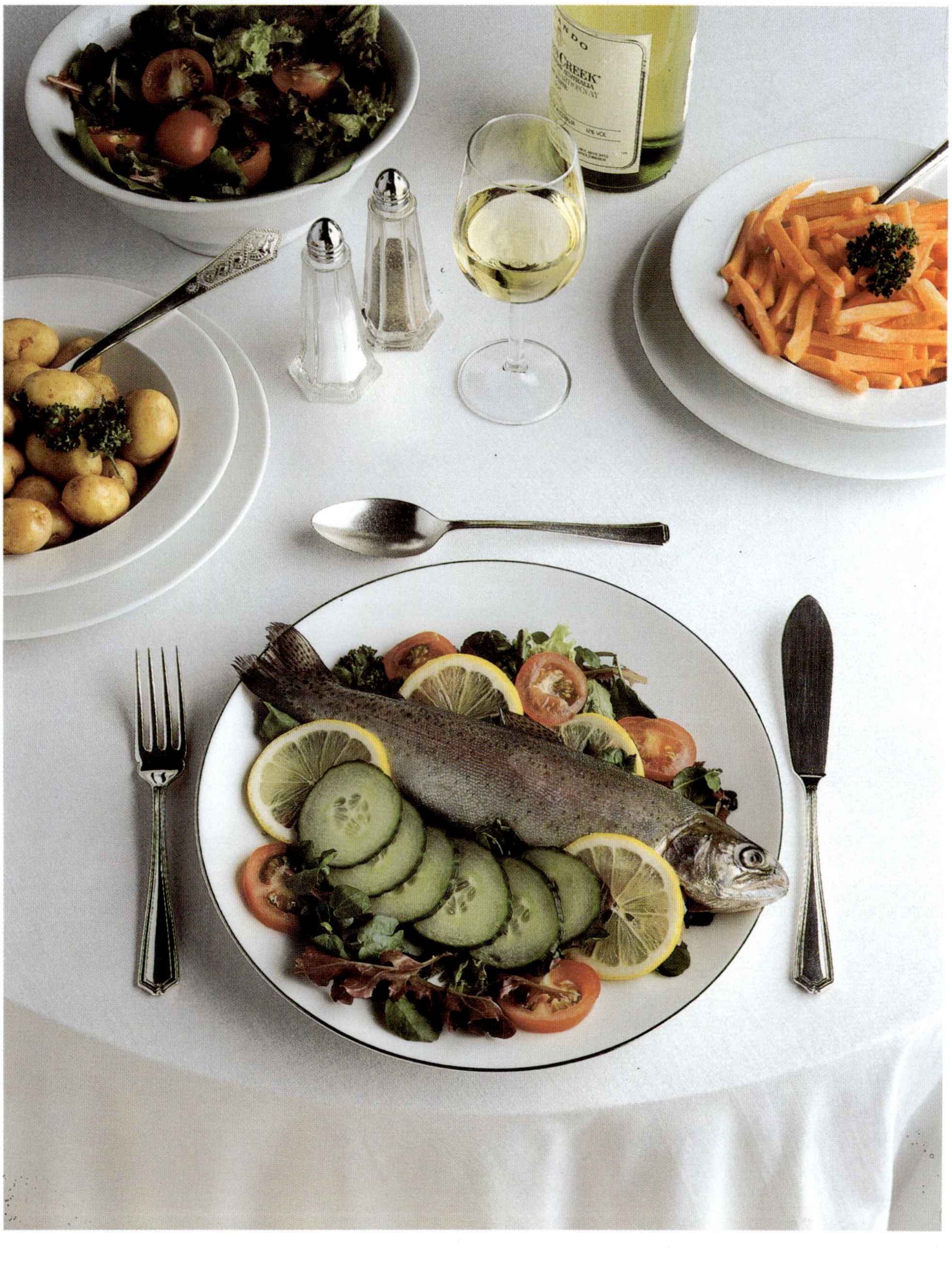

3 FILLING THE GAPS By adding the wine bottle, Seamus made the set up look more like a real meal. The bowl of salad filled a large gap at the rear and the spoon added to the foreground. To make the vegetables stand out, Seamus used two small reflectors to throw more light on to them.

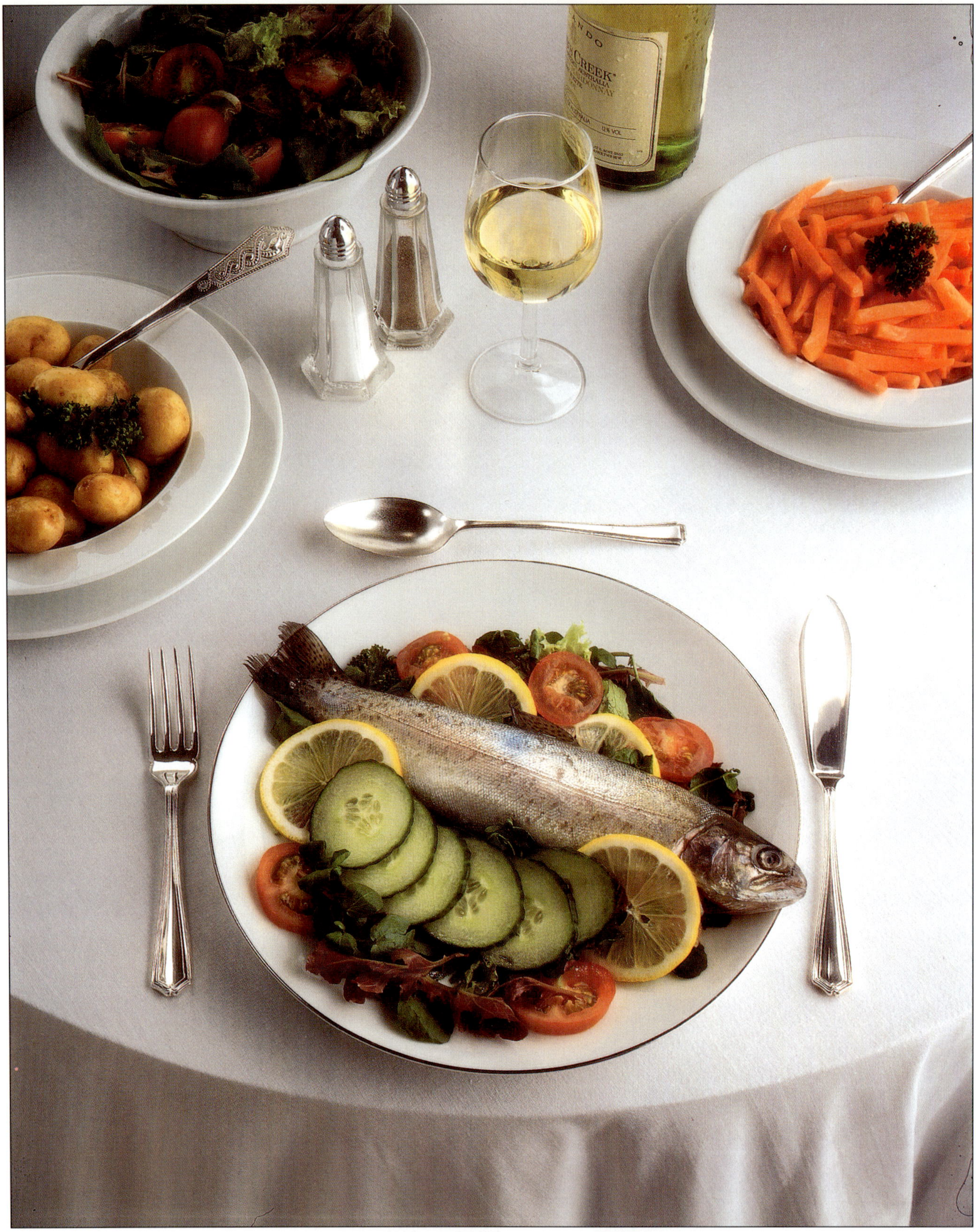

stand out he trained a spotlight on it from behind. Then he used mini-reflectors to throw some of the main light back on to the two bowls of vegetables. He even used a separate reflector to give the fish knife a nice glow. He took his final shot with a very fine soft focus filter in front of the lens to soften the image.

'Getting the lighting exactly right on a shot like this can take time', he concluded, 'so be patient.'

4 IN THE SPOTLIGHT
The fish still looked a little dull, so Seamus trained a spotlight with a warm up filter on it to pick out all the colour in its scales. He decided to try using a very subtle soft focus filter, which took all the hard edges off the set up and made the food look perfect.

SLR tip

Large format cameras are expensive to buy new, but you can hire them quite cheaply (though you have to leave a large deposit) and you can sometimes find used ones at very reasonable prices. Most 4x5 inch cameras made in the last forty or fifty years, and most lenses from this century, would have been adequate to take this picture.

Photographing a scale model

Photographing a scale model illustrates techniques used by professionals every day in lighting and arranging small sets. David Jones learns skills which can be applied to many other areas.

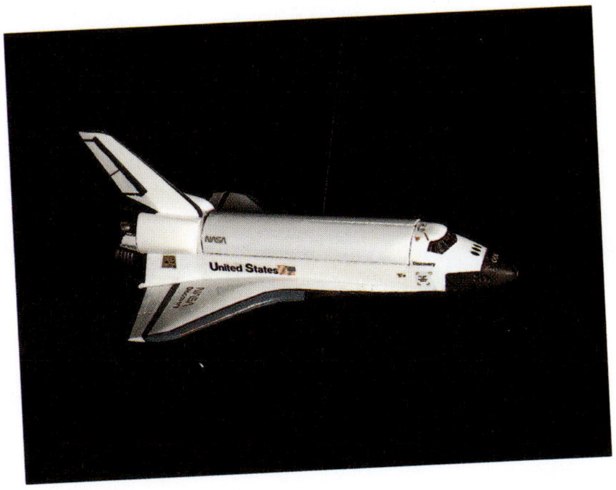

◀ ***David lit the spaceship with a single spotlight on the right of the set up to make it stand out against the plain black background. He used a 150mm lens and moved in as close as he could so the model filled the frame. But the close view really showed how badly the model had been painted, and the set up is very dull.***

My nine year old son Jimmy is a very keen model maker, and particularly enjoys building and collecting replicas of spaceships. He was so proud of making this model of a NASA space shuttle that he asked me to photograph it for him. I couldn't really think of an appropriate setting for it, so I asked professional still life photographer Seamus Ryan to give me a hand.

When we met up at his studio, I decided to have a go myself before Seamus took over. With all that professional equipment at my disposal, I thought I'd be able to come up with a fairly good photo. Seamus had decided the shot would look best on large format, so he set up a Sinar P 5 x 4in large format camera and loaded it with Ektachrome ISO 100 Plus colour slide film.

BUILDING UP A BACKGROUND

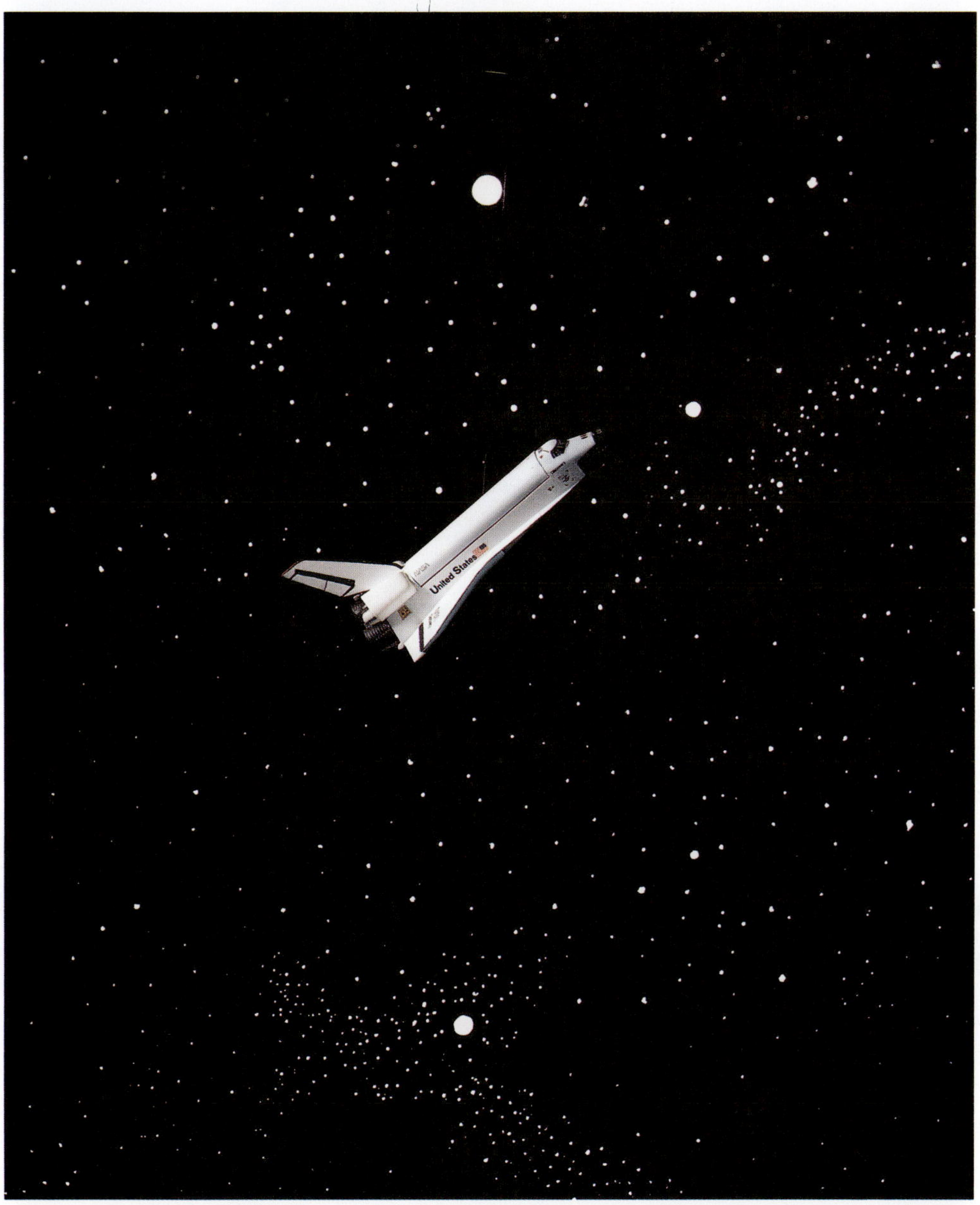

1 STARRY SKY
When Seamus took over, he switched to a 105mm lens and moved the camera away from the subject so he had a wider view of the set up. Then he hung the spaceship at a more dramatic angle and shone a diffused light through the perforated backdrop to create a starry sky.

A boring backdrop

Jimmy's model came with a plastic stand, but it wasn't very strong and broke the first time I placed the shuttle on it. As an alternative, Seamus suggested I try using some fine thread to suspend it in mid-air as if it was flying. I used Blu-tac to attach the string to the model and then suspended it from a metal stand.

I chose a sheet of thick black paper as a backdrop so that the white model would stand out clearly against it. I lit the ship with a single spotlight to the right of the set up, and used a 150mm lens to ensure that it filled the frame, but I wasn't very happy with the results. The lighting was alright but the set up looked really boring and unfortunately I couldn't think of anything better.

The stars come out

When Seamus took over he rehung the spaceship so it was travelling upwards and looked more dramatic. He stuck with the same camera and film as I had, but switched to a 105mm lens and moved the camera further from the subject for a wider shot of the whole set up. Then he turned to the backdrop.

Looking for a more suitable background, he decided to recreate the depths of outer space in the studio. He punched holes of various sizes in my black sheet of paper and shone a big softbox through it to create a background of stars and planets. The spaceship looked great in front of it, but Seamus thought the shot needed something extra.

A concrete moon

There was an old concrete ball lying around in the studio that Seamus had used as a prop several times before. When he put it on a workbench in the corner of the frame its pocked texture looked similar to the surface of the moon. He lit it from the left with a spotlight to accentuate the effect.

He lit the spaceship with another spotlight from the same side to suggest the presence of the sun. However, the strong light on the model revealed the imperfections in Jimmy's paint job. To conceal this, Seamus used a piece of stocking as a soft focus filter which

The set up

Seamus and David were photographing a model spaceship in a large commercial studio. David used a single spotlight to light the model, and a plain black background. Seamus used a pencil to punch holes in the black backdrop and shone a big softbox through it to create a starry night. He used one spotlight on the ship, and another from the same side to illuminate the concrete ball in the foreground. They both used a Sinar P 5 x 4in large format camera and Ektachrome ISO 100 Plus colour slide film.

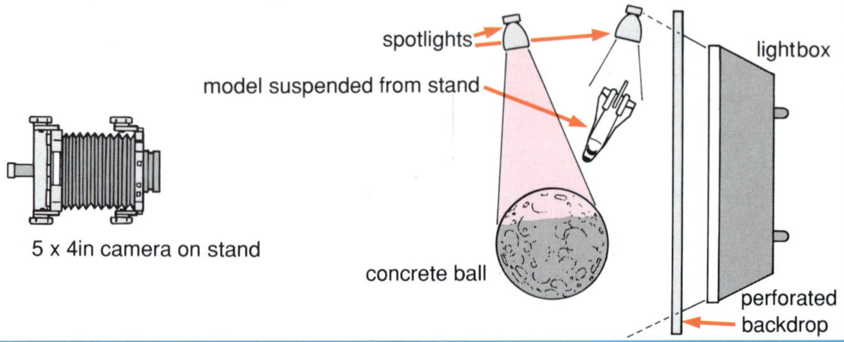

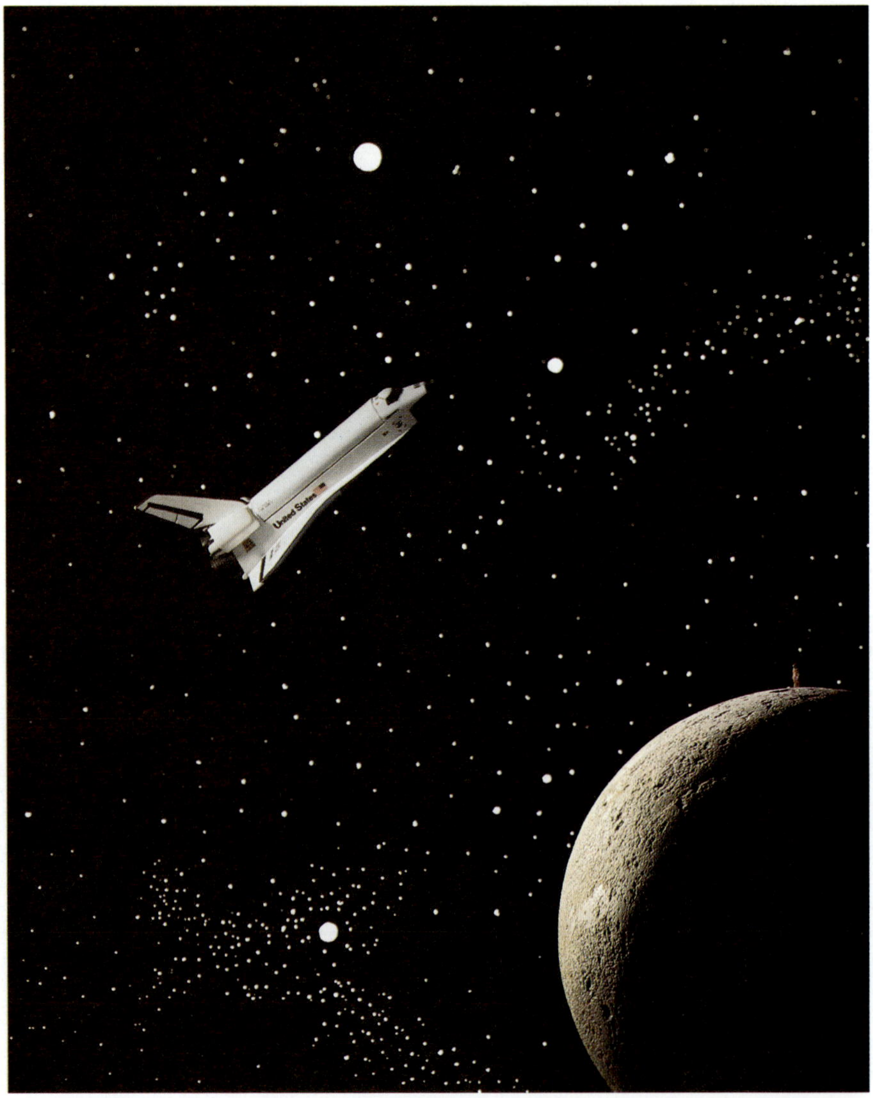

dulled the sharpness and gave the spaceship a nice glow.

A touch of colour

To add some colour to the picture, Seamus decided to experiment with coloured filters. He tried putting a blue gel in front of the light that was shining on the planet, then switched to a red one.

The red filter looked far more effective, and a miniature astronaut on the planet added a touch of humour that delighted my son Jimmy. Unfortunately, he wasn't quite so pleased with my efforts!

Compact tip

A close focus setting on your compact will help you tackle table-top set ups like this. First test your camera to check that subjects at the marked distance for close focus are sharp on film. Then arrange your still life so that the crucial elements are at precisely the right distance. Don't worry about the backdrop of stars: if they are slightly out of focus they will twinkle more effectively.

SLR tip

Take care if you decide to add a heavenly twinkle to your backdrop with a starburst filter, because it reduces sharpness. For best results use a double exposure: first shoot the starry backdrop with a starburst fitted and the other elements in place but not lit. Then extinguish the stars, remove the filter and make a second exposure of the foreground elements, this time lit exactly as you want them.

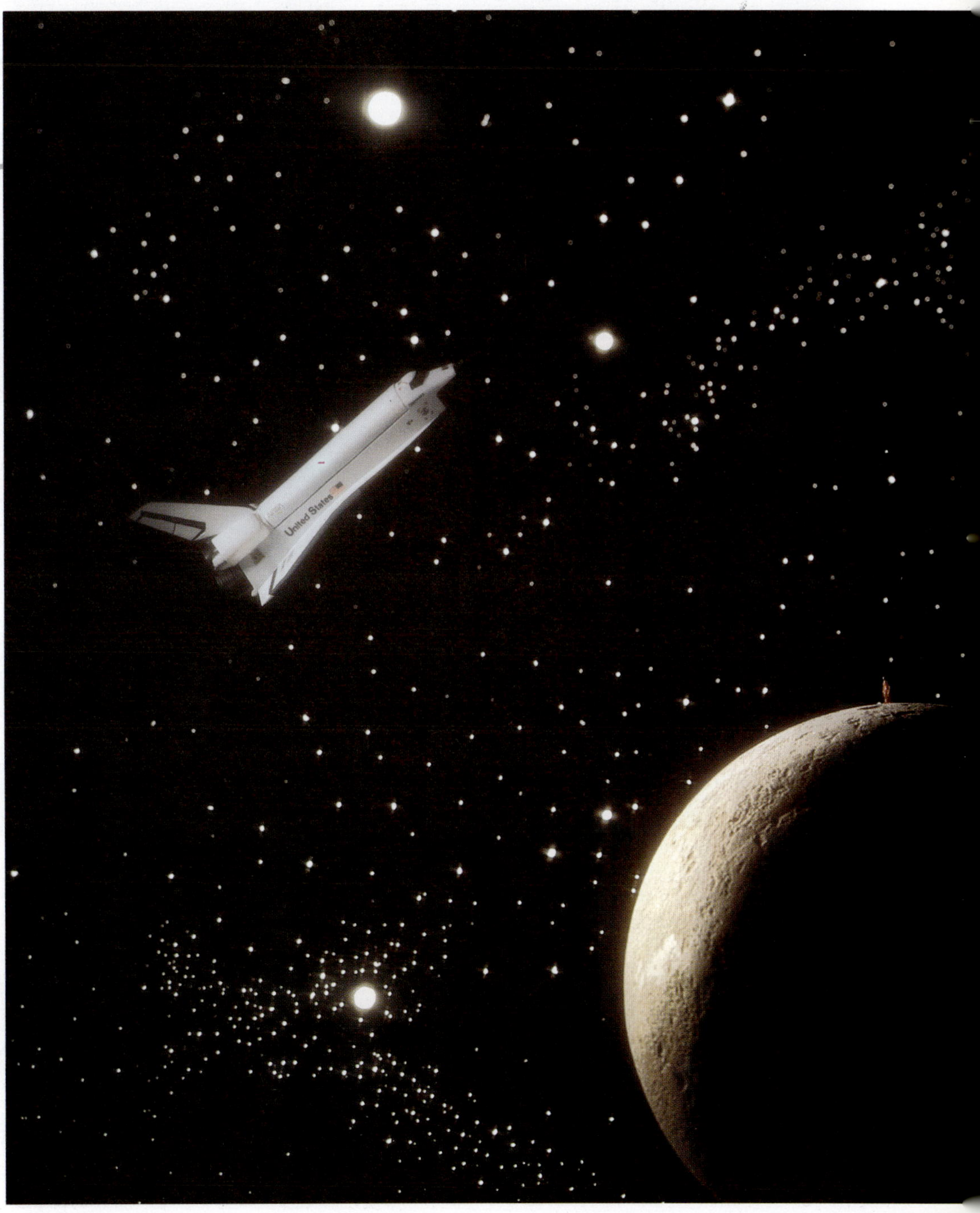

2 ◀ A LUNAR FOREGROUND
Seamus thought the model looked dull on its own, so he decided to add some interest to the foreground. He placed a large concrete ball on a workbench to the right of the set up, and lit up its pocked surface with a spotlight from the left.

3 ▶ SOFTENING THE IMAGE
The picture was now beginning to take shape, but Seamus was still unhappy with the way the model was painted. To disguise this, he tried using a piece of stocking as a soft focus filter. The soft effect gave the ship a nice overall glow and a sense of movement.

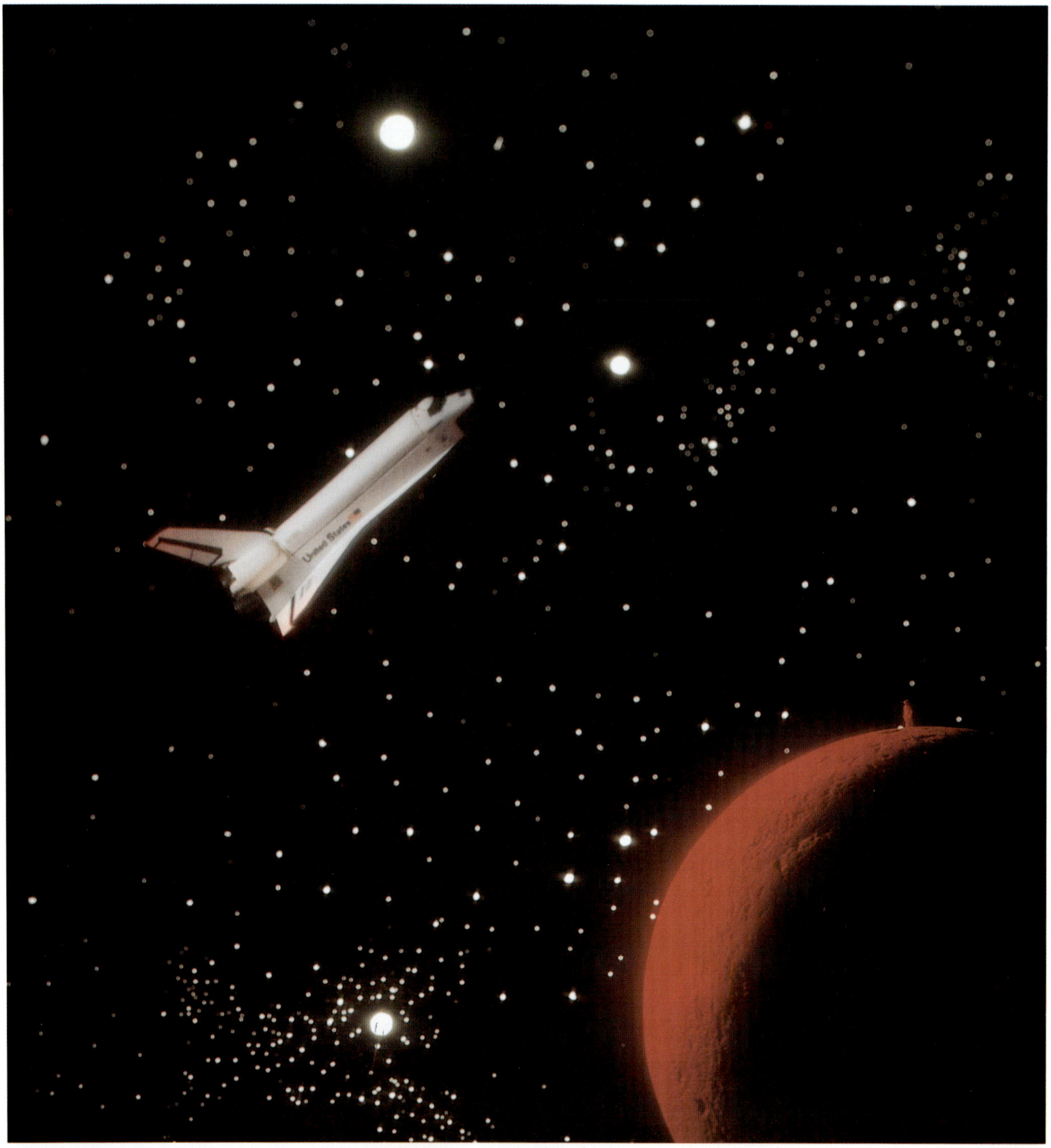

4 ADDING COLOUR

To give the image some extra colour, Seamus began experimenting by placing gel filters on the spot lighting up the concrete ball. He tried a blue filter first, but red looked far more effective. The spaceman standing on the moon adds a touch of humour to the shot.

Tip

The illusion of movement

If you want to experiment further when photographing your model, you could try creating the illusion of movement. This is done by exposing the same frame of film four or five times and moving the camera slightly each time.

With this shot, for example, you would expose the moon and background in the first shot. Then you would turn all the lights off except the one on the ship and keep shooting.

Moving the camera after each exposure will leave a trail of faint images on the film that should make the ship look as though it's travelling at speed. Be patient though – it's not an easy effect to achieve.

A creative double exposure

Seamus Ryan shows David Jones some more tricks of the trade, setting up a complex shot with several different kinds of lights and using multiple exposures. If you can handle this, you really understand studio photography.

Getting a double exposure right may seem difficult to begin with, but once you've mastered the technique, the creative possibilities are endless. I've always found the business of getting everything in exactly the right position over two exposures a bit tricky, so I asked advertising photographer Seamus Ryan to show me how it's done.

In the week before this shoot, Seamus and I thought hard about which subject to choose. We wanted something that would look unusual and convincing without being too elaborate, and we decided to build our shots around the theme of electricity. Our basic prop was an ordinary household light bulb, and I opted to shoot first.

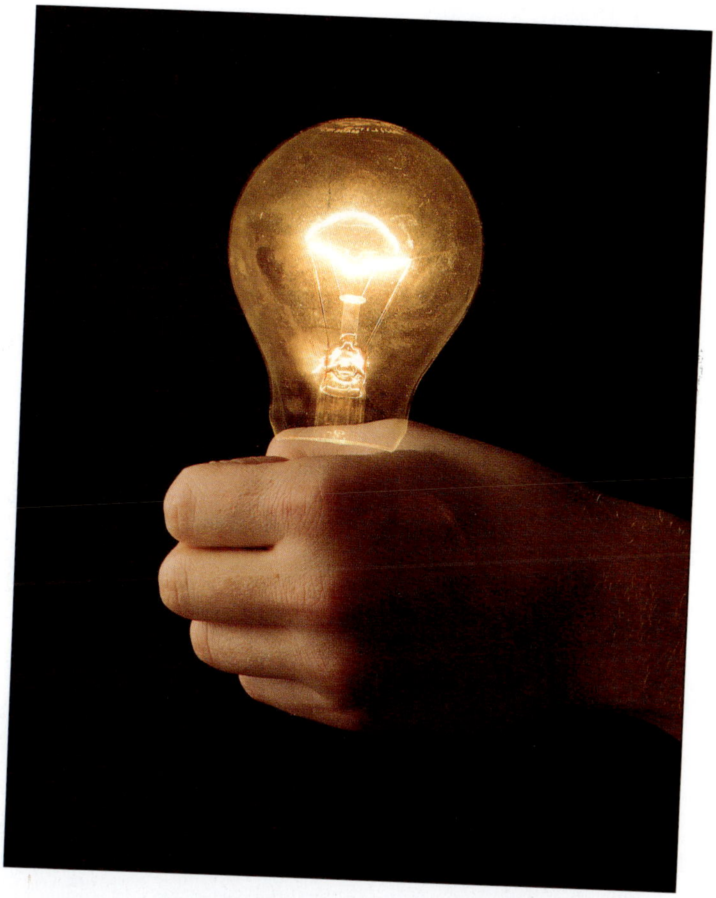

▶ David's original idea was to take a shot showing an apparently unconnected bulb lit up in a hand. Because his composition wasn't very accurate, however, the exposure of the bulb has overlapped with that of the hand and ruined the effect. A slightly overlong first exposure has left the bulb looking too bright, and the overall idea isn't a very ambitious one.

The set up

Seamus and David were shooting double exposures in a studio. David tried to photograph a hand holding a lighted bulb, but his composition wasn't accurate enough and the shot didn't work. Seamus laid the lighted bulb down on some soil against a cloudy backdrop. Then he drew the outline of a lightning bolt on a softbox and used black card and tape to fill in all the space around it. When he was sure he'd got the lightning exactly lined up with the bulb he combined both set ups on one frame. They both used Sinar P 5 x 4in large format cameras, 240mm lenses and Kodak Ektachrome 100 colour slide film.

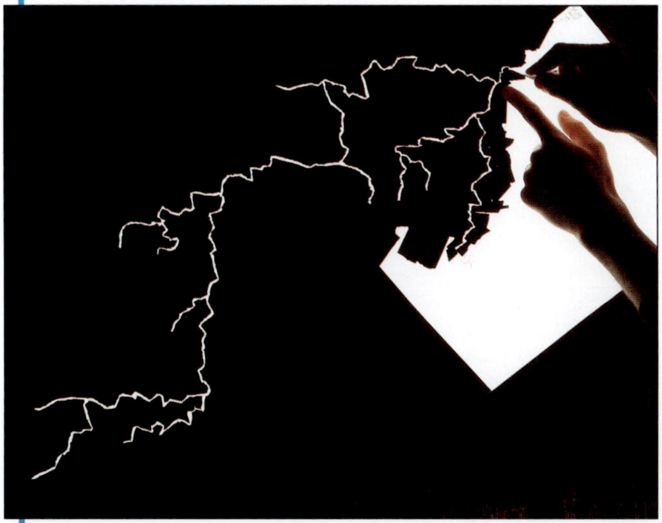

▲ Seamus created his lightning by masking a softbox with two jagged shaped pieces of black card. You could use a lightbox instead.

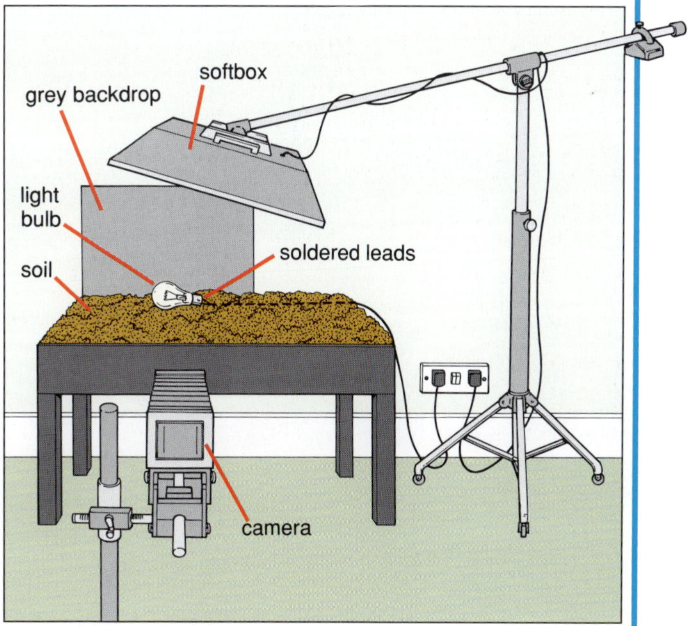

A simple start

I thought that the simpler my composition was, the more chance I'd have of getting my double exposure right, so after discussing a few alternatives with Seamus I chose to take what I thought would be a simple shot of a hand holding a lighted bulb. Seamus set up two Sinar P 5 x 4in large format cameras so I could shoot the two exposures separately, moving the film holder between the two cameras so that both images were on the same piece of film.

I set up the light bulb first, connecting it up by soldering wires to it that could be easily hidden. Then I sat the bulb upright in a cone of black velvet that would disappear easily in the second exposure. I used the other camera to photograph the hand of Seamus' assistant against a black background. I lit both shots with a single softbox.

I experimented first, using Polaroids, then shot three or four sheets of Kodak Ektachrome ISO 100 slide film with a 240mm lens (equivalent to about 90mm on 35mm format). Although I was careful to mark the relative positions of the hand and bulb, my best effort wasn't nearly accurate enough. I think I must have moved the camera slightly before taking my second exposure.

BUILDING UP A DOUBLE EXPOSURE

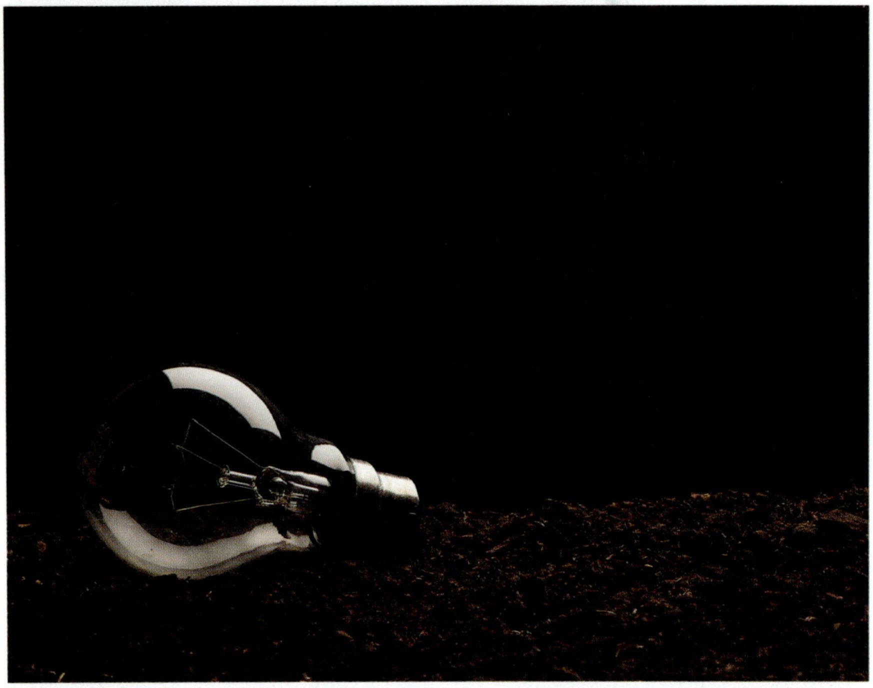

1 THE BASIC SET UP The first thing Seamus did was work out how he wanted the overall shot to look. He decided that some soil would make an interesting base, and positioned the bulb in the left hand corner of the frame so there would be plenty of room for the lightning. He lit the set up from the right with a single softbox.

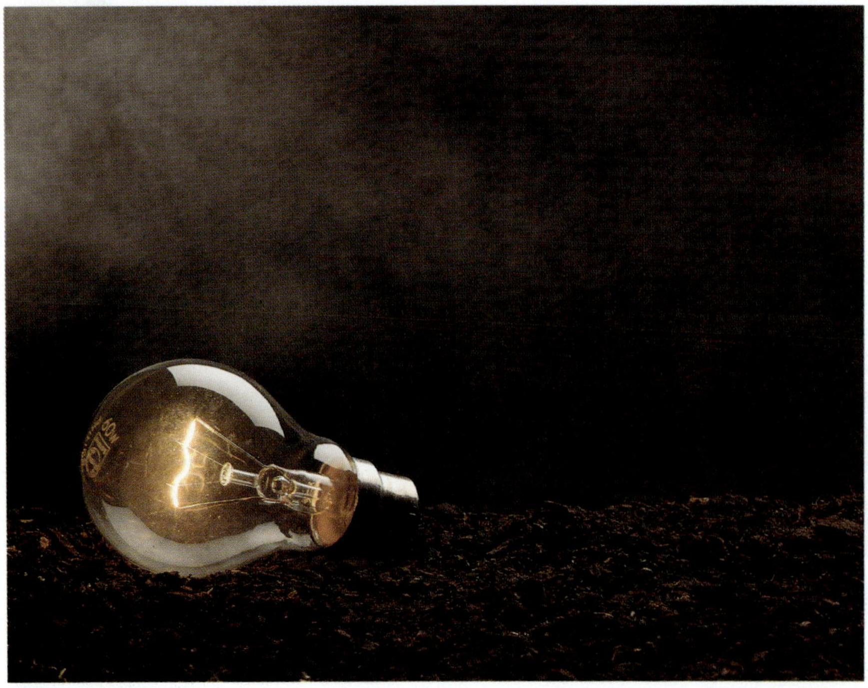

2 POWER AND BACKGROUND Seamus chose a grey, cloudy canvas as a backdrop, which he hoped would be subtle but effective. He soldered wires to the bottom of the bulb in order to light it, then hid the wires under the soil. He kept his exposure fairly short to make sure the bulb didn't end up looking too bright.

A more ambitious shot

When Seamus took over, he decided to try and produce a more adventurous shot. The light bulb would still be the centrepiece, but he wanted it to look as though it were being charged by a bolt of lightning. He also used two cameras so he could build up two separate set ups, and began with the bulb.

He spread some soil on a piece of card to form the base, and laid the bulb down on its side. Then he connected it up as I had and hid the wires in the soil. He lit the shot from above and slightly to the right with a single softbox, and was careful to keep his exposure quite short so the light from the bulb's element didn't end up looking too strong.

Making lightning

Once he was happy with the main shot, Seamus turned his attention to the lightning. He drew the pattern of lightning he wanted on to the face of a softbox, then used a mixture of black card and tape to block out the rest of the light so that only the fork remained.

He used bits of tape to make the edges look jaggedly realistic. When he took a colour Polaroid of the

Tip: Double exposures on 35mm

Although the large viewfinders on 5 x 4in and 10 x 8in cameras make them ideal for accurate double exposures, you can achieve good results on 35mm cameras. Some modern SLRs allow you to change the screen on your camera for a grid screen. When combined with a magnifying viewfinder extension, this will help you compose double exposures far more accurately.

If you want to check that a shot's working, a Polaroid Instant Processor will process 35mm Polaroid film in two to three minutes to show what you're getting. It will be very useful if you're keen on shooting more still life shots. If you're trying a double exposure without these aids, choose a shot with more margin for error than this one.

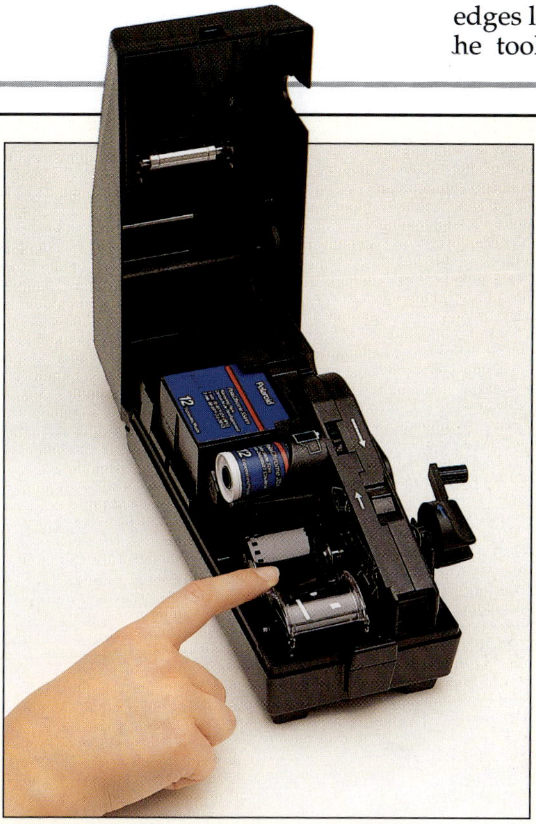

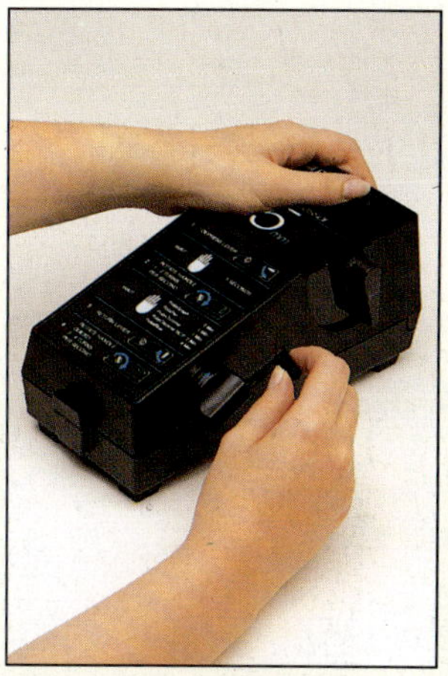

◀▲ To use a Polaroid Instant Processor, you simply load the exposed 35mm Polaroid film (left) and roll it through the processor (above) for instant results.

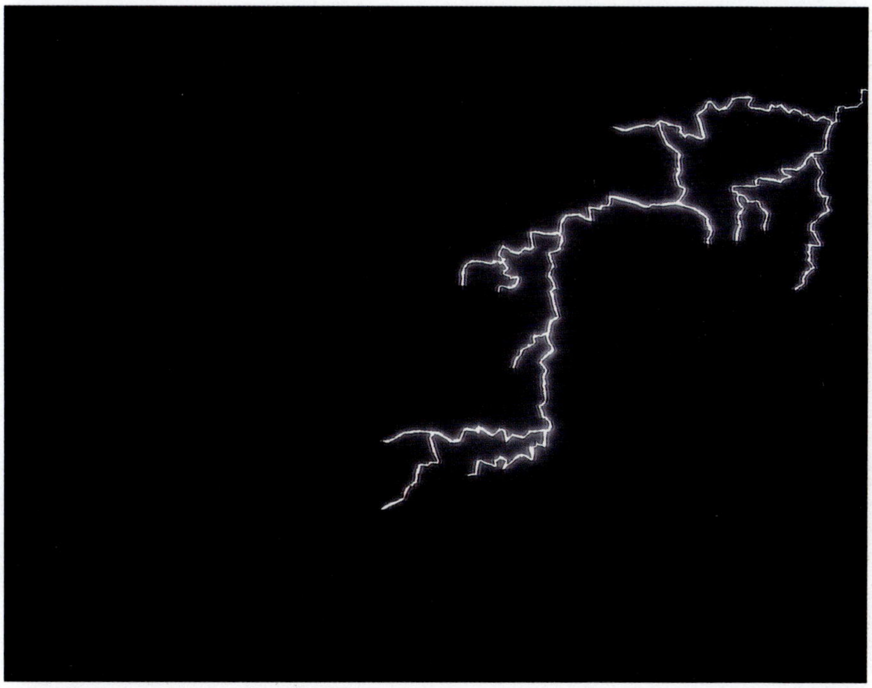

3 WHIPPING UP A STORM Seamus drew the outline of a fork of lightning on to the face of a softbox, then blotted out the surrounding light with black card and tape. He covered the lens with a blue gel to give the lightning a slight tint, and used a subtle soft focus filter to make it look slightly less distinct.

lightning, he didn't think it looked quite right, so he used a gel filter to give it a blue tint and a soft focus filter to blur its outline.

Pinpoint accuracy

Seamus used colour Polaroids to make a series of adjustments until he got the shot exactly right. When he was satisfied that the lightning was just touching the end of the bulb, he marked the position of everything on the viewfinder grid and weighted down both the camera stands to make sure they didn't move. He even taped the individual sheets of film into the film back to make sure they didn't move slightly between the two exposures. He used the same film and lens as I had.

The end result of all this caution was that Seamus' double exposure turned out exactly as he wanted it to. The cloudy grey canvas behind the bulb made an appropriate backdrop, and the subtle mix of colours looked extremely effective.

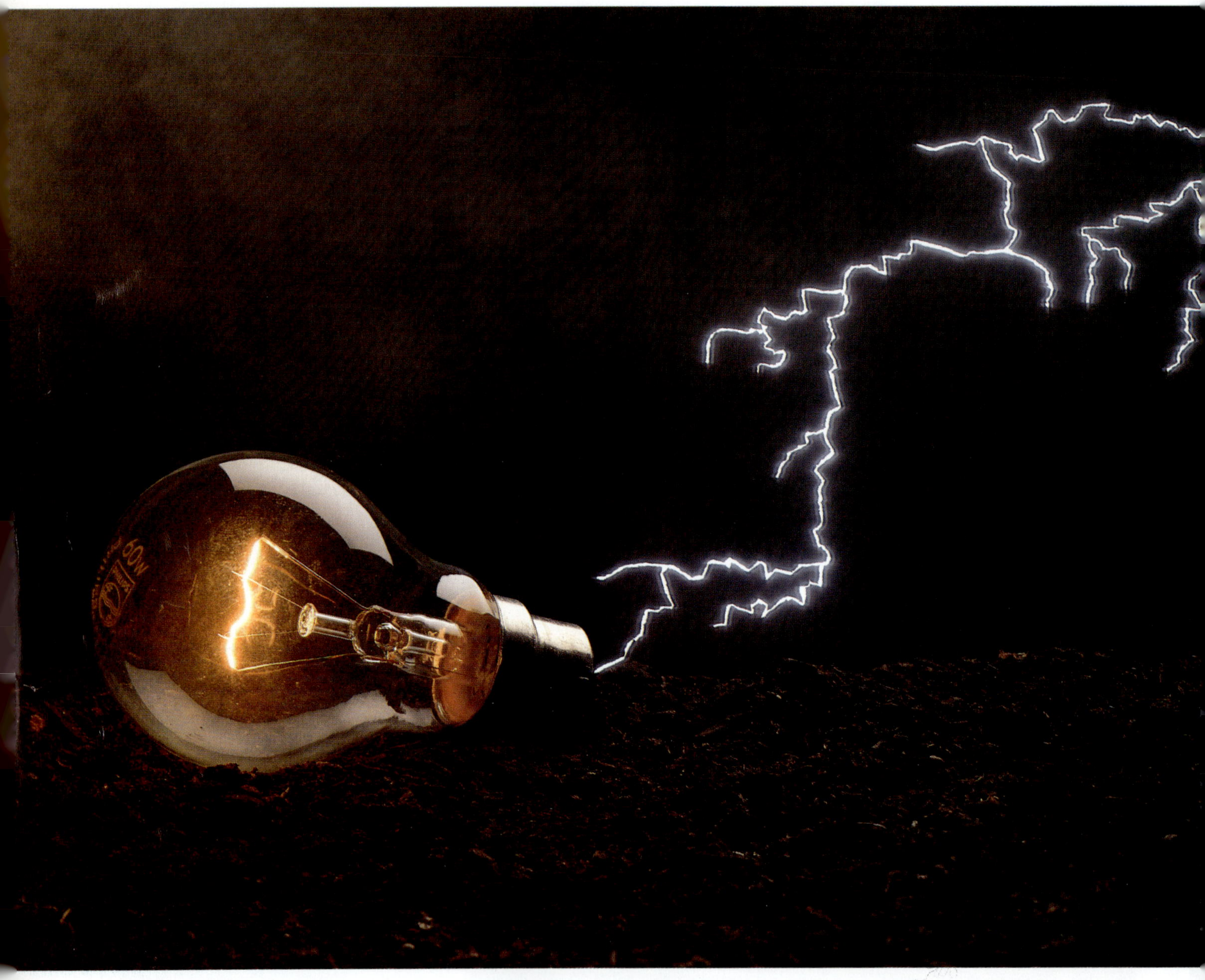

4 LIGHTNING STRIKES When Seamus was happy with both set ups, he combined the two on a double exposure. It was difficult to get the lightning to just touch the end of the bulb, but he was able to make fairly exact markings on the viewfinder grids and used colour Polaroids to make sure he was getting it right.

SLR tip

Some advanced SLRs have multiple exposure modes, but if you have an autowind camera that doesn't, you'll have to shoot the whole film and note which frames you want to double expose. If your camera winds on manually you can double expose individual frames at once. Shoot the first frame, then wind on the film while holding down the rewind button. Be careful you don't overexpose the frame when exposing it twice.